A LIBERAL WORLD ORDER IN CRISIS

A LIBERAL WORLD ORDER IN CRISIS

CHOOSING BETWEEN
IMPOSITION AND
RESTRAINT

GEORG SØRENSEN

CORNELL UNIVERSITY PRESS
Ithaca and London

First published 2011 by Cornell University Press

Printed in the United States of America

Library of Congress Cataloging-in-Publication Data

Sørensen, Georg, 1948-
 A liberal world order in crisis : choosing between imposition and restraint / Georg Sørensen.
  p. cm.
 Includes bibliographical references and index.
 ISBN 978-0-8014-5022-8 (cloth : alk. paper)
  1. Liberalism. 2. International relations. 3. World
politics—1989- I. Title.
 JC574.S59 2011
  327.1—dc22   2011017382

Cornell University Press strives to use environmentally responsible suppliers and materials to the fullest extent possible in the publishing of its books. Such materials include vegetable-based, low-VOC inks and acid-free papers that are recycled, totally chlorine-free, or partly composed of nonwood fibers. For further information, visit our website at www.cornellpress.cornell.edu.

Cloth printing   10 9 8 7 6 5 4 3 2 1

For the boys: Jacob, Jonas, and Tobias

◼ CONTENTS

 # PREFACE

Most of the 1990s was a honeymoon period for liberal thinking about international affairs and for liberal politics: the Cold War had ended with liberal victory, and that created great expectations for a long phase of sustained progress for liberal democracy, liberal international institutions, the liberal world economy, and liberal values. By the turn of the century, or even earlier, it was clear that any such hope for liberal progress rested on a much shakier foundation than most people had believed. It was at that point I began investigating the idea that tensions inside liberalism might be a major source of impediment to liberal progress. In particular, it became clear that liberal advance itself contains elements that may serve to undercut further liberal progress. I continue to believe that the progress that liberal theory talks about is possible in principle, but for reasons set forth in this book I am much more skeptical about any notion of facile advance toward a more liberal world order. Liberal progress is not merely predicated on formulating "good" policies; it is also dependent on dealing successfully with deep tensions in liberal principles themselves. I seek to explain why that is no easy task.

The overall argument has not appeared in print previously, but some of the themes contained in this book have been set forth in articles in scholarly journals and in book chapters. A number of ideas have also been presented at conferences and seminars. My thanks go to editors, reviewers, and participants; they have greatly inspired and enriched my understanding of the subject.

The relevant earlier publications are the following: "What Kind of World Order? The International System in the New Millennium," *Cooperation and Conflict* 41:4 (2006), 343–64 (chapter 1); "Liberalism of Restraint and Liberalism of Imposition: Liberal Values and World Order in the New Millennium," *International Relations* 20:3 (2006), 251–72 (chapter 2); "After the Security Dilemma: The Challenges of Insecurity in Weak States and the Dilemma of Liberal Values," *Security Dialogue* 38:3 (2007), 357–78 (chapter 3); "Antinomies of Liberal World Order: Liberal Dilemmas at 'History's

End,'" seminar paper, Danish Institute for International Studies, Copenhagen, 2009 (chapter 3); *Changes in Statehood: The Transformation of International Relations,* Basingstoke: Palgrave Macmillan, 2001 (chapter 4); "Free Markets for All: The Difficulties of Maintaining a Stable Liberal World Economy," in *Governing the Global Economy: Politics Institutions and Economic Development: Essays in Honor of Helge Hveem,* ed. Dag Harald Claes and Carl Henrik Knutsen, London: Routledge, 2011 (chapter 5).

Colleagues in the International Relations section at the Department of Political Science in Aarhus have provided help and encouragement. The Department, as well as Aarhus University Research Foundation, generously supplied economic support. A Guest Professorship at the WZB (Social Science Research Center), Berlin, during the spring of 2007 offered important input for the project. The WZB Research Unit on Transnational Conflicts and International Institutions was a very fruitful context for thinking about world order issues. My thanks to President Jürgen Kocka, Director Michael Zürn, and his colleagues, Martin Binder, Mathias Ecker-Ehrhardt, Susanne Fuchs, Kristina Hartwig, and Helmut Weidner. The BG Bank Foundation kindly made their Berlin guest apartment available for the stay.

Writing this book turned out to be a somewhat more difficult task than I had anticipated. I am deeply grateful, and much indebted, to colleagues who carefully read earlier drafts of the manuscript. They offered a large number of suggestions for improvements; my thanks to Francis Fukuyama, John Ikenberry, Peter Katzenstein, Judith Kelley, and Jan Zielonka. At Cornell University Press, Roger Haydon supported the project with unfailing help and advice. Susan Tarcov was a terrific copy editor and Susan Specter was a superb manuscript editor.

Martin B. Carstensen did an excellent job in putting together an overview of liberal world order literature. So did Jacob Hartmann Sørensen in reading and correcting the manuscript for typos and other errors. Annette Andersen once again expertly took care of all the technical details.

Thanks once more to my wife, Lisbet, for keeping me alive during the project. The book is dedicated to my grandchildren, Jonas and Tobias, and their father, Jacob. Thanks to the boys for engaging me in activities and appreciating my company in ways that had nothing whatsoever to do with whether or not I would eventually complete this book.

A LIBERAL WORLD
ORDER IN CRISIS

Introduction
The Argument

The current world order is more liberal than any previous order in history: it is dominated by free, democratic states, there is almost universal support for a state-market arrangement based on private property and free market exchange, and a vast network of international institutions articulate and support liberal doctrines. At the same time, progress is much less secure in many areas than it might seem at first glance; for example, democracy is not making significant progress in a large number of countries, and any global commitment to liberal principles and values remains thin and uncertain. In contrast to early "end of history" optimism, liberal principles compete with each other and there is no simple path to liberal progress. It is in this complex situation that liberal states are called upon to answer a fundamental question about the real content of world order: what is it that liberal principles have to offer peoples and countries, and what does it mean to have an order based on freedom and rights?

Liberal democracies offer two fundamentally different answers to this question. One affirms the universal validity of liberal values, as expressed in the United States' national security strategy of 2002: "the United States must defend liberty and justice because these principles are right and true for all people everywhere...the United States must start from these core beliefs and look outward for possibilities to expand liberty." I label this strategy a Liberalism of Imposition. It contains an imperialist element to the extent that

1

it employs power to secure the expansion of liberal principles; "imperialism," says Samuel Huntington, "is the necessary logical consequence of universalism." I demonstrate that Imposition offers no secure basis for a stable order.

The other answer stresses a different set of liberal values: pluralism, nonintervention, respect for others, moderation, and peaceful cooperation on equal terms. I label this strategy a Liberalism of Restraint. Several commentators argue that the United States and the other consolidated democracies successfully pursued a Liberalism of Restraint strategy during the Cold War and that a stable world order will be (re)established by returning to this posture. I demonstrate why there is no easy pathway to a stable Restraint order: because of recent economic and political developments, liberal states have been weakened and speak with less clout in the world. Furthermore, a Restraint order is simply not sufficient to address the core challenges that a well-functioning order must confront today.

Imposition is too much and Restraint is too little: that is the liberal dilemma. It is not new because the tension between Imposition and Restraint has been present in the liberal tradition from the beginning. But it is particularly pertinent today because the leading democracies must take on the responsibility for creation of a stable world order; no one else can, or will, shoulder the task.

Liberal states will probably not be able to agree on a set of coherent principles for world order. The tensions that lead to grave problems in the construction of order emerge in several areas: the core value of freedom is a highly complex entity that can be defined in very different ways; democracy leads to peace but liberal democracies can also be highly aggressive; liberal values are being advanced in ways that threaten to undermine what they seek to achieve; liberal institutions far from always serve liberal principles. This book analyzes the major problems and tensions facing the quest for a liberal world order.

For several centuries, liberal ideas about world order have been just that: ideas, aspirations, visions of what a better world might look like if it were constructed on the basis of liberal principles. After World War II, liberal democratic systems were consolidated in the OECD-world (Western Europe, North America, Japan, Australia, and New Zealand), but the international scene was dominated by the military competition between the two superpowers and their respective allies. A liberal order emerged in the OECD-world while liberal principles were barred from global dominance under Cold War conditions. This all changed with the breakup of the Soviet empire, the spread of liberal democracy to many more countries, and the true globalization of a liberal market economy. The post–Cold War hope for a liberal order was expressed by George H. W. Bush in 1990: "Until now, the world we've known has been a world divided—a world of barbed wire and concrete blocks, of conflict and Cold War. Now we can see a new world coming into view. A world in which there is the very real prospect of a new world order. In the words of Winston Churchill, a 'world order' in which 'the principles of justice and fair play protect the weak against the strong. . . .' A world where the United Nations, free from Cold War stalemate, is poised to fulfill the historic vision of its founders. A world in which freedom and respect for human rights find a home among all nations." Francis Fukuyama spoke of the "liberal moment"; he had already in 1989 predicted a "'Common Mar-ketization' of world politics," meaning that a peaceful liberal world would be more preoccupied with "economics than with politics or strategy."

But liberal triumph soon led to grave problems concerning both the sub-stance of liberal order and the appropriate strategy for promoting it. Prog-ress toward a genuinely liberal world order has proved much more intricate than expected when the wall fell in 1989 and the Soviet Union ceased to exist in 1992. Many different answers have been given as to why that is the case; some of the most important ones are discussed here. My argument is that current difficulties of creating a liberal world order have to do as much with the tensions in liberalism as with a renewed balance of power competi-tion between great powers, the existence of weak states, the phenomenon of international terrorism, or a confrontation between competing cultures. The competing views on world order, and the relevance of these views for the current analysis, are discussed in chapter 1.

World order can be defined as a governing arrangement among states with global reach.[1] Prominent observers claim that the current world order is defined by one major characteristic; however, they cannot agree on what that characteristic is, be it "the liberal moment," "the clash of civilizations," "the coming anarchy," "the return of history," or some other feature. As I shall explain in chapter 1, none of these analyses is entirely wrong or misleading, but all are insufficient because they fail to capture a key characteristic of the present order. That characteristic is tied in with liberal progress and liberal problems; there has been substantial liberal progress in creating a more liberal world: more liberal democracies, more liberal international institutions, and a liberal market economy with global reach. But that very progress is coming to a standstill today because of dilemmas and tensions in liberalism itself. In its finest hour, liberal world order is facing its gravest problems. Because the

---

1. The definition is indebted to, but not identical with, the one in Ikenberry (2001: 23).

problems connected with liberal world order are of decisive importance for the future of countries and peoples, this situation is a defining characteristic of the present world order. It has gone relatively unnoticed so far, probably because liberals have been too happy with liberal progress and nonliberals have looked elsewhere in their analyses; but it cannot and must not be hidden away any longer.

A liberal world order is based on domestic as well as on international change in a liberal direction, as explained in chapter 2. In the domestic realm, democracy, that is, sovereign states with liberal democratic institutions and practices, is the basis for a liberal world order. In the international realm, democracies cooperate at the transnational level; special emphasis is on free market economic intercourse and commercial relations. They also cooperate in international institutions. Liberals support strong international institutions regulated by common rules of international law. In the process of cooperation, liberal states help create an order based on liberal core values, such as freedom, responsibility, tolerance, social justice, and equality of opportunity. But liberal progress is much less impressive than many people think, and that presents a major set of challenges to liberal states. They do not have a clear answer to these challenges. The core conflict is about what it means for individuals to enjoy freedom and the good life. Classical liberalism embodies a Liberalism of Restraint, which concerns autonomy and the space to act unobstructed by others. Modern liberalism represents a Liberalism of Imposition, which requires active intervention to secure the proper conditions for real freedom.

Freedom is a highly complex entity for liberals because the concept of liberty can be interpreted in very different ways. Negative liberty is autonomy, self-determination, freedom of choice, and the ability to act unobstructed by others. Positive liberty, by contrast, is the liberty of being your own master. In order to be your own master you must not be held down by disease, poverty, ignorance, or tyranny. To secure positive liberty, comprehensive action is necessary in order to remove these grave obstacles to freedom; comprehensive action calls for intervention. To secure negative liberty, an entirely different behavior is warranted: leave people (and states) alone, and let them choose their own path. Therefore, the promotion of liberty is much more complex than would appear on first impression. The tensions in liberalism are identified in detail in chapter 2. Subsequent chapters discuss those tensions in relation to major aspects of the current world order.

The value foundation of a liberal world order is scrutinized in chapter 3. Liberal idealism holds a much too optimistic belief in universal progress. Progress is by no means assured; the obstacles to it may be insurmountable.

That creates a difficult situation for the promotion of liberal values. On the one hand, liberals must be respectful of the values of other cultures and societies; but liberals must also maintain that there are universal values, including human rights, valid for all. When outsiders attempt to promote such values, they are often conceived as imperialists, and that can call forth aggressive rejections by insiders. Since we live in a world where domestic preconditions for the promotion of liberal values are lacking in many places, the promotion of liberal values faces an uphill battle for a long time to come. At the same time, democracy is weak and frail in many countries, and the commitment to liberal values in international society is not strong either.

The analysis proceeds to focus on weak and failed states in chapter 4. There are a large number of weak states in the world, and in several cases an aggravation of their problems has led to complete collapse or state failure. These states pose a threefold challenge to a liberal world order: they are frequently humanitarian disasters, they represent a serious security problem, and they embody a development challenge in that it is difficult to promote political and economic progress in them. But neither the Liberalism of Restraint nor the Liberalism of Imposition represents a sustainable solution to the problems of weak and failed states, and liberal governments have not been able to set forth anything but problematic and unsuccessful compromises between these principles.

The economic dimension of a liberal world order is in focus in chapter 5. Today, there is more global support than earlier for open economies based on private property and free market exchange. But the neoliberal principles promoted by liberal states and the international financial institutions do not present adequate solutions to the problems faced by weak and modernizing states. At the same time, the advanced liberal states support one set of standards for themselves and another set of standards for their emerging competitors. They are now being forced to rethink their state-market setups in the midst of a profound economic crisis. The principles for a reformed liberal economic order are not in place, nor is there a country, or group of countries, able and willing to take the lead in economic policymaking. This bodes ill for any prospect of a stable economic order.

Liberals support an institutionalized, rule-based order. Chapter 6 examines whether the current conditions support the establishment of a stable institutional order; the answer is that they do not. The United States was a successful liberal hegemon after World War II: it was able and willing to establish a new order, and at the same time, bipolarity created a situation that prevented the abuse of hegemonic power. After the end of the Cold War that balance was destroyed; the hegemon was unconstrained. This led to aggressive U.S. leadership in the George W. Bush era, but such a one-sided order was largely rejected by both U.S. allies and other great powers. There is no easy path to a more stable order. Domestic changes in the United States raise questions about the support for liberal internationalism, and major international institutions are in need of fundamental reform, but liberal states cannot agree on how to move forward. Stronger, nonliberal great powers are pressing for more international influence. This all points to a loosely defined patchwork order that might not be able to meet the demands for regulation prompted by economic globalization, environmental degradation, and a host of other problems.

Against this background, the prospects for liberal world order are discussed in the conclusion. I argue that neither liberal Restraint nor liberal Imposition contains durable solutions to the world order challenges faced by liberal states. Is there a possible middle road that avoids both isolationist passivism and imperialist activism? There have been suggestions for a "realistic Wilsonianism" that would appear to move in the right direction; but durable solutions demand a rethinking of the liberal project and the tensions and contradictions it contains. That process of rethinking has barely begun, and therefore the prospects for liberal world order are probably much less bright than many people would like to think.

CHAPTER 1

The Debate on World Order

The lack of a general consensus on the major characteristics of world order has led to a considerable amount of confusion among scholars as well as among policymakers. What kind of order is emerging now? Is it the "liberal moment" (Fukuyama 1992); a multipolar balance of power and a new round of potentially hostile competition between states (Waltz 1993, 2002); a "clash of civilizations" (Huntington 1996); "Jihad vs. McWorld" (Barber 1995); "the coming anarchy" (Kaplan 2000); the "return of history" (Kagan 2007); or some combination of all this, or perhaps something entirely different, even a really "New World Order" (Slaughter 2004)?[1] The diversity of propositions demonstrates the confusion regarding the issue of world order. On the one hand, there are a significant number of radically diverging views about the makeup of the present order; on the other hand there are people who think that lack of order is what characterizes the present period.

None of the analyses of world order briefly mentioned here is entirely wrong or misleading. Each of them focuses on one or more important aspects of the current world order. There has surely been liberal progress, as indicated by Fukuyama; more or less hostile power balancing continues to take place,

---

1. For a vision of sustainable world order, see H. Müller (2009).

as Waltz emphasizes; the point made by Huntington, that confrontations between different civilizational value systems have increased, rings true. Economic globalization as well as religious and tribal fundamentalism can definitely present threats to (liberal) democracy, which is Barber's major point. Weak states threatening further decay and failure are a significant element in the current order. Finally, the liberal networks at the center of Slaughter's analysis do point to new forms of rule making and order creation.

Even if these analyses make valid points, they are insufficient or even partially misleading because they fail to capture a key characteristic of the present order. There has been liberal progress (Fukuyama, Slaughter), but that progress has exposed tensions in liberalism, which the above analyses do not identify or discuss. There is balance-of-power competition, but it has been constrained and moderated in new ways that traditional balance-of-power analyses (Waltz 2002, Mearsheimer 2001) do not recognize. Confrontations between value systems, especially among "the West and the Rest," are much more connected to tensions in liberalism than is acknowledged by Huntington and others. Weak statehood and state failure are not new occurrences, and any "coming anarchy" has much more to do with liberal apprehension than is noted by Kaplan. In short, my argument is that the present world order is more liberal than it ever was, but this has opened up tensions in liberalism that were much less pronounced in earlier periods. It is these liberal tensions that make up a fundamental characteristic of the present world order.

The present study makes use of the rival views of order briefly introduced above and attempts to integrate the relevant parts of their insights into the view of world order suggested here. My version of order does not reject all existing views. It is an alternative to them in the sense it suggests a different idea about a key characteristic of the present world order. Elements from the existing analyses are integrated into this view; they are not accepted *tout court* but only selectively.

The world orders that existed in the second half of the twentieth century were complex structures. They involved at least four major dimensions: a security dimension that revolved around the major security concern of that order; an economic dimension that embodied the major patterns of economic exchange; an institutional dimension that represented the most important institutional aspects of the order; and a value dimension that contained the ideas, or systems of meaning, that undergird the current order (Sørensen 2006a). I will further analyze these major dimensions in due course. The point in the present context is that even if a world order is a complex structure, it is also a mental construct that guides our understanding and influences or even determines our patterns of action.

These mental constructs are inevitably simplified; they attempt to express the decisive characteristics of a given order. We all make use of such images, which consist of a few simple ideas most often concerning the core difficulties of the present order. In that sense, any given world order is both a complex reality and a simple mental construct.

Most people could agree to the simple version of the Cold War world order. The foundation was the bipolar, military competition between the two superpowers and their respective allies. In addition to this East-West dimension there was also a West-West and a North-South order. The West-West order was based on American hegemony, liberal democracy, the Bretton Woods system, and other international institutions. The North-South order was based on the process of decolonization and the entry of the newly independent states into the system of United Nations organizations.

The simple versions of world order are important because they guide our actions and structure our thinking. After the end of the Cold War, and in particular after September 11, 2001, it has become increasingly difficult to agree on the simple and of course also on the complex version of world order. At the same time, the world order images—and especially the images held by key decision makers in leading states—are crucially important for the policies proposed and the courses of action taken. In that sense there is also an element of self-fulfilling prophecy in any conception of world order, because adopted policies help confirm the underlying image of the world that led to those policies. So it matters whether the current order is characterized by a "Global War on Terror," a "New Cold War," or an environmental crisis, because such views not merely reflect an aspect of global conditions but also contribute to shaping what those conditions will be in the immediate future. The following section further explicates the concept of world order.

The Concept of World Order

Focus in the present study is on world order in the second half of the twentieth and the early twenty-first century with major emphasis on the period since the end of the Cold War. This topic demands a clarification of the concept of world order. Order as opposed to disorder signifies some kind of pattern. The pattern can be more or less elaborate, it can be intended or unintended, and it may or may not promote a range of goals and values. At one extreme, a very slim and narrow concept of international order is offered by neorealist theory. Kenneth Waltz assumes that sovereign states seek their own preservation; they exist in a system of anarchy that requires them to practice self-help in order to survive. Given those conditions, states are compelled to balance against each other, and order, in the form of a balance of power between states, must emerge (Waltz 1979: 118).

A broader and more ambitious concept of order is offered by Hedley Bull (1995). He first notes that order in social life is not any conceivable pattern "but a pattern that leads to a particular result, an arrangement of social life such that it promotes certain goals or values" (3–4). The relationship between sovereign states, according to Bull, is not merely one of mechanic interaction; it is a social relationship, because it involves acts of recognition and of mutual obligation between states. Sovereign states make up an "international society" of states rather than a "system" of states. International order, then, is "a pattern of disposition of international activity that sustains those goals of the society of states that are elementary, primary or universal" (17). Bull identifies the major goals of the society of states as preserving itself, maintaining the independence of individual states, and peace.[2]

Perhaps the most ambitious set of goals for world order were elaborated by the World Order Models Project (WOMP). This project focused on an ambitious process of global reform in order to promote "peace, economic well-being, social and political justice, and ecological balance"; furthermore, the goal is to "demilitarize international relations within the existing framework of states and empires." An additional aspiration is to promote "a variety of structural reforms by way of an augmented United Nations, stronger regional institutions and the evolution of a variety of specialized regimes to handle growing complexity and interdependence" (Falk 1987: 17–18).

In sum, at one extreme we may envisage a slim and narrow, more or less stable variety of order that emerges because states are compelled to engage in a balance of power. At the other extreme is a regulated and institutionalized order that delivers an ambitious range of "world order values." In between, the order described by Bull focuses on preservation of the society of states, state independence, and peace. I shall argue below that ambitions for world order have indeed developed over time, from a narrow focus on a stable balance of power, toward a regulated order that incorporates a number of social values. As we shall see, it has been part of liberal progress that world order today involves an elaborate network of international institutions committed to liberal principles of freedom and rights.

The concepts of international and world order have been used interchangeably above. But any given international order can be more or less

---

2. Bull (1995) identifies a fourth set of goals for the society of states that are also the common goals of all of social life: "limitation of violence resulting in bodily harm, the keeping of promises and the stabilisation of possession by rules of property" (18).

inclusive in its geographical scope. John Ikenberry (2001) has studied the order arrangements emerging after major wars. He notes how the settlements expanded in scope, from a continental European settlement (Westphalia, 1648) to the Vienna settlement in 1815 that "brought the wider colonial and non-European world into the negotiations. In the twentieth century, the settlements were truly global" (8). In other words, states and other actors did not conceive of international order in strictly global or world order terms before political and other relations had developed between states on a truly global scale. This happened only in the second half of the nineteenth century; previous international orders were not world orders in a geographical sense.

Who are the entities that make up any given order? Are they sovereign states in the narrow sense of governments acting on behalf of each country, or do other actors (individuals, organizations, companies, institutions) play a role? Kenneth Waltz (1979) maintains that the core structure of international politics is defined in terms of states: "States set the scene in which they, along with non-state actors, stage their dramas.... When the crunch comes, states remake the rules by which other actors operate" (94). Robert Cox (1996) wants to emphasize the relevance of forms of power other than state power in international relations and seeks a definition of world order that is "neutral as regards the entities that constitute power" (494). Stanley Hoffmann (1998) agrees that world order and world politics are no longer purely dominated by states; on the one hand, states "are constrained by the world capitalist economy, which limits their domestic and external freedom of manoeuvre.... On the other hand, the various peoples of the world, as opposed to governments, are more turbulent than ever before" (123–24).

The disagreement reflects real world ambiguities. International society is a society of sovereign states; they are the members of international institutions, they form balances of power because they control the legitimate use of force, and they set most of the rules that other actors play by. At the same time, international institutions in today's world are not mere reflections of, or handmaidens of, states; they exert influence in their own right. Furthermore, the separation between an economic sphere of the market and a political sphere of the state is a feature of modern, capitalist society; the major actors in the market (managers, firms, workers, investors) influence the creation of order in the economic sphere. The emergence of international terrorism has questioned the states' monopoly even when it comes to the balance of power.

The relationship between states and other actors develops over time. For several centuries, states competed with the church for authority. The peace of Westphalia gave states the upper hand. The rise of state power was amplified by major wars; the leading states emerged more powerful than ever from World War II, but as we shall see, World War II also set the stage for a world order that was increasingly influenced by other actors. States are special actors in the construction of order, but they are not the only players, and there is no consensus on the privileged role of states. The question of what entities are relevant to world order is an integrated part of the discussion and disagreement about what kind of order there is.

As already indicated, the focus here is on world order since the end of World War II, with emphasis on the period since the end of the Cold War. Orders created in this period are global in geographical scope: they are world orders. The primary building block of world order is the sovereign state; at its core, a world order is a governing arrangement among states. In the context of decolonization, the institution of sovereignty became the universal principle of political organization. The United States took the lead in establishing a liberal postwar order based on sovereignty, common institutions, a liberal-capitalist world market economy, and a set of liberal values that concern both the preservation of the state system and the well-being of individual human beings. At the same time, the East-West confrontation meant that the balance of power continued to play a primary role in world order.

This order did not completely disappear when the Cold War ended and the Soviet empire folded. But the change was certainly sufficient to spark a new, large, and wide-ranging debate about the primary characteristics of the present world order. Several of these contributions chose one major aspect of world order as the defining characteristic of order in our time: international terrorism, clash of civilizations, or the balance of power are examples. Since the present study claims to develop an alternative to such views, it is relevant to comment upon them here. I begin with the realist view that focuses on the balance of power.

Balance of Power: a "Back to Basics" World Order?

With the end of the Cold War, the United States is the preponderant power in the world, especially in military strength. The distribution of military capability is at the center of neorealist theory (Waltz 1979), the spare version of realism that focuses on states in international anarchy, driven by fear and self-help. Neorealist logic dictates that other states will balance the United States, because offsetting U.S. power is a means of guaranteeing one's own security: such balancing will eventually lead to the emergence of new great powers in a multipolar system. The logic also dictates that NATO will not last and that there will be increased nuclear proliferation; intensified power competition will also emerge between European great powers. Leading neorealists

(Mearsheimer, Waltz, Layne) share these predictions (Fettweiss 2004; T. Paul et al. 2004; Ikenberry 2002a). In sum, neorealist theory anticipates that now that the common enemy has disappeared, the post–Cold War world order will be characterized by intensified balance-of-power competition between old friends, both across the Atlantic and inside (Western) Europe.

This has not happened. There has been no major balancing of U.S. power since the end of the Cold War. Kenneth Waltz (2002) has argued that it will happen "tomorrow" (see also Layne 2006), but after more than two decades the argument appears less and less persuasive. Other realist scholars propose to repair the balance-of-power argument in various ways. William Wohlforth (2002), for example, argues that U.S. power is so overwhelming that balancing is too costly; T. V. Paul (2004) contends that traditional hard balancing is to some extent being replaced by soft or asymmetric balancing.

Aggressive power balancing among states has not disappeared from the international system (Kagan 2007); it continues to take place in some major regions in Asia as well as in the Middle East. Such balancing is a consequence of the security dilemma, that is, the situation where "many of the means by which a state tries to increase its security decrease the security of others" (Jervis 1978: 169). In a self-help system, the creation of more security for one state is inevitably the creation of more *in*security for other states; power balancing is the result of that situation.

But neorealist analysis fails to recognize that the security dilemma can be significantly mitigated or even transcended. Neorealists see the security dilemma as inescapable because states have survival, understood as autonomy, as their primary goal. In John Mearsheimer's (2001) words, "specifically, states seek to maintain their territorial integrity and the autonomy of their domestic political order" (31). It is true that effective states pursue a number of basic social values, including security, freedom, order, justice, and welfare (R. Jackson and Sørensen 2010: 3–6). But in the quest for these values, states have often chosen to cooperate to an extent that has created a very high level of economic, political, and social integration among them. A number of modern liberal states have become so densely integrated that both their territorial integrity and the autonomy of their domestic political orders are no longer upheld (Zürn and Leibfried 2005). In that specific sense, state survival understood as autonomy is not the primary goal, and Mearsheimer's statement is misleading.

In the EU, the development of supranational authority and free movement across borders creates a new context where countries may continue to be formally independent but are at the same time deeply integrated in a cross-border community. Segregated modern states are transforming into integrated postmodern states.[3] Table 1.1 outlines the ideal types of modern and postmodern state.

That community cannot begin to be grasped with a notion of anarchy, because the community is densely framed by legitimate international and supranational authority. In such a framework, the use of organized violence to solve conflicts is no longer an option. The countries have become a security community (Deutsch et al. 1957; Adler and Barnett 1998) where states no longer resort to force as a means of conflict resolution. The adoption of nonviolent conflict resolution means that the security dilemma is eliminated; states do not fear each other in the classical sense that they fear attack, and war between them is not a possibility. In other words, the liberal view that the security dilemma can be transcended has been validated when it comes to the relations between the consolidated liberal democracies that are depicted as postmodern states in table 1.1.

The idea of a security community is relevant not merely for the EU. It is true that in the development of supranational authority the EU stands out,

Table 1.1   The modern and the postmodern state

	THE MODERN STATE	THE POSTMODERN STATE
Government	A centralized system of democratic rule, based on a set of administrative, policing and military organizations, sanctioned by a legal order, claiming a monopoly of the legitimate use of force, all within a defined territory	Multilevel governance in several interlocked arenas overlapping each other. Governance in the context of supranational, international, transgovernmental, and transnational relations
Nationhood	A people within a territory making up a community of citizens (with political, social, and economic rights) and a community of sentiment based on linguistic, cultural, and historical bonds	Supranational elements in nationhood, with respect to both the community of citizens and the community of sentiment. Collective loyalties increasingly projected away from the state
Economy	A segregated national economy, self-sustained in the sense that it comprises the main sectors needed for its reproduction. The major part of economic activity takes place at home	"Deep integration": a major part of economic activity is embedded in cross-border networks. The "national" economy is much less self-sustained than it used to be

3. See Sørensen (2001). The term was used by Robert Cooper in a 1996 article, and therefore many attribute it to him; I did, however, suggest the term in a book in 1995, edited with Hans Henrik Holm (Holm and Sørensen 1995: 204); but maybe Christopher Coker (1992) or Stephen Toulmin (1990) came first.

but the general level of integration is also high across the Atlantic;[4] in the triad relation between Europe, North America, and Japan (East Asia); and even in the OECD area.

These changes have been accompanied by increasing respect for the "territorial integrity norm," that is, "the proscription that force should not be used to alter interstate boundaries" (Zacher 2001: 215). According to Mark Zacher's detailed analysis, that norm emerged in the context of the League of Nations after World War I, it was generally accepted as an element in the UN Charter in 1945, and it has been strengthened since the mid-1970s. From 1976 to the present, "no major cases of successful territorial aggrandizement have occurred" (237). One might argue that a future independent Kosovo will be a partial exception here, but still, the general respect for territorial integrity has increased.

These normative and substantial developments have all but eradicated interstate war.[5] Few such wars have taken place since the end of World War II, fewer still since the end of the Cold War (Harbom and Wallensteen 2009).

Because of these developments, a back-to-basics world order centered on intensified balance-of-power competition is not emerging. Confrontational and belligerent power balancing remains a significant feature in some regions, but the retreat of the security dilemma means that power balancing is muted and constrained in major areas of international relations. My argument is not that the security dilemma has been completely eliminated but that the realist view posing the security dilemma as inescapable must be rejected (Sørensen 2007). Balance-of-power competition is not the core feature of the post–Cold War world order. At the same time, an important aspect of changes in the constellation of international power has gone relatively unnoticed: changes in power relations affect the policies of liberal states in the sense that an improved standing for liberal states tends to push their policies in new, more aggressive directions, as will be discussed in detail in the following chapters.

Weak Statehood and "Coming Anarchy" as the Core of World Order

Are major parts of the world descending into chaos and anarchy, with West Africa with its tyranny, lawlessness, crime, disease, environmental stress, and

---

4. A transatlantic security community is entirely compatible with a future stronger position of the EU vis-à-vis the United States, as predicted in Kupchan (2002).

5. Defined as armed conflict between governments in which at least one thousand people are killed, or killed yearly as a direct (or fairly direct) consequence of the fighting.

demographic pressures leading the way? According to Robert Kaplan (1994) the answer is affirmative, and for that reason the most important feature of the new world (dis-)order is that of "coming anarchy."

Kaplan's (1994) primary claim is that environmental problems are a key factor in the creation of disorder. Riots and other violent upheavals are not mainly due to ethnic and religious conflict but are ultimately caused by environmental problems such as "deforestation and soil erosion, water depletion, air pollution, and possibly, rising sea levels." Such factors are making "more and more places like Nigeria, India, and Brazil, ungovernable" (81). Kaplan extensively quotes Thomas Homer-Dixon's work (1991) on this point.

Kaplan and Homer-Dixon include demographic factors in the analysis. The problem of surging populations is acute because "95 percent of the population increase will be in the poorest regions of the world" (Kaplan 1994: 82). The worst environmental degradation tends to be found where the population increase is highest; such places include the West African coast, the Middle East, the Indian subcontinent, China, and Central America.

Environmental and demographic factors are surely important elements in many current violent conflicts. But such elements are rarely, if ever, direct or even primary causes of conflict. They always emerge as serious problems in a context where social factors such as weak political systems, ineffective institutions, and ethnopolitical tension between groups in the population are of great importance. A recent comprehensive analysis of what Kaplan would call "coming anarchy," that is, extensive violent conflict in weak states, concludes that this type of conflict is due to "a complex interplay of failing state structures, a set of material grievances, hostile social identities, and political entrepreneurs who are willing and able to mobilize groups" (Arnson and Zartman 2005: 262–70). Outside of such an enabling sociopolitical context, environmental and population problems do not automatically trigger or determine the emergence of violent conflict.

It follows that countries with a relatively high degree of political and social order would be much less prone to coming anarchy than indicated by Kaplan's and Homer-Dixon's claims. It does not appear likely, for example, that India will fall apart, which is what their analysis predicts. India has had a surprisingly stable political system for several decades; it is also substantially democratic as explained by Atul Kohli in the study *The Success of India's Democracy* (2001). Nor is it convincing to declare that China will fall apart because it is subject to "a crime surge like the one in Africa and to growing regional disparities and conflicts in a land with a strong tradition of warlordism and of central government—again as in Africa" (Kaplan 1994: 9). Economic growth in China has helped create severe environmental problems (Wen 2005), but unparalleled growth has also lifted large numbers out of poverty, a situation entirely different from the one in most African countries.

Coming anarchy is therefore not the core feature of the post–Cold War world order. The problem of violent, domestic conflict is not spreading like a prairie fire because of environmental and demographic factors. The problem is rather connected to the sociopolitical factors stemming from weak statehood.

Weak states are not a new feature of the post–Cold War world; they emerged in the context of decolonization after World War II, when international society decided that colonialism was no longer acceptable. The newly independent states—most of them in sub-Saharan Africa—failed to modernize and develop. The colonial past had not created a good starting point, but the elites that came to power after independence were no great help either: their way of ruling exacerbated state weakness.

Weak states have grave problems in three areas (Weinstein et al. 2004: 14–15):

- There is a *security gap:* These states are unable/unwilling to maintain basic order (protection of citizens) within their territory.
- There is a *capacity gap:* These states are unable/unwilling to provide other basic social values, such as welfare, liberty, and the rule of law.
- There is a *legitimacy gap:* These states offer little or nothing and get no support in return.

In sum, the existence of weak statehood is a core characteristic of the present world order, but this is no confirmation of Kaplan's analysis. Weak states emerged for reasons different from the ones given by Kaplan: they provide no indication that consolidated states such as India, China, and Brazil are on the way to breaking down, and they are not a post–Cold War phenomenon. Weak statehood was a significant, but much less noticed, problem during the Cold War. Weak states are a serious problem, but they do not replace the Cold War as a threat to the international system, nor are they an indicator of forthcoming global anarchy. Weak states loom extraordinarily large on the international agenda for two reasons: First, consolidated, liberal states have decided that widespread human suffering must be addressed. Second, liberal states are comprehensively unable to follow through on that view in a consistent manner. These aspects, which will be further discussed later, are absent from Kaplan's analysis.

The Threat from International Terrorism as the Principal Feature of World Order

Many people remember where they were and what they did on September 11, 2001. It was no ordinary day because of the attacks by international terrorists in New York and Washington. Scholars have suggested that "for years to come, if not decades, the 'war on terrorism' will be the defining paradigm in the struggle for global order" (Booth and Dunne 2002: ix). A number of influential politicians appear to support that claim. The George W. Bush administration defined the global war on terrorism as the "Long War" and explicitly compared it to the Cold War as "a similar sort of zero-sum, global-scale, generational struggle against anti-liberal ideological extremists who want to rule the world" (Buzan 2006: 1101)

But as mentioned above, there is an element of self-fulfilling prophecy in descriptions of world order: policies undertaken help confirm the underlying image of the world that led to those policies. The question, then, is whether this belief by some leading Western policymakers can be shown to have a substantial basis or whether it is a largely misleading image of world order. A few of the arguments in favor of considering terrorism a new, grave threat can be listed: a significant proportion of Muslims living in the Western world are not well integrated, and that makes them potential recruits for terrorist activity; Western societies are increasingly complex and therefore vulnerable entities; the wars in Iraq and Afghanistan and the conflict in the Middle East generate a blowback effect, drawing more people into terrorist activity; and the access to WMD (weapons of mass destruction) for terrorist purposes is easier today than earlier.

The reality of the threat from international terrorism hinges on the probability that terrorists will be able to acquire WMD and put them to use in terrorist attacks. Graham Allison suggested in 2004 that if new measures were not taken, a nuclear terrorist attack was likely to occur within the next decade. But there is no broad agreement about the imminence of such an attack. In a report to the U.S. Congress in 2002, Steve Bowman found that WMD "remain significantly harder to produce or obtain than commonly depicted in the press," and even were terrorists to get hold of an assembled nuclear weapon, "the built-in safeguards and self-destruction mechanisms would pose a serious challenge to detonating the weapon. In addition, the size of most nuclear weapons makes them rather hard to transport, especially clandestinely."

Another extraordinary feature of the al Qaeda attacks is the fact that they were acts of international terrorism. A very large number of terrorist groups have existed and continue to exist, but their ambitions remain primarily national, not international. That is to say, only very few groups move to become international terrorists, "attacking groups and states abroad whom they identify as allies of their local enemy" (Mann 2003: 160).

The threat from international terrorism has probably also risen to prominence because of the absence among liberal states of a serious classical security dilemma as discussed earlier. With old threats receding, new threats stand in sharper relief. At the same time, highly advanced societies are vulnerable in several ways and not easy to protect. Already in 1986, Ulrich Beck pointed out the significant extent to which such societies were organized around the management of risk. September 11 was a shock not least because the attacks could be executed with such relative ease, with plastic knives and a few hours of flying practice.

In sum, the threat from international terror is not new and is not likely to disappear sometime soon, because the complex set of factors that help produce this kind of terrorism will remain in place. In addition to the factors mentioned above, they include traditional Muslim elites in Saudi Arabia and elsewhere unable to accommodate processes of modernization and Westernization, weak states such as Afghanistan and Iraq, and socioeconomic inequalities pushed by uneven globalization. There is no simple relationship between these underlying causes and the emergence of international terrorism; they are structural conditions rather than immediate triggers of the terrorist actions.

But just like terrorism itself, these factors were in place well before September 11. A statement by the Clinton administration from September 1996 confirms this when it identifies the "greatest threats to our freedom and security" in the twenty-first century as "rogue states, terrorism, international crime, drug trafficking and the spread of weapons of mass destruction" (quoted from Buzan 2006: 1104). Terrorism can be defined as "premeditated, politically motivated violence perpetrated against innocents" (NSS 2002: chap. 3). In general, the scale of terrorist operations makes them more like crime than like organized warfare, and just as crime has existed in most or all types of societies, terrorism "has been around forever and will presumably continue to exist" (Mueller 2004: 199). At the same time, there can be organized crime and there can be organized terrorism. The al Qaeda network is a case in point, and the September 11 attack was highly unusual in its scale and intensity. During the entire twentieth century, "fewer than twenty terrorist attacks managed to kill as many as 100 people, and none caused more than 400 deaths" (Mueller 2004: 110). John Mueller (2006) has calculated the present risk for an American to become a victim of international terror;

he puts it at 1 in 80,000. This is based on the experience with international terrorism so far; precise future predictions are of course not easy to make. It would appear that recent international terrorism is specifically connected to a radical, fundamentalist version of Islam that is not representative of Islam as such (H. Müller 2003). Other cultural-religious belief systems (e.g., Confucianism, Hinduism, Buddhism, and Christianity) do not exhibit a similar kind of embittered anti-Westernism.

Although September 11 was an extraordinary event, what was novel for world order was rather the combination of such events with the forceful response pursued by some liberal states in the "global war on terror." In contrast to realism, liberalism is normally presented as an optimistic view of international relations because consolidated liberal democracies are at peace and cooperate intensely through international institutions. For such reasons Robert Keohane and Joseph Nye (1977) famously declared that the age of liberal interdependence would be accompanied by a significantly "declining use of force in international affairs" (24–26). The war on terror reveals a much more assertive side of liberalism: the leading liberal democracy went into this war "to save civilization itself. We did not seek it, but we must fight it and we will prevail" (G. W. Bush 2001, quoted from Kennedy-Pipe and Rengger 2006: 544). The U.S. National Security Strategy of 2002 vows to "defend liberty and justice because these principles are right and true for all people everywhere" (NSS 2002), and the same document declares that unilateral and preemptive action may be needed in the war on terror. At the same time, decidedly unliberal measures of surveillance and control have been taken in the domestic realm in the name of security against terrorist threat (Chalk 1998).

In sum, the threat from international terrorism is serious, but it is not new, and it cannot compare to the Cold War. The terrorist threat has helped bring forward an assertive, unilateralist side of liberalism that seriously calls into question what kind of world order liberal progress can and will bring. This aspect will be analyzed in detail in coming chapters.

The "Clash of Civilizations" as the Defining Feature of World Order

The analysis by Samuel Huntington first set forth in an article in *Foreign Affairs* (1993) and then in book form (1996) received wide attention from early on, and September 11, 2001, was seen by many as a confirmation of his prediction of intercultural conflict. Huntington's argument is as follows:

The fundamental source of conflict... will not be primarily ideological or primarily economic. The great divisions among humankind and the dominating source of conflict will be cultural. Nation states will remain the most powerful actors in world affairs, but the principal conflicts of global politics will occur between nations and groups of different civilizations. The clash of civilizations will dominate global politics. The fault lines between civilizations will be the battle lines of the future. (Huntington 1993: 24)

A civilization is considered "the broadest cultural entity." Huntington identifies "seven or eight" major civilizations. These are core entities in the post–Cold War world order. "The most important countries in the world come overwhelmingly from different civilizations. The local conflicts most likely to escalate into broader wars are those between groups and states from different civilizations.... The key issues on the international agenda involve differences among civilizations" (Huntington 1996: 29).

Is it possible to pick out a common cultural pattern across a wide range of societies and thus identify "civilizations"? Huntington is himself in doubt as to whether there is an African civilization, perhaps because he considers religion a central defining characteristic of civilizations and there is not a religion shared by all Africans. At the same time, he sees Confucianism as lying at the heart of the Sinic civilization, and that is not a religion in the ordinary meaning of the term. So one major objection to the analysis is that the complex patterns of cultures, religions, and civilizations are not spelled out with great clarity, and if they were, it would not be possible to summarize those patterns in terms of general civilizational identities. Such identities are much more diverse, and religion is not necessarily their primary core, whether in Europe, Africa, or China. Paul Berman (2003) argues that cultural boundaries are not sufficiently distinct to permit the designation of civilizations; he therefore rejects the notion that there is an Islamic civilization or a Western civilization.

Huntington identifies these civilizations at the macro level across large periods of time. But in order to do that, it is necessary to ascribe primordial qualities to cultural identifications. That is to say, what it means to be Orthodox, Islamic, Hindu, Japanese, or Western is highly consistent over time; empires may "rise and fall, governments come and go, civilizations remain" (Huntington 1996: 43). Such a claim of consistency does not fit the historical pattern; the exact qualities connected with cultural-religious-civilizational labels are dynamic and not static (Katzenstein 2009). They have developed and changed dramatically over time; cultural identities are always contested. What it means to be German, European, and eventually Western today is not the same as it was several decades ago. In order to set civilizations in opposition to each other, we must be able to attribute certain consistent qualities to them, and that is not possible because there is too much diversity and dynamic change within civilizations (Senghaas 1998).

These objections call into question the claim made by Huntington (1993) that "conflict between groups in different civilizations will be more frequent, more sustained and more violent than conflicts between groups in the same civilization" (48). A systematic empirical analysis of militarized interstate disputes indicates that "pairs of states split across civilizational boundaries are no more likely to become engaged in disputes than are other states *ceteris paribus.* . . . Contrary to the thesis that the clash of civilizations will replace the Cold War rivalries as the greatest source of conflict, militarized interstate disputes across civilizational boundaries became less common, not more so, as the Cold War waned" (Russett et al. 2000: 583).

Even if the clash of civilizations can be called off as the defining feature of post–Cold War world order, there remain valid insights in the analysis. Huntington (2007) would appear to be right in claiming that "in the coming decades, questions of identity, meaning cultural heritage, language and religion, will play a central role in politics." The broader identity issue was also raised by Benjamin Barber (1995); he used the label "jihad" but extended it to include all kinds of ethnic, religious, and tribal conflict.

The relevance of the identity issue has been demonstrated in a number of analyses (Gurr and Harff 2003), but the primary focus here will not be on various conflicts around the world that involve identity. With the victory of liberalism in the Cold War ideological struggle, the question of identity is increasingly directed at liberals.[6] Liberal democracy has progressed, a liberal market economy is globally dominant, international institutions based on liberal principles have proliferated, and these institutions have increasingly committed themselves to liberal principles, such as those expressed in the UN General Assembly's Millennium Declaration in September 2000 (United Nations 2000). At the same time, liberal progress is not secure, and the commitment to liberal values is frequently thin and superficial.

In sum, a number of conflicts in the world are related to identity issues even if they do not amount to a clash of civilizations. With no serious

---

6. This is, in part at least, in disagreement with Huntington (1996), who believes that "the power of the West relative to that of other civilizations will continue to decline" (82).

ideological rival in sight, the identity question is now posed to liberals with increased urgency: what is the real content of a liberal order and what kind of behavior can the rest of the world expect from liberals? The crucial identity issue at the moment emerges from this question, and the substance of any liberal order will depend on the answers given from liberal states, groups, and individuals.

Tensions in Liberalism as the Core Challenge to World Order

It may sound esoteric to claim that a core issue of the present world order is tensions in liberalism rather than the more colorful clashes and conflicts reviewed above. Let me therefore briefly indicate how the label "tensions in liberalism" ties together a series of the most pertinent current world order issues.

War and peace are the traditional focal point of world order. That is why realists focus on the balance of power emerging from the security dilemma. The maximum security, or order, one can hope for is a stable distribution (or balance) of power (Waltz 1979, 2002). It was argued above that the security dilemma has been significantly mitigated, in some places even transcended; therefore, a world order focused on the balance of power is not emerging. What then determines whether there will be war or peace among major states? The answer hinges primarily on what leading liberal states will do. Will they seek a rule-based, institutionalized, and cooperative order where the issue of war or peace is subject to common rules of international society? Or will they reserve for themselves the right to undertake preemptive or preventive strikes against perceived grave enemies? The issue of war and peace is increasingly connected to what liberal states choose to do; the advent of international terrorism has served to emphasize the tension between the cooperative and the assertive side of liberalism.

Does the threat from international terrorism warrant a global war on terror, or should the appropriate response rather be the creation of a special transnational network aiming at tracking down the perpetrators, their sources of finance, their training camps, and their support systems in different countries? Many liberals advocate a "network response" (Nye 2003: 65). In the United States, the "war on terror" view dominated the tenure of the George W. Bush administrations; in Europe, there has been more solid backing for the network response. Again, world order will be strongly influenced by what liberal states choose to do.

Comprehensive intervention by international society in order to address human suffering in weak states has become a real possibility after the end of the Cold War. Again, that returns us to leading liberal states. They are the ones who need to make the decisions about whether to intervene or not; nonliberal states do not take the lead. And when they do act, liberal states are compelled to evaluate how much outsiders really can do to establish order and safety, to promote democracy, and even to further development in the larger sense. Some liberals are highly optimistic in this regard; others are extremely skeptical. Both sides make strong arguments, so this tension in liberalism will not easily go away.

Finally, although, as stated above, identity questions are increasingly directed at liberals, liberals are not sure of the appropriate answers. For example, Tony Blair (2007) recently argued in favor of the universal validity of core liberal values and the strong need to promote those values all over the world. Samuel Huntington (1996: 310), by contrast, claims that Western belief in the universality of liberal values is "false, immoral and dangerous," and he advises Western countries to stay out of the affairs of other civilizations. These are, to put it mildly, extremely conflicting ideas about what it means to be liberal and what a liberal world order should look like.

In sum, the tensions in liberalism make up a core issue in the present world order. This book is about those tensions and what they portend for the emerging world order. My theoretical stance is that of a skeptical liberal: the progress in world politics that liberals talk about is in principle possible, but by no means assured or guaranteed. Liberal theory and liberal politics contain tensions and problems that have not been sufficiently recognized. My ambition is to analyze and evaluate these tensions and problems in order to consider the implications for liberal world order.

Who are the Liberals?

There are several debates about what it means to be liberal. In domestic politics in the United States, liberals are sometimes characterized as soft (bleeding-heart liberals) and ready to spend public funds (tax-and-spend liberals);[7] this is a rather narrow idea of what "liberal" means, unsuited for present purposes. In international relations research, the formula "U.S. power plus international cooperation" (Kupchan and Trubowitz 2007: 7) was recently presented as defining liberal internationalism. Such a concept

---

7. John F. Kennedy (1960) famously contested the claims of his opponents that "liberal" meant "someone who is soft in his policies abroad, who is against local government, and who is unconcerned with the taxpayer's dollar."

of liberal internationalism may be useful, but it is also too narrow for the purpose here. In the present context, "liberal" refers to the governments of consolidated liberal democracies (especially the leading liberal states) who are compelled to face the dilemmas involved in the construction of a sustainable liberal order. It should be noted that my analysis classifies the so-called neoconservative policies of the George W. Bush administration as one version of a "Liberalism of Imposition" order. John Ikenberry ascribed to this administration an extremist version of liberal internationalism: "They do not have the commitment to multilateralism and the norms of democratic community, but their ideas are nonetheless an outgrowth of liberal internationalism" (Ikenberry 2005: 14).[8]

The assumption is that all governments in consolidated liberal democracies (the OECD-world) are guided in their foreign policy behavior by what could be called a liberal impulse: they would like to support and promote liberty worldwide. This liberal impulse, however, is always conditioned by domestic and international constraints: what policies are possible at any point in time, given the perceived national interests on the one hand and, on the other hand, the situation in the international system (the balance of power, the interests pursued by other states in the system).

For example, Woodrow Wilson's Fourteen Points was the first comprehensive program for a liberal world order, as will be further discussed in chapter 2. In practice, the program was predicated on successful transitions to democracy in a large number of countries. Those transitions failed to take place, and the program faltered. At the end of World War II, conditions for a liberal order improved. It fell upon President Truman to concretely shape the vision set forth by Franklin D. Roosevelt in 1941; Roosevelt looked forward to a world "founded upon four essential human freedoms. The first is freedom of speech and expression—everywhere in the world. The second is freedom of every person to worship God in his own way—everywhere in the world. The third is freedom from want, which, translated into world

---

8. Condoleezza Rice (2005) reaffirmed the connection between interventionist policies and democratic ideals in 2005: "Since its creation more than 350 years ago, the modern state system has rested on the concept of sovereignty. It was always assumed that every state could control and direct the threats emerging from its territory. It was also assumed that weak and poorly governed states were merely a burden to their people, or at most, an international humanitarian concern but never a true security threat. Today, however, these old assumptions no longer hold. Technology is collapsing the distance that once clearly separated right here from over there. And the greatest threats now emerge more within states than between them. The fundamental character of regimes now matters more than the international distribution of power. In this world it is impossible to draw neat, clear lines between our security interests, our development efforts and our democratic ideals."

terms, means economic understandings which will secure to every nation a healthy peacetime life for its inhabitants—everywhere in the world. The fourth is freedom from fear, which, translated into world terms, means a world-wide reduction of armaments...anywhere in the world" (Roosevelt 1941). The actual construction of the postwar order did not fully meet these requirements. Most important, liberal goals could not be pursued globally— "everywhere in the world."

The containment order shaping relations with the Soviet Union was based on a balance of power and nuclear deterrence. At the same time, the creation of the United Nations system put in place an institutional framework within which the political and ideological competition between East and West could play out. This framework also made integration of ex-colonies into international society possible. The full ambitions of liberal order were realized only in the West-West relations among liberal democracies. That order comprised an economic order aimed at open markets, avoiding the protectionism of the 1930s, and a defense order that contained wide-ranging security cooperation across the Atlantic. Both of these elements required the construction of common institutions—the Bretton Woods organizations and NATO—that took on a comprehensive set of responsibilities. In addition, measures were taken to ensure support for liberal political and economic values in Japan and Germany. Part of these efforts included new initiatives aimed at close European cooperation.

This liberal democratic order has not gone away with the end of the Cold War (Ikenberry 1996), but it faces new challenges, partly as a result of its success. Liberal democracy and capitalism are in demand, even if capitalism is globally more popular than democracy, but weak states, international terrorism, environmental challenges, and a host of other problems need to be confronted. In this situation, liberal democratic governments must ask themselves how to respond to these challenges. I have argued that the major contending positions in this debate are the Liberalism of Restraint and the Liberalism of Imposition; a number of combinations or intermediate positions are also possible. When governments of liberal democracies suggest various policies in the context of the present order, they are simultaneously suggesting ways of further developing this liberal order.

My argument is that because of the tensions in liberalism, the construction of a stable and sustainable liberal order is exceedingly difficult, perhaps even impossible. Depending on the circumstances, liberal democracies lean toward either too much Imposition, which is not a stable basis for liberal world order, or too much Restraint, which is not a secure foundation either. Since there are no easy compromises between these extremes, the construction of a stable liberal world order under present conditions is a much more difficult project than assumed by many observers.

In sum, the governments of liberal democracies currently pursue some version of liberal order building even if these governments are not always connected with the label "liberal." Therefore, they face all the liberal dilemmas that are the subject of this book. The discussion in subsequent chapters will thus focus on the ways in which leading governments of liberal democracies have chosen to respond to those dilemmas. That will establish the basis for evaluating the prospects for a stable and sustainable liberal order.

CHAPTER 2

Tensions in Liberalism

Universal Values for All or a Pluralist World?

It is a core argument of this book that the liberal values that make up the foundation for a liberal world order are fraught with tensions and possible contradictions. The liberal difficulties are connected to the very core of the liberal creed: the complex entity of liberty. This chapter will demonstrate how the concept of liberty can be interpreted in very different ways. It also illuminates liberal tensions in the international sphere and the diverging opinions among liberal states about the best ways of promoting freedom.

World order was defined earlier as a governing arrangement among states. A liberal world order is an order permeated by liberal values, institutions, and practices, but what does that mean exactly? Even if liberals do not fully agree on the answer, there has been a solid element of continuity in the liberal conception of world order. Woodrow Wilson's program from 1918 and the doctrines set forth by the Liberal International in 1997 are very similar, and they correspond well with the principles formulated by the liberal theoretical and philosophical tradition. But in practice, there has also been change: the existing liberal world order has developed over time, and there is much less emphasis on sovereignty and nonintervention than was the case earlier (Ikenberry 2009). These developments will be briefly reviewed in what follows. First, however, liberal theory on world order must be clarified.

Liberal Theory and World Order

Liberals begin with the individual. Each individual is entitled to liberty; he or she has the right to freedom. In John Locke's (1632–1704) words, "*Reason*... tells us that men, being once born, have a right to their preservation, and consequently to Meat and Drink, and such other things as Nature affords for their subsistence"[1] (Locke 1965: 327). Every person therefore has a right to life and to the things necessary to sustain life; this is what Locke calls property. Every man has "*Property* in his own *Person*" (328). It logically follows that human beings have the right to property in the fruits of their own labor: "The *Labour* of his Body, and the *Work* of his Hands... are properly his. Whatsoever then he removes out of the State that Nature hath provided, and left it in, he hath mixed his *Labour* with, and joined to it something that is his own, and thereby makes it his *Property*" (329).

The overriding objective of creating a state—"Men's uniting into Commonwealths"—is the preservation of people's "Lives, Liberties, and Estates" (Locke 1965: 395). In contrast to realists, who see the state first and foremost as a concentration and instrument of power, a *Machtstaat,* liberals see the state as a constitutional entity, a *Rechtsstaat,* which establishes and enforces the rule of law that respects the rights of citizens to life, liberty, and property. The state needs power to take on the task of protecting life, liberty, and property. But state power must also be limited because too powerful rulers may abuse their power in ways that can harm the people. Periodical elections and separation of powers between the executive and the legislature are ways of limiting government. State power ultimately derives from the people, not from some higher might; the principle of popular sovereignty lets final authority rest with the people.

These few remarks already indicate how the liberal tradition takes a different path than realism in thinking about human beings and states. A brief comparison with the realist view will be instructive. First, realists tend to see individuals as self-seeking egoists in a state of permanent conflict with each other. According to Hobbes (1946), for example, in the state of nature, where such impulses are given a free rein, life is therefore "solitary, poor, nasty, brutish, and short" (Hobbes 1946: 82). Liberals take a more benign view of human nature. Individuals are to some degree self-interested and competitive, but they also share many interests, and the power of human reason stimulates human beings to engage in collaborative and cooperative social action.

---

1. Throughout the book, italics in quotes are in the original unless otherwise noted.

Second, the state of nature is not the state of war depicted by Hobbes. For Locke (1965), the state of nature is a condition of no government, but there is a "plain *difference between the State of Nature and the State of War*" (321). The state of nature is not lawless, because men are bound by natural law; human reason leads them to discover their obligation to respect life, liberty, and property (Nelson 1982: 165; Doyle 1997: 217).

Third, individuals are not driven by their passions to hand over power to an all-mighty sovereign; in contrast to what Hobbes claims, they are not "civilized by the fear of death" (Oakeshott 1975: 36). Locke instead depicts the state of nature as conflict-prone because laws may be poorly known and badly enforced. Therefore, men agree to enter the state of civil society, the commonwealth, but they do so knowing that bad government can be worse than the state of nature. Hence the demand that government must be constitutionally limited and democratic.

On the realist view, the pressure to get out of the state of nature leads to the creation of the (authoritarian and all-powerful) state. The result is that the state of nature is moved to the international level; the anarchy of the state system is a state of war: "In all times, kings and persons of sovereign authority, because of their independency, are in continual jealousies, and in the state and posture of gladiators; having their weapons pointing, and their eyes fixed on one another" (Hobbes 1946: 101). The liberal view is more benign. International anarchy is not a state of war; like the Lockean state of nature, it is a state of peace guided by natural law. Aggressor states may emerge and wars can break out, but that is not the ordinary condition of international anarchy.

It follows that liberals are more optimistic than realists in regard to the prospects for international cooperation and peace. Rational individuals take an interest in cooperation for mutual benefit; constitutional states may pursue narrow national interests, but they are compelled to respect life, liberty, and property. Jeremy Bentham, in *Plan for an Universal and Perpetual Peace* in 1789 (Bentham 1927) developed the idea that international law and international institutions would advance international peace and cooperation. Liberalism is a theory and philosophy of modernization and progress. Liberals believe that social and political institutions can be changed for the better (Gray 1995: xii); they "have a faith in the power of human reason and human action to change [the world] that the inner potential of all human beings can be more fully realized" (Howard 1978: 11).

Liberal theorists thus believe that human reason can triumph over human fear and the lust for power. In contrast to realists, they hold that international politics need not be "the same damned things over and over again";

cooperative anarchies and peaceful "security communities" are a real possibility (Deutsch et al. 1957). But they diverge on the magnitude of the
obstacles on the way to human progress. For some liberals, it is a long-term
process with many setbacks and success is not certain; for others, change
can go very fast.

Drivers and Facilitators of Liberal Progress

Liberals identify a series of different drivers and facilitators of progress.
Progress can come from individuals and groups in civil society, that is, from
below; or it can come from liberal governments, that is, from above. It can
come from primarily political or primarily economic sources, and it can
come from a transformation within states as well as from changing relations
between states. The principal drivers of progress are, first, social and economic relations across borders between individuals and private groups, and,
second, republican rule, that is, governments founded on liberal principles
and institutions. These stimulate international cooperation based on common moral values, and such cooperation is in turn significantly strengthened
by international institutions that incorporate relations based on liberal principles. Among the most important facilitators are technological change and
education. Liberals do not agree fully on the relative importance of all these
elements, but such diversity should not be overstated; for most liberals, each
of these factors constitutes a component in a larger process of modernization
and progress.[2]

Since liberals begin with individuals, it is appropriate to focus on progress from below first. Sociological liberalism (a term coined by Joseph
Nye 1988: 246) focuses on the interactions and communications between
individuals and groups in society. Several liberals support the notion that
relations between people are more cooperative and more supportive of
peace than are relations between national governments. Richard Cobden (1804–65) put the idea as follows: "As little intercourse betwixt the
Governments, as much connection as possible between the nations of the
world" (1903: 16). By "nations" Cobden was referring to societies and their
membership. In the 1950s, Karl Deutsch and his associates further developed the empirical study of transnational relations. Transnational relations

---

2. In addition to the original sources, the overview that follows draws on the excellent summa-
tions in Zacher and Matthew (1995) and Doyle (1997). Some formulations draw on R. Jackson and
Sørensen (2010: chap. 4).

are cross-border relations between individuals, groups, and organizations from civil society (nonstate actors). Deutsch and his associates attempted to measure the extent of communications and transactions between societies. Deutsch argues that a high degree of transnational ties between societies leads to peaceful relations that amount to more than the mere absence of war (Deutsch et al. 1957). It leads to a security community, that is, a state of integration where people have come to agree that their conflicts can be resolved "without resort to large-scale physical force" (5). Such a security community has emerged, argues Deutsch, among the Western countries in the North Atlantic area.

Another sociological liberal, John Burton (1972), suggested a "cobweb model" of transnational relationships. He tried to demonstrate that any nation-state consists of many different groups of people with different types of external ties and interests: religious groups, business groups, and other kinds of civil society groups. Because individuals are members of many different groups, conflict between groups will be muted if not eliminated (Nicholls 1974: 22; Little 1996: 72).

James Rosenau (1990, 1992) argues that new communication and information technologies combined with a much improved level of education and access to foreign travel have made individuals "important variables" (1992: 274) in global politics. Citizens increasingly make up a "multi-centric world...that is composed of diverse 'sovereignty-free' collectivities" (1992: 282). In some respects such a world will be more unstable, because the old order built on state power has broken down, but only rarely will conflicts lead to the use of force, because the numerous new cosmopolitan individuals that are members of many overlapping groups will not easily become enemies divided into antagonistic camps.

Several liberals put particular emphasis on the progressive effects of commerce and other economic activity across borders. Commercial liberalism sees economic intercourse as a basis for prosperity, cooperation, and ultimately for peace. According to Thomas Paine (1737–1809), "if commerce were permitted to act to the universal extent it is capable, it would extirpate the system of war" (1995: chap. 5). For Adam Smith (1976), the pursuit of wealth in the market could produce "a natural progress of things toward improvement" (443). In a nation of manufacturers, war would be very costly, creating a strong incentive to maintain peace. But Smith saw no simple relationship between market economy, free trade, and peace. Progress required industrial societies to be aware of the negative consequences of war, but some groups might continue to perceive violent conflict as beneficial. Norman Angell followed that view in his 1909 book *The Great Illusion*. The illusion

is on the part of many statesmen, who still believe that war serves profit-
able purposes and success in war is beneficial for the winner. Angell argued
that the exact opposite is the case: in modern times, territorial conquest is
extremely expensive and politically divisive because it severely disrupts international commerce.

Joseph Schumpeter further developed the argument that societies founded
on capitalism and liberal institutions would produce international peace and
nonaggressive behavior. The claim is that in a capitalist system citizens have
become "democratized, individualized, and rationalized" (Schumpeter 1955:
68). Rational materialists will reject militarism and aggression; such behavior
relies on atavistic instincts from earlier periods, furthered by traditional military forces and aristocracies. More recent analyses from Richard Rosecrance
(1986, 1999) provide support for this line of thinking. Modernization means
that the character of economic production changes. In an earlier age the
possession of territory and ample natural resources were the key to greatness. In today's world, it is no longer the case; now, a highly qualified labor
force, access to information, and financial capital are the keys to success.
Historically, states sought power by means of military force and territorial
expansion. But for highly industrialized countries economic development
and foreign trade are more adequate and less costly means of achieving
prominence and prosperity.

For a long time the very large countries, most notably the former Soviet
Union and the United States, pursued the traditional military-political
option, thereby burdening themselves with high levels of military expendi-
ture. But this is changing as well. According to Rosecrance, the end of the
Cold War has made the traditional option less urgent and thus less attractive.
Consequently, the "trading-state" option of participation in the international
division of labor is increasingly preferred even by very large states. There
remains a risk, however, that modern states will slide back to the military
option and once again enter into arms races and violent confrontations. But
according to Rosecrance it is not a likely prospect. It is in the less developed
countries that war now occurs, he argues, because at lower levels of economic
development, land and natural resources continue to be the dominant factors
of production.

These ideas about the progressive effects of social and economic interaction
have stimulated a general liberal theory of interdependence that was set forth
by Robert Keohane and Joseph Nye (1977). They argue that post–World
War II "complex interdependence" is qualitatively different from earlier and
simpler kinds of interdependence. Previously, international relations were
directed by state leaders dealing with other state leaders. The use of military

force was always an option in the case of conflict between national leaders. Under conditions of complex interdependence, this is no longer the case, for two reasons. First, relations between states nowadays are not only or even primarily relations between state leaders; there are relations on many different levels via many different actors and branches of government. Second, there is a host of transnational relations between individuals and nongovernmental groups. As a result, international relations are becoming more like domestic politics with different issues generating different coalitions. Welfare issues are increasingly important, and security issues are less important. This implies a far more friendly and cooperative relationship between states.

It will be apparent that even if these various analyses begin from "below" with relations between individuals and private groups, several of them move on to speculate about interstate relations. I return to that relationship in a moment; first, a brief introduction to the view from "above" that progress stems from governments founded on liberal principles and institutions.

How can sovereign states abolish war and promote peace? How can they escape the perils of anarchy and of the darker sides of human nature? This was the subject of Immanuel Kant's famous pamphlet "Perpetual Peace" from 1795. Kant argued that both domestic and international change were necessary. In the domestic realm, government must be based on liberal principles and institutions. What Kant (1992) called a "republican constitution" is based on three principles: "firstly, the principle of *freedom* for all members of a society (as men); secondly, the principle of the *dependence* of everyone upon a single common legislation (as subjects); and thirdly, the principle of *legal equality* for everyone (as citizens)" (99). From the principle of liberal republics, Kant draws implications both for individuals and for the international system. Liberal republics will further the moral progress of individuals: "by providing the framework within which moral progress is possible, republican government is an essential step on the road to perpetual peace" (Hurrell 1990: 196).

In the international system, liberal republics will gradually establish a federation of free states that will make up a pacific union. Democracy encourages peaceful international relations because democratic governments are controlled by their citizens, who practice peaceful conflict resolution among themselves and will not advocate or support war with other democracies. In a pacific union, individuals and states increasingly move toward sharing common moral values: "as culture increases and men gradually come closer together," there emerges "a general agreement on the principles for peace and understanding" (Kant, quoted from Hurrell 1990: n. 87). Peaceful ways of solving domestic conflict are seen as morally superior to violent behavior, and this attitude is transferred to international relations between democracies. Freedom of expression and free communication promote mutual understanding internationally and help to assure that political representatives act in accordance with citizens' views.

Peace between liberal democracies is further strengthened through economic cooperation and interdependence. "For the *spirit of commerce* sooner or later takes hold of every people, and it cannot exist side by side with war.... Thus states find themselves compelled to promote the noble cause of peace, though not exactly from motives of morality" (Kant 1992: 114).[3] In other words, for those involved in international economic cooperation and exchange, pacific union results in mutual and reciprocal gain.

Kant, like other liberals, was critical of the balance of power. He accepted that it could contribute to the creation of some form of international order, but it was also "too fragile an institution on which to base any hopes of perpetual peace" (Hurrell 1990: 189). Nor is existing international law sufficient. The long-term solution is a "general agreement between nations" (Kant 1992: 104). The general notion of far-reaching commitment to cooperation via strong international institutions is a significant element in liberal thought. Woodrow Wilson wanted an organization that could function as an overarching authority to regulate relations between nations, much as the U.S. constitution regulated relations among the states. The League of Nations was supposed to bring about "not a balance of power but a community of power; not organized rivalries but an organized common peace" (McKinlay and Little 1986: 186).

Even if Kant's starting point in "Perpetual Peace" is the call for liberal government, he manages to integrate other major strands of liberal thought in the notion of democratic peace. Republican government implies the moral improvement of individuals, and it implies a comprehensive form of interdependence between liberal states and liberal societies. A moral community established on common moral values emerges, interacting with the "spirit of commerce" that promotes economic cooperation. Furthermore, political liberty at home is significantly stimulated by the overcoming of anarchy in international relations. In that sense, perpetual peace is the "supreme political good" (Kant 1992: 175).

There is no full agreement in the liberal tradition about the appropriate view on the relationship between individuals and states. Some theorize

---

3. The modern interpretation of Kant's writing is in great measure reliant upon two seminal articles by Michael Doyle (1983). They have helped bring about a rich a varied literature on democratic peace. I shall return to some of those contributions later on.

individuals in opposition to states, so that transnational relations between civil society groups stand in opposition or make up an alternative to relations between states. Others think of civil society relations and interstate relations as mutually supportive, so that improved civil society relations help create positive interstate relations. By emphasizing government based on liberal principles, Kant helps solve the apparent disagreement among liberals concerning individuals in civil society and the state. In liberal states, transnational relations and interstate relations are mutually supportive in advancing cooperation and peaceful relations. In the case of nonliberal states, transnational relations between civil societies are progressive, whereas interstate relations are not.[4] Chapter 6 will argue that transgovernmental and transnational relations are an insufficient basis for a liberal world order.

In summary, change for the better is a real possibility for liberals; the state of war is not inescapable but can be replaced by peaceful cooperation. For that to happen, both domestic and international transformation is necessary. In liberal theory, there is no sharp separation between domestic and international. Domestic change toward liberal institutions and a free market economy are crucial elements in international change. And a more liberal international environment will help promote domestic change.

A liberal world order, then, grows from the following sources: First, transnational relations between individuals and private groups. All kinds of communication and exchange are relevant in this regard, but the economic intercourse of commercial relations is especially important. Noneconomic relations help create the integration that Deutsch and Rosenau emphasize; economic relations help create the interdependence that is central for Paine, Angell, and others. This is the "integration-interdependence" element in liberal world order.

Second, liberal world order grows from relations between states with liberal democratic institutions and free market economies. Kant argued that liberal states will embark on a process of establishing a pacific union. Schumpeter contends that a capitalist society promotes a rational materialism that furthers liberal pacifism. This is the "liberal democracy element" in liberal order.

---

4. Rosenau (1990, 1992) is an example of a recent liberal theorist who emphasizes the role of transnational relations in opposition to states. Moravcsik (1997), by contrast, focuses on states and sees the formation and interplay of state preferences as the core element in liberal theory. Keohane is an example of a liberal theorist who moved emphasis over time from transnational relations (Keohane and Nye 1971) to interstate relations (Keohane 1989). See also R. Jackson and Sørensen (2010, chap. 4).

Third, in a pacific union both individuals and liberal states will move toward the establishment of common moral values. The common "principles for peace and understanding" that Kant talked about were recently formulated by the association of liberal parties organized in the Liberal International. The Liberal International issued a manifesto in 1997 that singles out the following "central values of Liberalism": "Freedom, responsibility, tolerance, social justice, and equality of opportunity." This is the "common moral values element" in liberal world order.

Finally, international institutions provide a solid foundation for peaceful cooperation. In Woodrow Wilson's view, they make up the backbone of a collective security system. More recent liberal thought has been less ambitious concerning the role of international institutions, but it has been argued that these institutions significantly reduce the destabilizing effects of anarchy (e.g., Keohane 1989; Keohane et al. 1993).

In addition to these core elements liberals discuss a series of facilitators of liberal order, two of which will be mentioned here. First, technological change advances change in a liberal direction because new technology pushes interaction across borders in major areas. With improvements in means of transportation and communication as well as in possibilities for global organization of complex processes of production and exchange, the prospects for increased scope and depth of transborder relations at all levels improve dramatically. Second, education is also a facilitator of progress to which liberals have attached great importance. The faith in the power of human reason and rationality mentioned earlier gives liberals cause to believe that an educated public will embrace democracy and protect against sentiments of aggressiveness and war. At the same time, the belief in the potential of education has waxed and waned over time. It was strong in the 1920s and weak in the 1930s. With the end of the Cold War the hope for enlightened international understanding has reemerged with new vitality (Holbraad 2003: 42).

The notion of facilitators of liberal progress helps emphasize the relationship between liberal ideas and the general process of societal modernization unleashed by a revolution in science and the introduction of modern, efficient ways of producing goods and mastering nature. Modernization is a process involving progress in most areas of life, and it much enlarges the scope for cooperation across national boundaries. The various elements of liberalism will support each other in a process of liberal advancement; in that sense, the liberal tradition contains a notion of "all good things go together" (cf. Packenham 1973: 123–29), and there is not a relative order of merit between the various drivers and facilitators of liberal progress.

Liberal theory about progress toward liberal world order is complex and rich; it is also imprecise and tends to be overly optimistic. In order to develop this argument, the intricate concept of liberty is an appropriate place to start.

The Liberal Notion of Liberty

Freedom, according to *Encyclopaedia Britannica,* means "the quality or state of being free," which in turn involves "(a) the power to do as one pleases; (b) freedom from physical restraint; (c) freedom from arbitrary or despotic control; (d) the positive enjoyment of various social, political or economic rights and privileges; (e) the power of choice." Personal independence, then, the freedom to do as you please, the freedom of choice, is at the core of liberty; religious, political, and other freedoms flow from it. But how far can individual liberty go? John Stuart Mill emphasized that personal freedom does not mean the freedom to harm others or to put limitations on their freedom. As for religious or political freedom, there would appear to be limitations as well, but the degree of these limitations is a much-contested point among liberals. Personal independence leads to pluralism: for example, every person must have the right, as underlined by Roosevelt in 1941 "to worship God in his own way" (Roosevelt 1941). Such freedom can lead to the embrace of values—Christian, Muslim, Jewish, etc.—which are distinctly nonliberal. Pluralism thus turns against liberalism: since no one can claim that one culture or belief system is inherently better than any other, liberalism is reduced to an ideological position on a par with others, without any claim to universal authority (Crowder 2003: 6).

So on the one hand liberalism makes a universalistic claim that liberty is for all people; on the other hand liberalism's idea of freedom involves an emphasis on pluralism, of respect for the choice between different values as a core element in what liberty is. The Liberal Manifesto of 1997 has the following to say about liberal values:

> Freedom, responsibility, tolerance, social justice and equality of opportunity: these are the central values of Liberalism, and they remain the principles on which an open society must be built. The principles require a careful balance of strong civil societies, democratic government, free markets, and international cooperation. We believe that the conditions of individual liberty include the rule of law, equal access to a full and varied education, freedom of speech, association, and access to information, equal rights and opportunities for women and men, toler-

ance of diversity, social inclusion, the promotion of private enterprise and opportunities for employment. (Liberal International 1997)

The manifesto displays the tension between universalism and pluralism. It supports a set of values that are valid for any open society; at the same time it speaks of a "careful balance" between different principles. It emphasizes "tolerance of diversity," and it respects the rights of national and ethnic minorities. Liberal universalism points to a set of values that are not open to negotiation; liberal pluralism respects the choice between different values as a core element in what liberty is.

How serious is this tension in liberalism? According to John Gray, it is extremely serious. The two faces of liberalism, universal principles and value pluralism, cannot coexist. Accordingly, says Gray (2000), claims of universalism must be rejected and pluralism must rule: "if liberalism has a future, it is giving up the search for a rational consensus on the best way of life" (1). The consequences for liberal internationalism are potentially devastating; when liberalism cannot be "a prescription for a universal regime" (2), the embrace of pluralism would appear to involve the acceptance of the Soviet, Nazi, or any other illiberal regime with any claim to popular legitimacy.

But most liberals, even if they support value pluralism, reject such a perspective. They arrive at a position according to which pluralism and universalism can be combined even if they are not in full agreement about the relative emphasis on each. For Isaiah Berlin (1988), the starting point is pluralism—"that is, the conception that there are many different ends that men may seek and still be fully rational, fully men, capable of understanding each other and sympathizing and deriving light from each other" (14). Communication across cultural divides is possible only because there is a common element of humanity. We can certainly criticize the values of other cultures, even denounce them, "but we cannot pretend not to understand them at all" (14). There are a vast number of different moral principles, but "not infinitely many; they must be within the human horizon. If they are not, then they are outside the human sphere" (15).

Being "within the human horizon" defines something that is common between human beings even if their persuasions differ. Humans are diverse, but it remains meaningful to speak of a universal humanity; according to George Crowder (2003), "there is sufficient universality of human experience to make other cultures comprehensible to us, and through that comprehension to allow us to appreciate their values as genuine values that we might live by ourselves" (10). This ability to the values of others presupposes a "common 'human horizon' or shared field of moral experience.

Our ability to understand other cultures implies a set of universal values"
(10). Pluralism, as it were, is predicated on a universalistic idea: the principle of "tolerant coexistence between differing cultural traditions" (Hardy
2003: 7).

Gray (2000) recognizes the notion of a "common human horizon" but
claims that although this is a "minimal universalism" leading to the rejection of, e.g., Nazi ideas, it does not provide a basis for privileging liberalism
over other ideologies in general. His argument is that there are "minimal
standards of political legitimacy" that must be "applied to all regimes" (106);
they include the "rule of law and the capacity to maintain peace, effective
representative institutions, and a government that is removable by its citizens
without the recourse to violence" (107). These would appear to be liberal
principles (Talisse 2000: 455), but they might not be, so for most liberals
they are not enough. George Crowder (2003), for example, maintains that
the hard choices required by pluralism can be made only on a basis of liberal
virtues, because without the personal autonomy that liberal freedom con-
veys, the hard choices of pluralism are not possible to make: "value pluralism
imposes on us choices that are demanding to a degree such that they can be
made rationally only by autonomous agents" (13). It follows that pluralism
"implies a case not only for liberalism but specifically for that kind of liberalism under which the promotion of personal autonomy is a legitimate goal of
public policy" (13).

In sum, freedom of choice is the core element in the liberal notion of
liberty. Freedom demands pluralism: there are many different values and
different ends; selecting among them in one's own way is what freedom
of choice is all about. Tolerance, empathy, and moderation are core liberal
values in a world that must necessarily adhere to conflicting principles. At
the same time, all people are members of the great community of mankind;
pluralism can exist only if universal liberal principles are respected. In that
sense, liberalism is morally superior to other ideologies; the full expression
of pluralism is possible only within a liberal framework that promotes personal autonomy. This is liberal universalism: the values supporting personal
autonomy must be promoted everywhere or freedom is not possible. In
other words, the liberal understanding of freedom contains a moderate side
where tolerance of diversity, compassion, and understanding of others are
central elements; and it contains an aggressive side, seeking to promote the
appropriate conditions for freedom everywhere. In the absence of those
conditions, people cannot be free; liberalism is morally superior to other
ideologies because only liberalism supplies the appropriate framework for
freedom to bloom.

The tensions in liberalism do not end there. What does it actually mean to promote the appropriate conditions for freedom? What are those conditions? In order to approach this question, it is helpful to introduce the basic distinction between negative and positive liberty suggested by Isaiah Berlin (1969; some of what follows draws on Sørensen 2006b). Freedom, in the classical liberal tradition, is an individual sphere of autonomy, of noninterference by authorities of any kind. The core element is property rights. Liberty is a right that flows from property in one's own person. Property of person and possessions is a crucial condition for liberty and happiness. The critical task of government is to ensure these rights. This autonomy of individuals was defined by Berlin (1969) as "negative liberty": "the area within which a man can act unobstructed by others" (122). Negative liberty ensures self-determination or freedom from outside interference. Classical liberalism thus fundamentally embodies a liberalism of moderation and self-control; "there is a sphere of action which is one's own" (R. Jackson 1993). Interference with that sphere of liberty can be justified only if the purpose is to prevent harm to others.

Modern liberals, however, have pointed out that the unconditional protection of property rights advocated by classical liberals has in fact led to debasement of large sections of the populations. T. H. Green (1941) argued that "a man who possesses nothing but his powers of labour and who has to sell these to a capitalist for bare daily maintenance, might as well, in respect of the ethical purposes which the possession of property should serve, be denied the rights of property altogether" (219). Unrestricted property rights come in the way of competing basic values for liberals, such as social justice and equality of opportunity.

Green's solution to the problem was to claim that the state has the responsibility to provide for a distribution of property that is to the benefit of all citizens. This requires the state to take "positive steps to see that the national wealth does not become concentrated in so few hands that others are deprived of its moral benefits" (Nelson 1982: 84). This is "positive liberty" in Berlin's terms: the liberty of "being one's own master." Positive freedom is possible only when certain conditions are met: one must have a substantial basis for being free; people who are poor, destitute, and insecure cannot be free.

Modern liberalism thus fundamentally expresses a liberalism of intrusion: it requires active intervention by the state to secure the appropriate conditions for real freedom. The degree of required intervention is disputed among liberals. Green (1941) was at pains to emphasize that the state's role remained limited; it should only remove "the obstacles to the realization of the capacity for beneficial exercise of rights" (210). But he offered no clear-cut way of deciding the precise limitations for the state's intervention, and there is no liberal consensus as to how far the state can go.

The tension between active interventionism and holding back can be seen in several different areas. "Free markets," for example, may impede social justice and equality; they may even work against the goal of a "strong civil society" (Scholte 2005). The goals of "economic development worldwide" and "economic sustainability," mentioned in the Millennium Declaration adopted by the UN in 2000, may work against each other. In a large number of areas, liberals are required to strike a balance between different objectives that may compete with each other. Berlin (1988) considered the collisions of values an inescapable part of the human condition. They cannot be made to disappear because "every solution creates a new situation which breeds its own needs and problems, new demands.... We are doomed to choose and every choice may entail an irreparable loss" (15–16). Choice is forced upon us as individuals, but also collectively, as groups, peoples, and states (Beran 2006: 4).

In sum, the promotion of liberty is much more complex than would appear on first impression. This complexity is exacerbated by the fact that liberals cherish both positive and negative liberty. For freedom to bloom there must be room for choice; in order to make such room a sphere of autonomy is needed. That calls for self-determination, the ability to act unimpeded by others. That is the value of negative liberty. However, for freedom to bloom, certain preconditions are also necessary. Oppression, poverty, ignorance, and tyranny stand in the way of liberty. They must be removed in order to create the appropriate conditions for freedom to thrive. Such removal calls for activism, for intervention, for moving in and clearing away the obstacles to freedom. That is the value of positive liberty.

Let me try to summarize the tensions in liberalism discussed here. The first tension discussed was between universalism and pluralism. Universalism points to a set of nonnegotiable liberal principles that are valid for all people and societies; pluralism emphasizes the tolerance of diversity leading to the understanding and even acceptance of different principles, including values that are nonliberal. The second tension flows from the distinction between negative and positive liberty. Negative liberty is the principle of self-determination and freedom from outside interference; positive liberty is about the active creation of the substantial conditions for all people to be free.

Liberals will disagree on the appropriate combination of relative emphasis on these principles. A large number of different combinations are possible,

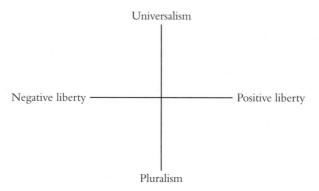

FIGURE 2.1.   Major dimensions of liberalism

as is shown in figure 2.1. As far as practical policy is concerned, however, it will be helpful to identify two major modalities of a liberal posture. One can be called Liberalism of Restraint: it emphasizes tolerance of diversity, moderation, holding back, empathy, nonintervention, and peaceful cooperation. Pluralism rather than universalism will be at the heart of this posture, and negative liberty will be preferred over positive liberty although there can be different priorities in domestic and international politics. The other posture can be called Liberalism of Imposition: it accentuates that liberal principles are morally superior to other principles and universally valid. It supports activism, intervention, and, in the international realm, the change of nonliberal regimes to liberal regimes, not excluding the possible use of force. It stresses universalism over pluralism, but there is not necessarily agreement among impositionists on the relative importance of negative versus positive liberty.

This section has given an overview of the possible tensions to which the pursuit of liberal freedom leads. As we shall see below, the tensions first and foremost concern what liberal states *should* do: what is the best way of promoting liberal principles in the world? But any such choice will also always be related to what liberal states *can* do: what are the advantages and drawbacks of pursuing a policy of Imposition versus a policy of Restraint? Before addressing these questions, however, it will be helpful to provide an overview of the political programs for a liberal world order.

Political Programs for a Liberal World Order

The first comprehensive program to establish a liberal world order was formulated by American president Woodrow Wilson in 1918. The carnage of

World War I had thoroughly discredited the balance of power as a reliable instrument of order creation. Wilson "spoke for internationally minded Americans and for many Europeans who regarded the prewar international society as an anarchy of sovereign states; to rely only on the restraint of statesmen and the balance of power seemed to them a recipe for disaster" (Watson 1992: 283). Wilson's vision of order was based on making the world "safe for democracy." His ideas influenced the Paris Peace Conference in 1919, which followed the end of hostilities.

Wilson's peace program calls for an end to secret diplomacy: agreements must be open to public scrutiny. There must be freedom of navigation on the seas, and barriers to free trade should be removed. Armaments should be reduced to "the lowest point consistent with domestic safety." Colonial and territorial claims must be settled with regard to the principle of self-determination of peoples. Finally, "a general association of nations must be formed under specific covenants for the purpose of affording mutual guarantees of political independence and territorial integrity of great and small nations alike" (Wilson in Vasquez 1996: 40). This latter point is Wilson's call to establish the League of Nations, which was instituted by the Paris Peace Conference.

Four major points in Wilson's program deserve special emphasis because they constitute the central pillars in a liberal conception of world order. First, there is a call for democracy and self-determination. Behind this point is the liberal conviction that democratic governments do not and will not go to war against each other. It was Wilson's hope that the growth of liberal democracy in Europe would put an end to autocratic and warlike leaders and put peaceful governments in their place. Liberal democracy should therefore be strongly encouraged.

The second major point in Wilson's program concerned the creation of an international organization that would put relations between states on a firmer institutional foundation than the realist notions of the Concert of Europe and the balance of power had provided in the past. Instead, international relations would be regulated by a set of common rules of international law. In essence that was Wilson's concept of the League of Nations (Ikenberry 2001: 139).

Third, Wilson emphasized an economic aspect of order; his program calls for "the removal, so far as possible, of all economic barriers and the establishment of an equality of trade conditions among all the nations consenting to the peace and associating themselves for its maintenance" (Wilson in Vasquez 1996: 39). This element connects to the liberal tradition of commercial pacifism expounded by Adam Smith and Joseph Schumpeter. The core claim is that liberal commerce brings peace. For Schumpeter (1955), it was "beyond controversy that where free trade prevails *no* class has an interest in forcible expansion as such" (55).[5] Ludwig von Mises taught that in a world of privatized economic activity and free trade, international peace and prosperity will be created, not by government, but by free men who will "naturally pursue peaceful intercourse through economic and cultural exchange" (quoted from Ebeling 1991).

Fourth, Wilson's whole project is to promote an order based on liberal values, both in the domestic affairs of states and in their international relations. In Wilson's words, "an evident principle runs through the whole program I have outlined. It is the principle of justice to all peoples and nationalities and their right to live on equal terms of liberty and safety with one another, whether they be strong or weak. Unless this principle be made its foundation no part of the structure of international justice can stand" (Wilson in Vasquez 1996: 40).

All major elements in Wilson's vision proved problematic and eventually unrealizable in the post–World War I context. "Self-determination" was supposed to be applied to the whole area between Switzerland and Persia, previously dominated by the Habsburg and Ottoman empires, but there was no clear idea of how that principle should be implemented, so the Western allies eventually ended up supporting the status quo. The League of Nations never got the full support of Germany, Japan, or the Soviet Union, and, most important, the United States never joined the League. Instead of open markets and free trade, economic crisis helped introduce protectionism and self-sufficiency. Finally, the spread of liberal values fell on hard times; instead of democracy, authoritarianism bloomed, not merely in Germany, Italy, and Spain but also in Poland, Hungary, Romania, and Yugoslavia.[6]

So attempts at a liberal world order—always halfhearted anyway—failed to take off during the interwar period. The balance of power failed as well; no one stood up to Germany and Japan before it was too late. World War II, however, created a new context with much better possibilities for a liberal order. With the end of the Cold War, a liberal order with truly global reach became a possibility for the first time in history.

---

5. Doyle (1997: 230–50) and Keohane (1989: 165–94) have fine discussions of commercial liberalism.

6. Wilson was a much more moderate liberal than his ambitious program might suggest. He favored a Liberalism of Restraint, leaving to "indigenous peoples themselves the option of changing their governments as times permitted and conditions allowed" (Skowronek 2006: 398). At home, he defended racial hierarchy and "did nothing to liberate race relations in his time" (398).

1997 Liberal International Manifesto

The Liberal International is the world federation of liberal political parties, founded in 1947. In November 1997, 475 representatives met in Oxford Town Hall to celebrate the fiftieth anniversary of the Liberal International and reconfirm its commitment to liberal values; the 1997 Congress adopted a "Liberal agenda for the 21st century," and the four major points made by Wilson reappear in the manifesto:

- Democracy: "We reaffirm that...liberty and individual responsibility are the foundations of civil society; that the state is only the instrument of the citizens it serves; that any action of the state must respect the principles of democratic accountability...and that a peaceful world can only be built upon respect for these principles and upon cooperation among democracies. We reconfirm that these principles are valid throughout the world."
- International organization: "We believe that close cooperation among democratic societies through global and regional organizations, within the framework of international law, of respect for human rights and of national and ethnic minorities...is the necessary foundation for world peace."
- Free trade and market economy: "We believe that an economy based on free market rules leads to the most efficient distribution of wealth and resources, encourages innovation and promotes flexibility.... We welcome...the consolidation of an open international economy, within an agreed framework of international regulation....Resistance to economic protectionism...remains a key Liberal commitment."
- Liberal values: "Freedom, responsibility, tolerance, social justice and equality of opportunity: these are the central values of Liberalism, and they remain the principles upon which an open society must be built. These principles require a careful balance of strong civil societies, democratic government, free markets, and international cooperation." (All quotes from Liberal International 1997)

In sum, both Wilson in 1918 and the Liberal International in 1997 are convinced of the real possibility for a peaceful, democratic, and prosperous world order based on liberal values. Some contemporary scholars will, like Wilson, emphasize the special importance of liberal democracy and democratization as the core of liberal progress (Doyle 1997). Stanley Hoffmann (1998), by contrast, notes that even with the successful spread of liberal democracy, "we would still be left with a number of major sources of disorder" (219). The Liberal International calls upon both "governments and peoples" to promote changes in a liberal direction (Liberal International 1997). These elements of debate among liberals indicate some of the tensions in the liberal project. Restraint and Imposition in relation to liberal internationalism will be discussed below. First, however, it is relevant to briefly discuss the current status of liberal world order.

Liberal World Order: Progress and Problems

The major elements in a liberal world order can be summarized as follows:

- Democracy: states with liberal democratic institutions are the basis for liberal world order.
- Transnational relations between individuals and private groups: special emphasis on free market economic intercourse and commercial relations.
- International institutions: cooperation via strong international institutions regulated by common rules of international law.
- Common moral values: support for central liberal values, such as freedom, responsibility, tolerance, social justice, and equality of opportunity.

On first impression, there has been substantial progress toward a more liberal world order. Let us briefly consider each of the four dimensions in the list. First, measuring democratic progress is a complicated task because many indicators have to be estimated and weighed together. I shall rely on the annual survey provided by Freedom House, in which democratic countries are rated free, countries with some democratic elements are rated partly free, and nondemocratic countries are rated not free. Democratic progress has been significant. In 1976 there were 42 free countries, composing 26 percent of the world's population. In 2010 there were 89 free countries with 46 percent of the world's population (see table 2.1.). Close to fifty countries made transitions toward democracy between 1976 and 2010. The transitions began in southern Europe (Greece, Spain, and Portugal). The next wave was in Latin America (Argentina, Uruguay, Peru, Ecuador, Bolivia, Brazil, and later Paraguay) and in Central America (Honduras, El Salvador, Nicaragua, Guatemala, and later Mexico). Then came the transitions in Eastern Europe (Poland, Czechoslovakia, Hungary, Romania, Bulgaria, and the former

German Democratic Republic). The most recent wave has been in Africa and in the former Soviet Union. Finally, transitions toward democracy have taken place in Asia over the entire period since the early 1970s (Papua New Guinea, Thailand, Pakistan, Bangladesh, the Philippines, South Korea, Taiwan, Mongolia, and Nepal).

No single factor can account for the significant moves toward democracy in this period. There are complex patterns of internal and external elements, of various conditions that interplay with different groups of actors. Ideally, the movements should be untangled country by country, but that is not necessary here. Michael Mandelbaum (2003) has offered a general explanation for the democratization process in terms of three related causes: "democracy was the political system of the world's most powerful states; the political systems that had opposed liberalism in the modern era were discredited; and the features of social life historically conducive to democratic politics spread" (252).

Transnational relations and the free market economy make up the second major aspect of liberal progress. Processes of modernization have surely led to a dramatic expansion of transnational relations between individuals and private groups, as predicted by liberals. The general connection between a high level of modernization and a high level of interconnectedness is documented by the Globalization Index published annually by *Foreign Policy*. The ten countries that top the list as the world's most integrated for 2007 are Singapore, the Netherlands, Switzerland, Ireland, Denmark, the United States, Canada, Jordan, Estonia, and Sweden. The index measures integration on four dimensions: economic, personal, technological, and political. There are considerable variations, of course. For example, smaller countries tend to be more integrated than larger countries; the United State takes the lead in "technological connectivity" but scores much lower in "economic integration" and "personal contact." In any case, the growth of transnational relations is well documented by recent analyses (e.g., Beisheim et al. 1999; Held et al. 1999).

Table 2.1 Global trends in democratization by number of countries and percent of world population

YEAR UNDER REVIEW	FREE COUNTRIES	PARTLY FREE COUNTRIES	NOT FREE COUNTRIES
1976	42 (26%)	49 (31%)	68 (43%)
1986	57 (34%)	57 (34%)	53 (32%)
1996	79 (41%)	59 (31%)	58 (28%)
2010	89 (46%)	58 (30%)	47 (24%)

Source: Freedom House (2010).

With the end of the Cold War, nearly all countries are capitalist market economies, increasingly integrated in a globalized economic network (Sørensen 2004). In the former Soviet Union and in other planned economies, private economic activity was forbidden by law; the state was in absolute economic control. The emergence of free market economies on a global scale does not mean that the role of the state is terminated. States and markets are tied together; they make up an "integrated ensemble of governance" (Underhill 2000: 13). Any free market depends as much on the development of a permissive regulatory framework as on the behavior of the economic actors proper (i.e., producers, consumers, financiers, etc.).

What have been discredited are two extreme models of political-economic organization. The Soviet model gave full economic power to the state; the system was capable of basic agrarian and industrial reform, and it also mastered a process of extensive industrialization, supplying manufactured goods at a decent level even if there were always quality problems and shortages when it came to consumer goods. But the system was comprehensively unable to sustain an intensive process of economic development with emphasis on innovation and flexible specialization. And it was open to takeover by powerful elite groups who exploited it to their own narrow advantage.

The other discredited matrix is one with very little or no state at all. Very weak states in the least-developed Third World countries are not capable of providing the necessary institutional conditions for a market economy to function properly. One influential analysis (North 1990) set forth four institutional conditions that states need to provide in order to secure an appropriate framework for economic growth and development: (a) secure property rights; (b) an efficient and unbiased juridical system; (c) a clear and transparent regulatory framework; and (d) an institutional framework promoting impersonal forms of exchange and interaction, including rules of contract and regulations of entry/exit for private firms.

These necessary institutional conditions for a market economy are frequently not sufficiently present in the least developed states. One of the most serious problems is the lack of secure property rights. People often cannot document ownership of the house they live in or the land they cultivate. The reason is that the road to legal ownership has been bureaucratized in the extreme, and there are vested bureaucratic and other interests in keeping it that way (Sørensen 2004: 46–58).

In sum, there is almost universal support for a capitalist state-market arrangement based on private property and free market exchange. Only very few countries have not adopted this model. Near universal support for free markets "strengthens the foundation for a liberal world order" (Buzan

2004). (The impact of the recent global financial crisis on this situation will be addressed in chapter 5.)

International institutions make up the third major element in liberal progress. International institutions are sets of rules, formal and informal, that states and other international actors play by (Keohane 1990: 732). Liberals generally favor a rule-based international order with a strong role for international institutions. To what extent has such an order emerged? The leading liberal power after World War II, the United States, took the initiative in creating an institutionalized postwar order. If we focus on institutions formalized in international organizations, the United Nations is supposed to help stop violent conflict between states by allowing wars only in case of self-defense and in case of collective security measures against aggressors. The larger family of UN organizations is supposed to help promote development and prosperity on a worldwide basis.

The emerging Cold War confrontation between East and West got in the way of a comprehensive collective security arrangement. The leading powers used their Security Council veto right to prevent UN measures against their respective allies (Rittberger and Zangl 2003: 54). The larger development goals were promoted in different ways within the respective camps.

In this situation the liberal states gave priority to close institutional cooperation within the liberal camp. NATO was not merely a mutual defense arrangement; it locked the dominant U.S. military power into an institutional arrangement of joint force planning, coordinated military command structures, and a network for taking political and military decisions (Deudney and Ikenberry 1999).[7] The Bretton Woods institutional system created an environment of "embedded liberalism" (Ruggie 1982) where liberal democracies could pursue growth and welfare in the context of comprehensive economic linkages.

The end of the Cold War should, in principle, increase the possibility of stronger and more comprehensive globally and regionally oriented international institutions. This has to some extent already been the case; the UN assumed a much more active role in humanitarian emergencies in the 1990s because intervention was no longer completely blocked by the Security Council. The International Criminal Court (ICC) was created in 1998 in order to address crimes against humanity and genocide.

---

7. For the view that the building of an order among liberal states helped lead to the outbreak of the Cold War, see Latham (1997).

In the economic area, the General Agreement on Tariffs and Trade (GATT) became the World Trade Organization (WTO) in 1995. Trade in services and intellectual property rights was added to the area of regulation, and the organization was given new powers in the area of dispute settlement. In the financial area, the International Monetary Fund (IMF) had been prominent for some time, but the financial crises in Asia and elsewhere in the 1990s gave it a new role as financial crisis manager.

This is cooperation with a global reach. A further strengthening of cooperation confined to liberal states has also taken place. NATO expanded to include a large number of East European countries that had embarked on a transition to liberal democracy. Most of these countries also became members of the European Union. These liberal institutions involve much closer cooperation than, for example, the more comprehensive institution of security and cooperation in Europe (OSCE).

The terrorist attacks of September 2001 surely led the United States away from a policy of strong support for global international institutions, especially in the area of security. But in the areas of economic and social exchange between countries, there are other forces in play that point to a prominent role for international institutions. Processes of globalization and market integration create a need for cross-border coordination, which serves to increase the demand for international institutions. When societies are increasingly interconnected, the mutual requirements for regulation of common problems grow (Zürn 2002). Even if the WTO can be seen as an example of such coordination, it is, again, the liberal states that have developed such cooperation the furthest. The European Union, in particular, has developed into the most ambitious and far-reaching example of regional cooperation. The EU contains a significant element of supranational governance, meaning that EU institutions in some areas have the powers to write the rules for member states. The European Court of Justice, the European Commission, and the Council of Ministers can make decisions going against single members. Rulings by the European Court take priority over rulings by national courts. Member states have bargained with their sovereignty to achieve influence over the domestic affairs of other member countries. In return, they allow these other states to influence the regulation of their own domestic affairs (Sørensen 1999).

In overall terms, the post–World War II period has seen a significant increase in the number of international governmental organizations (IGOs). There were 100 such organizations in 1946; by 1985 there were 378 (Rittberger and Zangl 2003: 86). The number decreased somewhat in the following decades, probably owing to the death of organizations connected to the Eastern bloc. The number of INGOs (international nongovernmental organizations) went from around 800 in 1950 to nearly 6,000 by the turn of the century.

In sum, the liberal states led by the United States did establish an institutionalized order after World War II. In both scope and depth, institutions within the liberal camp—the OECD-world in general and the EU and the transatlantic relations in particular—are the most elaborate and ambitious compared with the universal institutions. Since the end of the Cold War, liberal states have spent relatively more time on the further development of interliberal cooperation—e.g., the expansion of the EU and NATO—than on the further development of universal institutions. Significant parts of the United Nations system, especially the Security Council, are in need of reform because they reflect the world of the late 1940s rather than the world of the twenty-first century.

At the same time, the end of the Cold War has unleashed economic globalization on a truly worldwide scale for the first time. The push of globalization increases the demand for institutional coordination in areas of "low politics" (Zürn et al. 2006). Liberals generally favor an institutionalized international order, but at the present time leading liberal states appear to be highly hesitant supporters of universal institutions, both in the high-politics area of security and the low-politics areas of economic and other exchange. Chapter 6 will discuss this in detail.

Common moral values make up the fourth and final dimension of liberal progress. A liberal order draws strength from states that are based on liberal principles. In the absence of such states, and with many groups contesting liberal values, such an order would be hard to sustain. This then raises the question of the existence of common values and the extent to which such values are being called into question by different groups.

There are various approaches to estimating the existence of universal values (Bok 1995). One is to look at the endorsements of the human rights conventions. They signal a strong support for universal values. In Vienna in 1993, representatives of 171 states adopted the Vienna Declaration and Programme of Action of the World Conference on Human Rights. The Declaration "reaffirms the solemn commitment of all States to fulfill their obligations to promote universal respect for, and observance and protection of, all human rights and fundamental freedoms for all. . . . The universal nature of these rights and freedoms is beyond question" (United Nations 1993). Another relevant example is the Millennium Declaration adopted by more than 150 states at the UN General Assembly in September 2000. It also confirms a great commitment to universal values of freedom, equality, solidarity, and tolerance.

Liberal values have also been strengthened from below, that is, at the societal level. The key claim here is that modernization—the social changes linked to industrialization and economic growth—penetrate many aspects of life. The process involves, for example, higher levels of education, longer life expectancies, urbanization, and specialization. In the long run, "modernization brings democracy" (Inglehart and Welzel 2009: 35), that is, modernization supports the emergence of liberal values in the population. These claims emerge from global surveys of values and attitudes carried out between 1981 and 2007 covering almost 90 per cent of the world's population. The surveys demonstrate that the value systems of people living in high-income countries differ systematically from the value systems of people living in low-income countries. The differences run along two basic dimensions: traditional versus secular-rational values and survival versus self-expression values. The transformation from agrarian to industrial societies marks the shift from traditional to secular values: "Traditional societies emphasize religion, respect for and obedience to authority, and national pride. These characteristics change as societies become more secular and rational" (Inglehart and Welzel 2009: 39). The transformation from survival to self-expression values is linked to the rise of postindustrial societies. Survival values emphasize conformist social norms and physical security. Self-expression values underline tolerance, participation, gender equality, and freedom of expression. The survey thus confirms modernization theory's claim that the dominant values in a given society reflect its level of economic development.

But this brief overview of liberal progress looks almost too good to be true. I shall argue in detail in coming chapters that this is indeed the case. Each of the recorded elements of liberal progress comes with significant drawbacks. Democracy has not taken firm hold in many states, and major nonliberal great powers exist. Weak states are unable to supply the basic institutional conditions for a market economy, and there is no global agreement on the appropriate state-market matrix. Global institutions are relatively weak and in need of reform. The support for common liberal values is shallow and fragile in many places and insecure even where such values have a firmer grip. Rather than an increasingly liberal world, we are facing a more complex order where liberal voices are often not listened to or respected. The analysis of this world begins below, with the introduction of the concepts of Liberalism of Restraint and Liberalism of Imposition, followed by a clarification of the major dilemmas in liberal internationalism.

Restraint and Imposition in Liberal Internationalism

Liberal ideas about the international sphere are less developed than liberal ideas about domestic politics. It is an essential liberal conviction that once states become democratic and are ruled in accordance with liberal principles, international relations between them will more or less automatically be amiable, peaceful, and cooperative. But the happy prospects for liberal relations among democracies leave a major issue uncovered: what about the relationship between liberal and nonliberal states? That was the major issue among classical liberal thinkers; one camp essentially favored restraint, the other imposition.

Immanuel Kant represents a Liberalism of Restraint in the sense that he explicitly endorses a policy of nonintervention. The Fifth Preliminary Article of "Perpetual Peace" says that "no state shall forcibly interfere in the constitution and government of another state" (Kant 1992: 96), a principle that applies "regardless of circumstances." The principle of nonintervention is connected to the core principle of freedom; people cannot decide for themselves how to organize their way of life if they are subjected to outside interference. Kant "made a strong case for respecting the right of non-intervention because it afforded a polity the necessary territorial space and political independence in which free and equal citizens could work out what their way of life would be" (Doyle 1997: 395). A society of states respecting each other's independence and autonomy will be the best way of securing the conditions for progress.

Kant (1992) indicates, however, that intervention can be justified if a state is characterized by domestic chaos and lawlessness: "But it would be a different matter if a state, through internal discord, were to split into two parts. . . . For it could not be reckoned as interference in another state's constitution if an external state were to lend support to one of them, because their condition is one of anarchy" (96). Following on this, some contemporary interpretations of Kant point out that regimes may be so despotic that they deny any rights to the population. For example, governments that commit massacres or genocide "lose their status as moral persons and thus their right of self-determination. The perfect duty of non-intervention does not apply to them" (Cavallar 2001: 243). This qualification raises the further question of how to decide the conditions under which intervention in nonliberal states can be acceptable; it also indicates that there can be vastly different types of regimes in the nonliberal category.

John Stuart Mill argued that nonintervention applies to relations between civilized nations. But not all nations are civilized; there are "culturally inferior peoples," who cannot be subject to the same rules of equal treatment and reciprocity that apply to civilized nations: "In the first place, the rules of ordinary international morality imply reciprocity. But barbarians will not reciprocate. They cannot be depended on for observing any rules. . . . In the next place, nations which are still barbarous have not got beyond the period during which it is likely to be for their benefit that they should be conquered and held in subjection by foreigners" (Mill 1984: 118).

This is a forceful statement of the Liberalism of Imposition. It contains a liberal version of imperialism: civilized people may rule over barbarians because that is the best way to prepare for the graduation toward civilized society. Liberal values can be promoted by illiberal means (Jahn 2005). The Liberalism of Imposition involves an element of knowing what is best for others, of knowing what others *ought* to want. "Once I take this view," warns Isaiah Berlin (1969), "I am in a position to ignore the actual wishes of men or societies, to bully, oppress, torture in the name, and on behalf, of the 'real' selves, in the secure knowledge that whatever is the true goal of man . . . must be identical with his freedom' (132–33).

In sum, classical liberal philosophy covers the entire space between the Liberalism of Restraint and the Liberalism of Imposition. A policy of non-intervention with no exceptions stands against a policy of intervention and rule over "inferior peoples." A variety of contemporary liberal positions can be found between these extremes. Most of them want to allow intervention under certain conditions. Disagreement primarily concerns what those conditions are. Michael Doyle has made an instructive distinction among three major views. "Right-wing cosmopolitan Liberals" want to promote liberal democratic regimes that respect free speech, privacy rights, private property, and freedom from torture. Violation of those rights "should be resisted everywhere and whenever it occurs, provided that we can do so proportionally, without causing more harm than we seek to avoid" (Doyle 1997: 398). "Left-wing cosmopolitan Liberals" include subsistence rights (e.g., food, shelter, clothing) and security rights (freedom from arbitrary killing, torture, and assault) in the list of rights that states have the duty to protect in order to qualify for freedom from intervention. "National Liberals," finally, emphasize the principle of nonintervention but still want to allow intervention under special circumstances. This includes intervention in order to prevent "gross violation of the rights to survival" (Doyle 1997: 401) of a population. But such interventions to mitigate human suffering on a large scale must be a last resort, and the humanitarian motive must not be a mere cloak for national interests.

Applied to the international realm, the Liberalism of Restraint and the Liberalism of Imposition embody different notions of freedom. Georg

Schwarzenberger noted this in his book on the League of Nations; he commented on a remark by one of the delegates at the conference establishing the League. The delegate spoke of admission to the League as being open to "free" states. Schwarzenberger (1936) noted that the word *free* was "somewhat ambiguous, as it does not necessarily refer to the internal conditions of an applicant state, but may be read as synonymous with 'independent' or 'sovereign'" (88).

On this latter view, "freedom" is the autonomy that allows states to conduct their affairs without outside interference. Gerry Simpson (2001) has labeled this view "Charter Liberalism" because its principles "find their highest expression in the UN Charter. The point of this approach is to treat all states equally, to allow them each the same rights afforded to individuals in a liberal society (i.e. domestic jurisdiction, equality, nonintervention) and to, if not celebrate, at least tolerate the diversity produced by these norms. . . . Undemocratic or illiberal states are admitted into international society so that society might be universalized and those states domesticated" (541).

This is not a liberal endorsement of illiberal states; the hope is rather that inclusion of such states in an international community creates the best context for domestic changes in a liberal direction. Furthermore, such changes remain the primary responsibility of insiders, the citizens of the state (Franceschet 2001). Outsiders can help, but they are secondary; if they take over, liberal imperialism threatens, and that is not freedom.

The Liberalism of Imposition adopts a different view; it focuses on the rights of the individual in any state: liberal universalism rather than pluralism. Freedom is freedom for individuals, not for states. This leads to much less tolerance of illiberal states, because of their lack of respect for individual rights. Emphasis is on democracy and the rights of individuals (Simpson 2001: 541). Freedom, then, is individual freedom based on universal liberal rights; sovereignty resides with the people, not with the government; international legitimacy is conditioned on domestic legitimacy. In the absence of the latter, states cannot be fully legitimate members of the international community, and in cases of severe violations of basic human rights, such states are legitimate objects of intervention.

Dilemmas in Liberal Internationalism

How, then, to pursue liberty in the world? Democracy means self-determination, but who are the selves that are going to decide? Every ethnic or religious community cannot qualify for self-determination, as became clear in the troublesome dismantling of empires in Eastern Europe after World War I and in the process of decolonization after World War II. The UN declaration of 1960, which paved the way for colonial independence, talked about the right of "all peoples" to self-determination. But the formulation did not mean that individuals and groups were to decide about which communities they wanted to belong to. Declaration 1514 explicitly declared that "any attempt aimed at the partial or total disruption of the national unity and territorial integrity of a country is incompatible with the purposes and the principles of the Charter of the United Nations" (quoted from R. Jackson 1993: 77). The "nations" that were entitled to self-determination were not nations in any community sense. They were the people living within colonial borders. The "right of peoples" effectively meant the right to independence of existing colonies even if such colonies contained a variety of ethnic groups that were not nations in any meaningful sense of community.

Once the issue of political community or nation is decided, new problems emerge. Some nations may not be particularly democratic; they may support religious or political projects that are distinctly undemocratic, as in the Soviet Union after 1917 or in Germany in the 1930s. For example, Woodrow Wilson welcomed the fall of the czar in 1917, but not the Bolshevik revolution that followed. Wilson indicated that before a government of Russia could be recognized, "we must bind them to a procedure which will lead to the formation of a regular democratic government. If they resist, we can break off relations with them" (quoted from T. Smith 1994: 98). In other words, the people should decide, but within limits that secure democracy and order.

Furthermore, if democracy is self-government, can outsiders come in, take over, and install self-government in a meaningful way? Democracy, in a basic sense, is allowing domestic political processes to operate; outsiders taking over is quite the opposite (Chandler 2006). Even with the best of intentions, there is a risk of paternalistic behavior, of knowing what is best for others and acting on their behalf. Immanuel Kant (1992) thought that paternal government was the "greatest perceivable despotism," because subjects are treated as "immature children who cannot distinguish what is truly useful or harmful to themselves" (71). At the same time, a policy of imposition will most probably mean that some groups turn toward nonliberal religious or ethnic values, as demonstrated by the current situation in Afghanistan and Iraq.

Outsiders promoting democracy face the additional task of defining the exact features of the democracy they want to promote. A stress on the liberal side of liberal democracy means emphasis on individual rights, autonomy, self-regulating markets, and a minimalist state; a stress on the democratic side of liberal democracy means emphasis on popular participation and a high degree of state intervention in order to secure substantive benefits and entitlements for all rather than merely formal rights and liberties (Sørensen 2008: 10–18). One charge against the United States is that the promotion of "low intensity democracy" has been given priority over more fundamental political and social change (Robinson 1996); the allegation underlines that democracy is no simple entity.

This, then, is the liberal dilemma: on the one hand, a strict Liberalism of Restraint may help very little in promoting freedom because it respects the principles of sovereignty and nonintervention in nonliberal states. A vigorous Liberalism of Imposition, on the other hand, risks undermining what it seeks to achieve, because it invokes a liberal imperialism that removes the local responsibility that is the very condition of freedom; it also risks calling forth illiberal counterreactions. And it must make difficult choices concerning the model of democracy it wants to promote.

Liberal intervention in illiberal states may be connected with goals other than democracy promotion in a narrow sense: it might be humanitarian interventions to address the suffering of civilians in the midst of violent conflict, it might be state-building interventions with broad aims of institution building, or it might be connected with security concerns. In each case, the relationship between insiders and outsiders must be negotiated. To be sustainable, any change must build firmly on local conditions. Only insiders can effectively do that; outsiders cannot. But locals, insiders, emerge from a context of norms and habits that need to be transformed in order for real changes for the better to take hold. The evidence indicates that insiders cannot or will not easily perform that transformation on their own.

The tensions discussed here have implications for the liberal view of international institutions. We saw earlier that liberals favor a rule-based order with a strong role for international institutions. But there is a further question: should international institutions be universal in character, that is, open to membership for all sovereign states? Or should they be distinctly liberal in character, allowing only members who meet certain liberal standards? The Liberalism of Restraint favors pluralism, the equal treatment of all sovereign states, liberal or not. The Liberalism of Imposition leans toward antipluralism; it emphasizes the universal relevance of liberal principles, and that calls for unequal treatment of liberal and nonliberal states. Only the former are valid candidates for full membership of international institutions.

In the late nineteenth century European international lawyers stipulated that international law was closely connected to the "special civilization of modern Europe." Therefore, countries "differently civilized" could not be expected to understand it; "such states can only be presumed to be sub-ject to it" (William Hall, quoted by Wight 1977: 115). In other words, full membership in the international community was predicated on a "standard of civilization" that included "the respect for basic rights, an effective state machinery, and the adherence to international law" (Gong 1984: 14–15). Woodrow Wilson had similar ideas about the League of Nations; states had to be democratic in order to qualify for membership: "A steadfast concert for peace can never be maintained except by a partnership of democratic nations. No autocratic government could be trusted to keep faith within it or observe its covenants. It must be a league of honor, a partnership of opinion.... Only free peoples can hold their purpose and their honor steady to a common end and prefer the interests of mankind to any narrow inter-est of their own' (Wilson 1917, quoted by T. Smith 1994: 94). But a league of democracies soon turned out to be an unrealistic goal, and the growth of authoritarianism in Europe in the interwar period made it even less feasible. Only half of the thirty states that joined the League in 1919 were democra-cies. When League membership had increased to fifty-seven states in 1938, the proportion was even smaller (T. Smith 1994: 94).

Wilson wanted an international institution with ambitious goals; it should make up a collective security system committing members to defend each other in case of aggression. For this to work, members had to be democracies; when that turned out to be impossible, the League could not maintain such ambitious goals, and domestic U.S. support for commitment to the League was not forthcoming (Ikenberry 2001: 117–63). Liberals are torn between the support for institutions with universal membership that will—so it is hoped—slowly but steadily help create domestic change in a liberal direction among their members and institutions with democratic membership and far-reaching commitments among members with a high degree of mutual trust and dedication to common liberal values.

The formation of the United Nations raised the issue of universality anew. The United States indicated that membership should be open only to "properly qualified states," and the Netherlands wanted new members to "have political institutions which ensure that the state is the servant of its citizens" (Simpson 2001: 552). In the end the principle of universality pre-vailed, and in the following decades institutions with a global reach became open to all: "It is possible to see the period 1945 to 1989 as one marked by a rejection of standards of civilization, culture and democracy as criteria for membership of the international community" (Simpson 2001: 556).

With the end of the Cold War the emphasis on universal human rights has grown stronger compared with the traditional principles of sovereignty and nonintervention. An influential report has proposed a "responsibility to protect," which permits military intervention for human protection in cases of large-scale domestic violence (International Commission 2001). This is also a step away from equal treatment of states in international institutions; states who blatantly abuse rights and liberties of their citizens forfeit the right of nonintervention. And in addition to the debates about reform of the UN system there are new proposals for creating a community or "concert of democracies"; "If the United Nations cannot be reformed the Concert would provide an alternative forum for liberal states to authorize collective action, including the use of force, by a supermajority vote" (Princeton Project 2006: 7).

In sum, liberals strongly favor setting up international institutions as a framework for cooperation, peaceful resolution of conflict, and the promotion of democratic governance. On the one hand, liberals support a pluralist approach to international institutions: a community of both liberal and nonliberal states is an appropriate framework for the promotion of liberal democracy worldwide. On the other hand, liberals favor a nonpluralist approach to international institutions: only a concert of democracies will be able to act decisively for the defense and promotion of a liberal democratic world; nondemocratic states cannot be trusted in this regard, and their lack of democratic qualities makes them unreliable partners.

Turning to the area of transnational economic exchange, Ludwig von Mises taught that in a world of privatized economic activity and free trade, international peace and prosperity will be created, not by government, but by free men who will "naturally pursue peaceful intercourse through economic and cultural exchange" (quoted from Ebeling 1991). In the real world, however, liberals have had a more complex relationship with the notion of free trade. One of the U.S. founding fathers, Alexander Hamilton, was a strong proponent of mercantilism in the form of protectionist policies aimed at promoting domestic industry in the United States. Liberal democracies did not generally practice open markets and free trade during the 1930s. Economic relations during that period were characterized by nationalistic, self-interested, protectionist competition where countries pursued "beggar your neighbor" policies.

World War II elevated the United States to a position of nearly unrivaled world leadership. A majority of U.S. politicians recognized that the United States had to take on the responsibility for creating a liberal world market economy. The institutions of the Bretton Woods system (the IMF, the World Bank, the OECD, and the GATT) were also inspired by the domestic experience of New Deal liberalism. They helped set in place regulatory mechanisms that could guard against market failures. Free market aspirations were combined with attention to broader social goals. This was "embedded" liberalism (Ruggie 1982).

By the 1960s Western Europe and Japan had been rebuilt. Gradually, U.S. policies became more oriented toward national interests. The United States began to act as a "predatory hegemon," losing sight of its role as defender of an open world economy. It was an era characterized by "increasing protectionism, monetary instability, and economic crisis" (Gilpin 1987: 351). In the 1980s, Ronald Reagan and Margaret Thatcher strongly promoted a neoliberal approach that turned against state regulation and defended the virtues of the market (Toye 1987). At the same time, such policies did not necessarily abandon special favors to domestic producers (L. Weiss 2005a).

So in the real world liberal support for free trade and open markets was always tempered by perceived national interests concerning the benefits they would bring to certain countries and groups. The general tendency is for free market support to grow stronger in tandem with increasing competitiveness and efficiency of the national economy. But even in the case of highly competitive economies, liberals can continue to support pockets of protectionism, in particular in agriculture and some sectors of manufacturing.

Liberals continue to disagree about the appropriate social measures needed to mitigate market failures. Neoliberals find that state intervention most always does more harm than good; social liberals recognize that markets and states are both necessary and that special measures are needed to confront problems of poverty and stark inequality (Sørensen 1991).

Finally, neoliberals tend to downplay the framework of rules and regulations needed for the free market to function properly. Free trade, deregulation, and privatization measures undertaken in weak states have not fostered development; it is rather the case that these countries are increasingly marginalized in a global economy where "difficult" markets are avoided (Hoogvelt 1997); the prospects for weak states have worsened in the current financial and economic crisis. In sum, free markets do not necessarily bring the benefits claimed by neoliberals; their success depends on the context and the conditions under which they function. Realizing this, liberal states have far from always adhered to the principles of open economies and free trade, and they sometimes preach liberal economic principles to others that they do not follow themselves.

Social relations across borders between individuals and private groups are principal drivers of progress for liberals; all kinds of transnational relationships among people help create overlapping networks of interdependence that function for mutual benefit and understanding. Globalization can be defined as the expansion and intensification of economic, political, social, and cultural relations across borders. It is certainly true that forces of globalization tie people and countries closer together; this is especially true for the liberal democracies that are among the leading participants in the process. But it is not true that such relations bring only "transnational goods" to people. To a large extent they also bring "transnational bads." The liberal view that transnational relations between people and groups always bring benefits will have to be replaced by a more complicated consideration of transnational goods versus transnational bads.

There are a number of different kinds of transnational bads: for example, diseases, environmental pollution, international terror, ecological imbalances, crime, drugs, and economic crisis. An influential sociological analysis has termed this state of affairs "risk society" (Beck 1986), indicating that sovereign borders provide little protection in a globalized environment where social problems and risks emerging from single societies can quickly be transmitted elsewhere. On this view, there has been a movement away from external, natural risk toward "manufactured risks" that are manmade; we have started to worry "less about what nature can do to us, and more about what we have done to nature" (Giddens 1999: 26). There is less historical experience with meeting the challenge of manufactured risk and large uncertainties in evaluating it. A recent analysis, for example, claims that 40 percent of all deaths are due to environmental pollution and degradation (Lang 2007).

Another example concerns the increased exodus of citizens across borders. The liberal view of the beneficial effects of connections between people construes such movement as weakening national loyalties and making citizens "more ready to rethink the collectivities with which they identify and to redefine the balance between their own and society's interests" (Rosenau 1992: 286). But large-scale migration has also caused fears and anxieties that have led to xenophobic reactions and nationalistic movements stressing a very exclusive definition of national identity. Such reactions see transnational integration and increased interdependence as a two-pronged threat. On the one hand, it threatens the social and economic well-being of "original" citizens because of the new claims made on the state by immigrants and other types of outsiders. On the other hand, it threatens a historically specific, narrow conception of national identity in which there is no room for newcomers.

On the whole, closer relations between people across borders bring transnational goods but also contain a number of real or perceived transnational bads. Liberals have traditionally concentrated on the former and downplayed or entirely disregarded the latter. As a consequence, liberals are not well prepared to consider how to make sure that goods outweigh bads in strengthening transnational relationships among people.

In sum, liberals cannot agree on the concrete substance of principles. Two fundamental liberal postures were identified above: the Liberalism of Restraint, which emphasizes pluralism, tolerance, moderation, and nonintervention; and the Liberalism of Imposition, which underscores the universal validity and moral superiority of liberal principles and supports intervention and the active struggle for regime change. These postures are connected to a pluralist and a nonpluralist approach to international institutions. At the same time, we saw that liberals were not in agreement about economic principles surrounding free markets and paid little attention to the problem of transnational bads.

Are these merely problems that can be successfully confronted through intelligent policies that avoid unnecessary extremes by defining credible compromises that can pave the way for additional liberal progress? Or do they constitute a real dilemma, defined as a problem that "seems incapable of a satisfactory solution" (Wheeler and Booth 1992: 29)? It is my claim that for the time being, the choice between restraint, nonintervention, tolerance, empathy, and understanding on the one hand, and imposition, intervention, the validity of universal values, and the superiority of liberal principles on the other, remains a dilemma. This leaves no clear path to a more liberal world order.

The liberal dilemma has been present ever since liberal democracies began to play a major role in the world. It is particularly acute today because of the fluctuations in the international system of power: the end of the Cold War elevated Western countries, and in particular the United States, to an unrivaled position of power and influence in the international system. U.S. primacy pushed toward an activist Liberalism of Imposition; "the forceful and unilateral exercise of U.S. power," says Robert Jervis (2003), "is the logical outcome of the current unrivaled U.S. position in the international system" (82).[8] But this was not an appropriate formula for a stable liberal world order, as will be explained in chapter 6. With the financial crisis and the wars in Afghanistan and Iraq, liberal preponderance is again in question. Writing in 2008, Fareed Zakaria (2008a) diagnoses the end of global dominance by the United States: "We are now living through the third great power shift of the modern era—the rise of the rest" (42). Zakaria and other commentators find that the United States can adapt to the new situation through a

---

8. The primacy of the United States sparked a large literature on the United States as a new form of empire. See the overview in Tønnesson (2004) and the analysis in Münkler (2005).

pragmatic liberal strategy—a version of the Liberalism of Restraint in the vocabulary of this book. I shall argue that there is no simple path to a stable liberal Restraint order.

The choice between Imposition and Restraint cannot be determined from the relative power of liberal states in the international system. It is also connected to particular political coalitions in power and to dominant ideas (strategic beliefs) in particular liberal countries.[9] During the first presidency of George W. Bush, these elements came together in support for a particularly virulent Liberalism of Imposition. Some European countries strongly encouraged that stance; others were more hesitant. Today, there is a renewed debate about the appropriate liberal strategy. Most of what follows will stress the principal positions in the liberal posture combined with a focus on the leading liberal country, the United States.

Conclusion

Liberals face the serious challenge of devising a coherent set of principles for liberal world order: How can further democratic transitions and democratic consolidation be promoted? Which liberal state-market matrix can sustain a liberal world economy, and how are the conditions for a functioning market economy brought about in weak states? How is an effective liberal institutional order to be established? And can real support for liberal values be improved?

Unfortunately, liberals do not have clear answers to these questions. This chapter traced the tensions in liberalism to the very heart of the liberal concept of freedom. Liberals make a universalistic claim of liberty, freedom for all people; they also emphasize pluralism, respect for the choice between different values. Liberals support negative liberty, the ability to act unimpeded by others; they also support positive liberty, the creation of the appropriate conditions for freedom to thrive. These postures can be condensed in the Liberalism of Restraint and the Liberalism of Imposition. They help define a number of dilemmas in liberal internationalism: to pursue liberty in the world, should outsiders leave other peoples alone or are they obliged to intervene in order to support the promotion of freedom? Should international institutions have a global reach, embracing both liberal and nonliberal states, or should focus be on a concert of democracies? Free markets bring benefits, but only under certain conditions. What are those conditions and how

---

9. As demonstrated in the detailed analyses by Jonathan Monten (2005, 2007). See also Ikenberry (2009, 2011).

are they established? Transnational goods are accompanied by transnational bads. Is it possible to make sure that goods outweigh bads in the development of transnational relationships? Given the conflict between different ends that are all desirable, how can we promote liberal values in the world? The governments of liberal democracies must confront these questions and come up with answers that can claim legitimacy while also creating the basis for further, much-needed liberal progress. The following chapters will demonstrate both the difficulties involved in this undertaking and how little has been achieved so far.

■ CHAPTER 3

Values and Liberal World Order

The support for liberal values was identified earlier as a central element of liberal world order. At the same time, any endorsement of liberal values must confront the tension between a Liberalism of Restraint and a Liberalism of Imposition, as clarified in chapter 2. What does that mean for the promotion and status of liberal values in the world? The Liberalism of Imposition was accompanied by a strong optimism concerning the prospects for liberal progress: if evolutionary change for the better is secure, why not give history a helping hand and accelerate the tempo of an already predestined evolution?[1] I shall reject idealist liberal optimism: there is no certain path to progress.

Where does that leave the attempts by liberal states to further liberal progress in the world? It leaves them in an ambiguous situation where neither a clear policy of Liberal Imposition nor a clear policy of Liberal Restraint presents an attractive solution. Liberals are used to confronting nonliberals

---

1. According to Stephen Walt (2005), "the Bush team was firmly convinced that history was on America's side and the U.S. power should be used to reinforce what... Condoleezza Rice termed 'the powerful secular trends moving the world toward...democracy and individual liberty'" (58). At the same time, many supporters of the administration, including Robert Kagan and Charles Krauthammer, were not animated by any liberal optimism about progress; theirs was rather a "let's do it while we can" attitude driven by an optimism about U.S. power. I owe this point to John Ikenberry.

of all stripes with identity questions, requesting or demanding their commitment to universal liberal values. But it is increasingly necessary for liberals
to direct such identity questions at themselves: What does it mean to be
liberal? Which precise values do we support? What is our concrete vision for
a liberal world order? The profound liberal optimism that bloomed after the
end of the Cold War is not warranted, and a major part of the problem is
that liberal states have attempted to promote liberal values in ways that risk
undermining these values because they can easily be shown to suffer from
hypocrisy and doubletalk.

The central dilemma facing liberals is this: The promotion of liberal
values, including human rights, must be respectful of other cultures and
societies, including their traditions and their values. At the same time, it
must maintain that there are universal values valid for all, irrespective of
local traditions and customs. There can be no denial of rights to life, liberty,
security of the person, and protection against torture and racial discrimination (cf. Donnelly 1993: 36; Beitz 2009). In the vocabulary of this book, the
undertaking cannot adopt a strategy of radical Restraint because that equals
radical relativism, and it cannot adopt a strategy of Imposition because that
will be received as imperialism. Further, I shall argue that there are no facile
compromises between these principal postures. The argument leads to a
pessimistic view of the possibilities for strengthening liberal values in the
world.

Liberalism and Progress

The belief in progress toward an ever more liberal world is a core component
in liberal philosophy, theory, and politics (Pollard 1971). Liberal optimism
reached a new high after the end of the Cold War, emblematically formulated in the notion of "the end of history." The last decade, however, has not
lived up to these profoundly optimistic expectations. This chapter first discusses the notion of progress in liberal thinking. The idealistic optimism of
the end of history is not representative of the liberal tradition. Major voices
among liberals have always been unsure of progress, and for them the current
problems come as much less of a surprise.

The end of the Cold War was celebrated by Francis Fukuyama (1989)
as "the unabashed victory of economic and political liberalism," leading to
"the end of history as such: that is, the universalization of Western liberal
democracy as the final form of human government" (3, 4). It was an elegant
and eloquent argument that captured the high hopes and liberal spirits of
the time; but the idealist belief in undiluted progress was never as prevalent

in the liberal tradition as Fukuyama's first formulation claimed.[2] The path
to progress was frequently viewed as more complex, uncertain, and filled
with reversals than was assured in "the end of history." The liberal tradition
contains an uneasy balance or tension between an idealistic optimism (with
Fukuyama's 1989 essay as a recent peak) and a more cautious, defensive pragmatism (represented by such thinkers as Isaiah Berlin, Raymond Aron, and
Karl Popper). The position of strong liberal idealism is critically discussed in
the following, and I shall argue that a less idealist version of liberalism is the
better guide to analysis of the prospects for a liberal world order.

What triumphs at the end of history, according to liberal idealism, is not
a liberal reality but the liberal *idea*. The triumph of the idea is so hugely
significant because "the idea will govern the material world *in the long run*"
(Fukuyama 1989: 4; italics in original). Ideas should be understood in the
larger sense of comprehensive worldviews, that is, ideas as ideology. Hegel's
Phenomenology of Mind is the primary source for this idealism; for Hegel,
history ended in 1806 with the battle of Jena: "at that point the *vanguard* of
humanity... actualized the principle of the French revolution. While there
was considerable work to be done after 1806... the basic *principles* of the
liberal democratic state could not be improved upon" (Fukuyama 1989: 5).

For Hegel, the end of history was embodied in the Prussian absolutist
state; for Alexandre Kojève, Hegel's modern French interpreter upon whom
Fukuyama strongly draws, the democratic, peaceful, and cooperative state
emerging at the end of history is the typical member of the Common
Market (today the European Union); for Fukuyama, the current version
of the liberal end of history is the Western systems on both sides of the
Atlantic, with "liberal democracy in the political sphere" combined with
"the abundance of a modern free market economy" in the economic sphere
(Fukuyama 1989: 8). Thus, even the "pure" idealism of Fukuyama, Kojève,
and Hegel makes political commitments. It engages with the real world in
pointing out the systems that are the embodiment of the ideals. In doing so,
of course, idealism also underwrites and justifies those systems; it is at this
point that liberal ideas are connected to liberal ideology.

This is perhaps most apparent in the case of Hegel, who was known as the
"royal Prussian court philosopher." "We must... worship the State as the
manifestation of the Divine on Earth" (Hegel in Loewenberg 1929: 447). For
that reason, "in civilized nations, true bravery consists in the readiness to give

---

2. The many recent contributions by Francis Fukuyama do not share this strong belief in progress. My focus here, however, is on the early version of the "end of history" thesis.

oneself wholly to the service of the State so that the individual counts but as one among many. Not personal valor alone is significant; the important aspect lies in self-subordination to the universal cause" (465). Idealism turned into ideology, then, implies knowing what is best for others and knowing what others ought to want.

In the political process, the splendid idea may be captured and transformed into an instrument of oppressive rule. Robert Nisbet (1979) makes the point: "from Fichte's *Addresses to the German Nation,* through Hegel's *Philosophy of History,* down to the spokesmen, Left and Right, of the twentieth century's totalitarianisms, there has been a continuing philosophy of progress in the West rooted in the transforming, redemptive uses of power" (18). The German philosopher Ernst Cassirer observed that "no other philosophical system has done so much for the preparation of fascism and imperialism as Hegel's doctrine of the state—this 'divine Idea as it exists on earth'" (quoted from Bovard 2005: 3).

Kojève and Fukuyama present different and more strictly liberal ideologies at the end of history. For Kojève, the end of history is the everyday politics of the Common Market—he worked as a bureaucrat in the European Economic Community; for Fukuyama, it is "liberal democracy and easy access to VCRs and stereos" (Fukuyama 1989: 8). Not very dramatic, but that is the whole point: there is an eerie silence at the end of history because all the great confrontations are over; "all prior contradictions are resolved and all human needs are satisfied. There is no struggle or conflict over 'large' issues, and consequently no need for generals or statesmen; what remains is primarily economic activity" (Fukuyama 1989: 5).

But it would appear to be only on an abstract level that political strife and major struggle died at history's end, where "there will be neither art nor philosophy, just the perpetual caretaking of the museum of human history" (Fukuyama 1989: 18). Ideology in the hands of power can be used and abused; the greater the power, the higher the risk of abuse in the domestic as well as in the international sphere. In the hands of power and interest, liberty is always in danger. Ideological principles, no matter how pure, can always be used as justification to bully, oppress, and torture. Consequently, "you must remember, my fellow citizens, that eternal vigilance by the people is the price of liberty, and you must pay the price if you wish to secure the blessing. It behooves you therefore, to be watchful in your States as well as in the Federal Government," said Andrew Jackson in his 1837 farewell address.

For that reason, liberalism "is not at the tail end of a necessary process of social evolution—i.e. it is not the winning ideology—but needs constantly to struggle against opposing ideologies and theories in order to make and remake its case" (Freeden 2008: 14). There will always be new reasons to question liberal principles: the war on terror (security versus liberty); the influx of immigrants (equal rights for all versus nation first); the promotion of democracy in the world (we know what is best for all versus autonomy and self-determination). In a pessimistic comment to Fukuyama, Allan Bloom (1989) even argues that "fascism has a future, if not *the* future" (21). The ideological struggle does not suddenly die away; conflicts over large issues do not evaporate. A vibrant liberalism must make its case against old and new challenges every day. And these challenges emerge not merely from the outside, from rival ideological systems, but also and significantly from domestic sources, because the powerful groups that support liberal principles may eventually betray them in pursuit of power and interest.

The idealist version of liberalism, then, begins and ends with the liberal idea, because the ideal governs the material world in the long run. When the vanguard of humanity endorses the ideal, history ends. In ideal terms, we can go no further, perfection has arrived, and the theoretical truth of liberal ideals is "absolute" and cannot "be improved upon" (Fukuyama 1989: 8). It remains to defeat ideologies pretending to represent different and higher forms of human society. They were fascism and communism; two world wars and the Cold War took care of them. Religion and nationalism are current problems but not sufficiently significant to challenge liberalism. There awaits a process of extending liberal principles to countries and peoples who have not yet fully embraced them. The world has first and foremost accepted the free market principles of a capitalist economy. While advanced capitalism and political democracy do not always go hand in hand, human beings are driven by a "desire for recognition" (Fukuyama 1992: xvi), which will eventually push toward liberal democracy as the superior solution to the problem of recognition. We can then look forward to the "Common Marketization" of world politics because the great struggles are over and the large issues are all settled.

The nonidealist version of liberalism begins with liberal principles of reason, tolerance, and liberty and also hails them as superior and universally relevant. It, however, immediately moves on to view the ideological development of liberalism in concrete historical context. Liberalism is an extraordinarily complex set of principles and propositions that are not always in harmony. It developed dramatically over time in the hands of many different theorists and practitioners, and in relation to shifting material conditions. Liberalism emerged as "a narrative about civilized growth and about the spread of reason, tolerance and liberty itself" (Freeden 2008: 10). But liberalism "is not a static set of beliefs and practices but an adaptable and mutating set of propositions, allowing us to address it in the plural" (Freeden 2008: 14).

The different faces of liberalism are connected to its ideological role as a *via media* between left and right.[3] At the same time, different convictions have led to different versions of liberalism. A leading figure on the right, Friedrich von Hayek, makes a distinction between liberalism and democracy. Hayek calls the former a doctrine about what the law ought to be and the latter a doctrine about the manner of determining what will be the law. For Hayek democracy is of secondary importance. The highest political end is liberty, which can be achieved only if there are strict limits on government activities. Government intervention in civil society must aim at protecting life, liberty, and estate, which basically means creating the best possible framework for the operation of the free market. There is no room, for example, for redistributive measures because they would jeopardize the free choice of individuals in the free market. In this view democracy is desirable as a mechanism for ensuring that the majority will decide what the law should be. It is vital, however, that democratic majorities respect limitations on government activity. If they do not, democracy will be in conflict with liberty, and if that happens, Hayek "is not a democrat" (quoted from Held 2006: 204).

In more general terms, a large number of different versions of liberal principles including models of democracy—left, right and center—can be identified in the course of liberalism's development. In that sense, the basic principles of the liberal democratic state were not formulated once and for all in 1806. They have been contested and discussed from the very beginning to this day (Sørensen 2008). Consequently, when we talk about liberal values in the current world order, the issue is less about the position of one single, fixed model of liberalism and much more about the unequal advance or retreat of different configurations of liberal values and the extent to which they can serve as a basis for a liberal world order.

It follows that liberal progress is not secure. In the idealist versions of liberalism there is a tendency to see the road to progress as an easy journey with few obstacles leading to a goal of near-perfection. The nonidealist versions are much less certain about progress and emphasize the large number of obstacles on the road forward. Many early liberals were inclined to be thoroughly optimistic. For example, Herbert Spencer, inspired by Darwin, identified laws of progress in nature as well as in human society: "Progress, therefore, is not an accident, but a necessity. Instead of civilization being artificial, it is part of nature; all of a piece with the development of the embryo

---

3. "[T]o the Right, it preached concessions; to the Left, it preached political organization. To both it preached patience: in the long run, more will be gained (for all) by a via media" (Wallerstein 1995: 255).

or the unfolding of a flower." Bad developments were seen by Spencer as maladaptations, which would disappear through evolutionary processes, so that "all unfitness must disappear; that is, all imperfection must disappear" (Spencer, quoted from Nisbet 1979: 17).

But not all early liberals shared Spencer's optimism; Immanuel Kant (1992) was confident that "all capacities implanted in a creature by nature are destined to unfold themselves completely and conformably to their end, in the course of time," but he emphasized that "reason does not itself work instinctively, for it requires trial, practice and instruction...one stage to the next" (42). For Kant, progress was predicated on the existence of a pacific union among republics (democracies). But no such union would emerge automatically; it would be formed in a slow process where earlier results of cooperation would eventually lead to further cooperative efforts. The pacific union is a possibility rather than a certainty; Kant speaks of "an infinite process of gradual approximation" (130).

The liberal tradition contains several complex debates about how best to proceed in order to secure liberal progress. A major element in such debates concerns the relationship between change from "below" and change from "above." Before World War I, for example, liberals would emphasize the importance of change from below so that enlightened and rational human beings would be the major force for change. With the Great War a different view emerged. "The older internationalism, based on belief in humanitarian ethics on the one hand, and in the peaceful tendencies of commerce on the other, is dead," L. T. Hobhouse declared in 1916 (189). Such forces were no longer sufficient to constrain sovereign states from coming into violent conflict. Instead, powerful international institutions were required. Alfred Zimmern (1918) argued that "if the world wishes to organise its life on a peaceful basis, it must habituate itself to the idea of international governmental organization" (279). John Hobson (1915) went one step further: "Nothing short of a representative international government, involving a definite diminution of sovereign rights of the separate states will suffice" (639).

Fukuyama's essay marked a new high point of idealist liberal optimism in recent times. During the Cold War period, leading liberal voices were much more cautious and defensive. The liberalism of Karl Popper, Raymond Aron, and Isaiah Berlin was skeptical and defensive, concerned with "avoiding the worst, rather than achieving the best" (J.-W. Müller 2008: 48). At the same time, this liberalism was more concerned with rejecting any determinist view of the future, liberal or Marxist. Instead of certainty of progress, it emphasized uncertainty and clashes of values. History, said Berlin, has "no libretto," and for Popper we would always live in an imperfect society, because "there always exist irresolvable clashes of values: there are many moral problems which are insoluble because moral principles may conflict" (quoted from J.-W. Müller 2008: 53).

In sum, both the early liberal tradition (Kant) and later liberal thinking (Aron, Berlin, Popper) are highly skeptical of a deterministic view of assured progress. Yet these thinkers do endorse human reason as the basis for the social world and progress as a real possibility. Liberal thinking about international relations (IR), then, must be understood against the background of a liberal tradition that has an idealist extreme where progress toward an end-state of perfection is almost secure, and a nonidealist extreme where progress is a much more remote possibility and imperfection is a condition from which there is no escape.

Liberal *theories* of IR contain elements of both, but they have a tendency to lean toward the idealist extreme; there is strong focus on the good things connected with transgovernmental and transnational relations, democracy, international institutions, and economic and social interdependence. In contrast, issues concerning inequality, exploitation, dominance, subordination, dependence, resistance, and conflict are played down. Insofar as these aspects are covered, there is an inclination to see them as minor items that can be peacefully resolved in the larger process of liberal globalization and modernization.

In sum, there are theoretical flaws in liberal IR theory, connected with an insufficient analysis of the downsides of liberal development and in particular with lack of analysis of the role and position of nonliberal states, some of which are weak and less developed, with no immediate or even long-term prospect of becoming part of a liberal community.[4] It is an essential liberal belief that once states become democratic and ruled in accordance with liberal principles, international relations between such states will more or less automatically be cooperative and peaceful. This line of thought is behind Stanley Hoffmann's (1995) claim that liberal internationalism is "little more than the projection of domestic liberalism worldwide" (161). Cooperation between democracies, however, does not say anything about the relationship between liberal and nonliberal states.

In the idealist version of liberalism this omission is rather easily taken care of by the process of historical transformation in which an increasing number of countries and peoples will embrace the liberal ideal. But as we have seen, the idealist version of liberalism is not a fully reliable guide to history or to

---

4. For a discussion of liberal IR theory, see R. Jackson and Sørensen (2010), chap. 4.

current events. Therefore, it is necessary to rely more on the nonidealist tradition of liberalism. This leads toward a less sanguine view of liberal progress and a more unsafe position for liberal values in the world. Progress is possible but so is regress, and the emergence of a liberal world order is neither predetermined nor assured.

Progress Based on Liberal Values

We now know that liberal philosophy and liberal theory have a tendency to be too optimistic about the prospects for liberal progress in the world. The argument in this and the following section is that any liberal progress on a global scale is unequal and fragmented. Political systems may import some facets of liberal institutions and practices and still be illiberal democracies. Countries may embrace varieties of a market economy and still preserve nonliberal economic practices. People may accept some aspects of liberal values but in such a way that their overall worldviews cannot be considered liberal. In sum, what uneven and contradictory progress there may be does not add up to a stable and uniform value basis for liberal world order.

A primary argument for the advancement of liberal values concerns the progress of liberal democracy (Mandelbaum 2003: 251–65). As reported in chapter 2, the number of free countries in the world according to the Freedom House rating increased from 42 in 1976 to 89 in 2010; the number of countries classified as not free went from 68 to 42 over the same period. That is indeed considerable liberal progress. But the democratic advance must not be overestimated. It might appear as if there is an inexorable trend toward an increase in the number of democracies while authoritarian systems become ever fewer. But regime transition is not a smooth process always moving in the "right" direction, toward more democracy. Many countries today are in a gray zone between full democracy and outright authoritarianism, and they show few signs of becoming more democratic. These countries conduct more or less democratic elections, yet they are not democratic in other important respects; they remain merely electoral democracies.

A large number of states in the gray zone are also weak states. Such states lack national community; instead, ethnic identities connected to tribal, religious, or similar characteristics dominate over the national identity (Sørensen 2008). A further major characteristic of many countries in the gray zone is domination by elite groups that interfere in the democratic process in order to protect their own interests. Such groups as the military, traditional economic elites, and leading politicians may insist that any process of democratization does not go against their vital areas of interest. When some narrow coalition of elites dominates the political scene, the consolidation of democracy may be impeded.

What can we then say about current regimes in the gray area? Consider the 2010 survey by Freedom House. Countries with an average score of 2.0 or less are considered full-blown democracies, and countries with an average score of 6.5 or worse are considered authoritarian.[5] Countries between these averages are in the gray zone. On this view roughly half of the countries in the world—97 out of 192—are situated in the gray zone. There are vast differences between them, of course; if we divide the 97 countries into two groups (the middle range being the average Freedom House score of 4.25), the half with better scores could be called "electoral democracies," whereas the half with the worse scores could be called "electoral authoritarian" systems. The two groups are identified below.[6]

Electoral democracies (Freedom House average score above 2.0 and less than 4.25)

Argentina, Benin, Brazil, Bulgaria, Dominican Republic, Mauritius, Mongolia, Namibia, Romania, Samoa, Sao Tome and Principe, Serbia, South Africa, Trinidad and Tobago, Vanuatu, Antigua and Barbuda, Botswana, El Salvador, Guyana, India, Indonesia, Jamaica, Mali, Mexico, Montenegro, Peru, Ukraine, Albania, Bolivia, Ecuador, Lesotho, Macedonia, Paraguay, Senegal, Seychelles, Sierra Leone, Turkey, Bangladesh, Bosnia-Herzegovina, Colombia, Comoros, East Timor, Liberia, Malawi, Maldives, Moldova, Mozambique, Papua New Guinea, Philippines, Solomon Islands, Tanzania, Zambia, Burkina Faso, Georgia, Guatemala, Guinea Bissau, Honduras, Kenya, Kuwait, Lebanon, Malaysia, Nepal, Nicaragua, Sri Lanka, Tonga

Electoral authoritarian systems (Freedom House average score 4.25 and above, but less than 6.5)

Bhutan, Burundi, Haiti, Kosovo, Morocco, Niger, Nigeria, Pakistan, Singapore, Thailand, Togo, Uganda, Venezuela, Armenia, Central African Republic, Djibouti, Ethiopia, Fiji, The Gambia, Madagascar, Algeria, Angola, Azerbaijan, Bahrain, Brunei, Cambodia, Congo (Brazzaville), Cote d'Ivoire, Egypt, Gabon, Iraq, Jordan, Kazakhstan, Kyrgyzstan, Mauritania, Oman, Qatar, Russia, Rwanda, Tajikistan, United Arab

---

5. This procedure follows the one suggested by Larry Diamond (2002).

6. Calculated from Freedom House (2010). Countries arranged with lowest (i.e., most democratic) scores first.

Emirates, Yemen, Afghanistan, Cameroon, Congo (Kinshasa), Iran, Swaziland, Tunisia, Vietnam, Zimbabwe

Therefore, liberal democracy has progressed in the world, but progress is less secure than it may immediately seem, and the large number of countries in the gray zone will continue to represent challenges to the quest for a liberal world order. Such systems will not easily become consolidated democracies; they very frequently lack the five conditions that Robert A. Dahl (1989) has identified as promoters of stable democratic rule:

> Leaders do not employ coercion, notably through the police and the military, to gain and maintain their power.
> A modern, dynamic, organizationally pluralist society exists.
> The conflictive potentialities of subcultural pluralism are maintained at tolerable levels.
> Among the people of a country, particularly its active political stratum, a political culture and a system of beliefs exists that is favorable to the idea of democracy and the institutions of polyarchy.
> The effects of foreign influence or control are either negligible or positively favorable. (314)

The problem, then, is that in many cases frail liberal progress has introduced some elements of democratic rule, but there are few prospects for further democratic consolidation, the process by which democracy becomes "the only game in town" (Linz 1990: 158). The three most important impediments in this respect are the lack of legitimacy of political rule, the lack of institutionalized political parties, and the weakness of civil society (Sørensen 2008: 160). Consolidated democracies are based on a type of legitimacy that Max Weber called "rational-legal": the population accepts the authority of rulers, not because of their individual personalities but because the system under which these rulers won and now hold office is accepted and supported. For this type of legitimacy to prevail, the source and the agent of legitimacy must be separated. Such separation is especially difficult in systems in which the regime's legitimacy rests on people's faith in a personal leader—what Weber called "charismatic legitimacy." The personal rule systems in Africa, for example, are based on charismatic legitimacy; democratic consolidation is difficult in these countries because the whole basis for legitimate rule has to be changed.

Political parties are crucially important for democratic consolidation. Democracy introduces an element of uncertainty into the political process; a stable party system helps reduce uncertainty because "actors know the rules and have some sense of how to pursue their interests.... Democracy has generally thrived when party systems have been institutionalized" (Mainwaring and Scully 1995: 27). Institutionalization of political parties means that they emerge as valued and stable elements in the political process. Many countries in Africa, Asia, Latin America, and the Middle East do not have institutionalized party systems, and this hinders the process of democratic consolidation. Countries possessing such a system—for example, Uruguay and Chile—have much better prospects for democratic consolidation.

Finally, an effective civil society—a dense network of associations, interest groups, civil rights groups, and so forth—is the best basis for the consolidation of democracy. In many new democracies, including those in Eastern Europe and Russia, an effective civil society is only in the process of being established, and thus these countries face additional problems for democratic consolidation. In sum, there are numerous unconsolidated democratic openings in the world, but very few countries present favorable prospects for democratic consolidation on the three major dimensions considered here. These impediments will also constrain the current democratic openings in the Middle East, including Egypt, Tunisia, and Libya. That bodes ill for the solid advancement of liberal democracy.

What about the well-established democracies in the OECD-world? They too face new challenges to their democratic vitality; two tendencies are especially problematic in this regard. First, Robert Putnam (1995) has argued that there is a loss of "social capital" in the United States, which has negative implications for the quality of democracy. The leading indicator of social capital is the rate of membership in voluntary associations such as amateur soccer clubs, choral societies, or hiking clubs. The rate of membership has dwindled in the United States. Putnam argues that a decrease in social capital will undermine the vitality of democracy in many established, wealthy democracies; a crucial element in maintaining a democracy is the active participation and support of a large majority of the population. With the decline in social capital, the conditions for such popular participation and support are increasingly adverse.

The other great challenge to established democracies comes from globalization. Processes of globalization tend to intensify cooperation between countries in order to face common challenges. But such governance across borders is not based on a clear constitutional framework. Therefore, core decision makers are not subject to sufficient democratic accountability and control. Decisions are made behind closed doors, frequently by high-ranking bureaucrats without a clear democratic mandate. Citizens are not sufficiently informed about the issues because there is little public debate and discussion about them (Dahl 1999). Dahl believes that international organizations can never become democratic; other scholars are less pessimistic (Sørensen 2004: 71–79). The debate demonstrates how new developments present new challenges to democracy, even in well-consolidated systems.

A particular aspect of globalization concerns the threat from international terrorism. There is a delicate balance between security and freedom. On the one hand, freedom depends on a sufficient amount of security; on the other hand, security measures involving unrestricted surveillance and control threaten individual freedom. At the same time, terrorist suspects may be subjected to interrogation techniques and other forms of treatment that violate basic human rights. Some observers think that the USA Patriot Act (Uniting and Strengthening America by Providing Appropriate Tools Required to Intercept and Obstruct Terrorism Act), passed in October 2001, goes too far in defense of security. That is because individual freedom is violated in the process, and in the longer term, so they claim, the measures may even stimulate radicalization and create more insecurity (Donohue 2008; Waldron 2003).

In sum, democracy can never be taken for granted, not even in those parts of the world where it appears to be most firmly entrenched. Ways must be found to strengthen and deepen democratic processes, in both "new" and "old" systems. In many places, today's fragile democracies are a step ahead compared with yesterday's authoritarian systems, but real, sustained democratic progress cannot be taken for granted; it will require further democratic consolidation.

Great powers are more important than others to world order. There is a leading group of liberal democracies in the world at the present time: the G7, made up of the United States, Germany, the United Kingdom, France, Japan, Italy, and Canada. The major great power contenders, however— China, Russia, and India—are a much more mixed group. India is a mature democracy even if challenged by radical Hindu nationalism, elite dominance, and weak state institutions, especially at the level of single states. At the same time, regional concerns—especially the relationship to Pakistan—continue to be the defining axis of India's approach to international order.

China is an authoritarian political system; the Chinese Communist Party (CCP) has a monopoly on political power. The ruling elite is concentrated in the CCP's politburo and its standing committee of nine members. At the same time, private firms have replaced state-owned enterprises as the dominant economic force. Even if capitalists can now become members of the CCP, there is an increasing tension between a more open economy and a closed political system. Rising inequalities, rampant corruption, and emerging environmental pressures contribute to instability. Despite the policy of economic openness and political participation in international institutions, Chinese decision makers continue to "view the world as essentially conflict-prone, interstate relations as zero-sum power struggles, [and] violence as by no means a less common solution" (Deng 1998: 316). China is not likely to become a member of the liberal community of states devoted to close cooperation anytime soon (chapter 6 further develops this argument).

There were high hopes for the democratization of Russia after the end of the Cold War. They have not been met; under Vladimir Putin, power has been concentrated in the executive authority, leaving little room for political pluralism and representation of diverse interests. The strengthening of presidential powers is combined with shrinking opportunities for opposition voices; all national television networks are controlled by the government. Presidential power has also extended to the two remaining major groups in Russian society, the oligarchs and the regional political elites. Putin has gained control of the appointment of regional governors, and a compromise has been struck with the oligarchs: they pay more tax and reduce their meddling in government while in return they retain their fortunes made from privatization deals. Russia does seek a cooperative relationship with the West, but it does so "on equal terms and will not toe the Western line in international organizations" (Bluth 1998: 325). As in the case of China, Russia is no enthusiastic member of international society. It is strictly focused on its national interests and jealously guards its special role in the former Soviet area, the Commonwealth of Independent States (CIS). Russia may be a G8 member, but its relationship to the liberal community of states is not at all close.

In sum, democratic progress has been significant, but the quest for a liberal world order still faces the challenge of how to promote democracy and effective statehood in a very large number of countries. The continued existence of nonliberal great powers is another major challenge. As indicated earlier, there is a tendency among liberals to think that all good things go together, so that, for example, the establishment of a liberal economy will quickly be followed by the emergence of a liberal polity. Real world developments have not supported such optimism. Consolidated liberal democracies will continue to face a world with a large number of semidemocratic or outright authoritarian countries, and that group will include some of the great powers.

Progress Based on Liberal International Society

Another major argument in favor of the progress of liberal values concerns the principles respected by sovereign states as members of the international society of states. The values of peace, freedom, social progress, equal rights, and human dignity are enshrined in the Charter of the United Nations and in the Universal Declaration of Human Rights, as was briefly reported in chapter 2. But the mention of these values in the charter is of course no guarantee that member states actually endorse or respect them. The same goes for the Declaration of Human Rights. For many years it had no practical importance; there was no monitoring of human rights violations and no enforcement activity against offenders. The limited range of activities "reflected a very strong conception of sovereignty, that is, a narrow reading of the range of international human rights permitted by the principle of non-intervention. It also reflected the ambiguous position of intergovernmental human rights bodies" (Donnelly 1993: 58).

In 2006, the United Nations Commission on Human Rights was replaced by the UN Human Rights Council; the latter has improved procedures for scrutinizing every UN member state's record on human rights. Even so, the extent of real progress remains in question. The old human rights commission was dominated by nonliberal countries, and the new council has not changed in this regard. When Cuba came up for examination in the beginning of 2009, its allies on the council showered "paeans of praise" on the regime's achievements in health care and education, "leaving little time for critics to ask questions about political prisoners or freedom of speech" (*Christian Science Monitor,* February 9). China sent a large delegation to Geneva in the spring of 2009 to defend its own human rights performance. When the "Outcome Report on China" was debated in the council in June 2009, the Chinese government rejected, without exception, all seventy recommendations by the UN member states concerning human rights abuses in China. A sharp critique from Human Rights Watch (2009) followed: "Amid heightening repression of China's human rights lawyers, a tightening chokehold on freedom of expression, and an ongoing crackdown in Tibet, the Chinese government has tried to whitewash its human rights record in the hope that the UN will just look the other way. Its statement and denials bordered on farce."

In other words, consensus in principle can be combined with considerable deviation in practice. In non-Western societies the human rights conventions and declarations are part of what Hedley Bull (1995) called a diplomatic or elite culture, that is to say, a common intellectual culture that exists only at the elite level with roots that are shallow in the wider society. Furthermore, even at the elite level, such common values are not deeply ingrained (305). So the formal existence of universal liberal values as basic principles for a society of states says little about the actual status of these values or about the ways in which such values may be promoted to the largest effect.

The principles that make up the framework for the society of states concern the promotion of common values from above. The final major argument in favor of the progress of liberal values to be discussed here shifts the perspective to the emergence of common values from below. Again, the progress reported in chapter 2 can be seriously questioned. Modernization need not always lead to democracy and the embrace of liberal values. Samuel Huntington and others have argued that the relationship between modernization and Westernization is complex because processes of modernization can lead to de-Westernization in two ways. On the one hand, increasing economic, political, and military capacities give people a boost of confidence, making them more "culturally assertive." On the other hand, modernization animates feelings of alienation "as traditional bonds and social relations are broken" (Huntington 1996: 76). Both processes stimulate crises of identity.

Modernization in the context of uneven globalization thus frequently tends to strengthen local identities and to produce "resistance identities" (Castells 1998), including religious (fundamentalist) movements and ethnic movements. This has been the case, for example, not merely in Muslim countries, but also in places such as India, one of the few Third World countries with a long liberal political tradition. The Bharatiya Janata Party (BJP) asserts the preeminence of unique Hindu values, rejecting cultural pluralism (Chandra 1997: 142). The shift toward secular-rational values connected with the transformation from agrarian to industrial society is open-ended: the rural masses who become significant political actors may choose to support non-liberal and nondemocratic systems such as fascism or communism. That was the major insight in Barrington Moore's classic analysis from 1966.[7]

Ronald Inglehart and Christian Welzel (2009) are obviously optimistic: "the emergence of postindustrial society makes the democratic alternative increasingly probable" (160). Several other observers are much less optimistic. They question the idea that modernization involves secularization or that modernizers more or less automatically become secular and proceed to separate religion from politics. Peter Berger (1999) wrote that "the assumption that we live in a secularized world is false. The world today . . . is as furiously religious as it ever was, and in some places more so than ever. This means that

---

7. This means that the turn toward liberal values is primarily connected to the emergence of what Inglehart and Welzel call postindustrial society (see chapter 2). But even here competing inclinations continue to weigh in. According to the Inglehart and Welzel (2005) cultural map of the world, the following countries are at roughly the same stage in terms of the transformation from survival values to self-expression values: Egypt, South Africa, India, Poland, Slovakia, Taiwan, South Korea, and China. These countries are obviously very differently placed in terms of the development of liberal democracy.

a whole body of literature by historians and social scientists loosely labelled 'secularization theory' is essentially mistaken" (17). George Weigel (1991) speaks of the "unsecularization of the world" as one of "the dominant social facts of the late twentieth century" (27).

This brief survey of liberal values on a world scale emphasized the skeptical view. Liberal democracy has progressed in that there are a substantially higher number of free countries today than three decades ago. But in a very large number of cases, democratic consolidation is impeded by the lack of institutionalized party systems and the weakness of civil societies. Established democracies face new challenges from globalization and from the struggle against international terrorism. There has been some progress of liberal values "from above" in that almost all countries have signed the UN Charter and other declarations expressing liberal principles. But in practice there is frequently less support for such principles. Finally, if there is a strong trend toward secularization, there is also a strong trend toward desecularization; the coming dominance of liberal values can by no means be taken for granted. In sum, there is no firm development toward a universal cultural homogeneity dominated by liberal values. Supporters of such values have to steer a course across a more complex and uneven terrain where full commitment to liberal principles can never be taken for granted. The next section will argue that the tension between liberal Restraint and liberal Imposition makes such navigation an even more complicated task.

Liberal Ambiguity in an Uncertain Order

It was argued above that liberal values do not amount to a "winning ideology," once and for all formulated in Europe more than two centuries ago and from then on set to conquer the world. Liberal values are a set of principles, "an adaptable and mutating set of propositions" (Freeden 2008: 14) that always have to state their case in concrete historical circumstances where they are challenged by competing principles and ideologies. Liberal principles, such as human rights, should rather be seen as constantly evolving standards related to concrete struggles against various kinds of domination and repression. They are not "rooted in some fixed human nature or condition" (Peterson 2004: 22).

The distinction between timeless Western principles and principles that emerge in the course of historical struggles is not trivial because it defines the nature of the challenge that liberal principles pose to nonliberals. On the one hand, when liberal values are seen as inherently Western, they question others on their identities; other peoples are basically called upon to replace their commitment to nonliberal values with a commitment to Western, liberal values (Peterson 2004: 25). The promotion of liberal values can then become a case of identity politics where the West promotes its principles and the receiving society must appear as second-rate when it cannot meet Western normative standards. "What is lost is nothing less than the identities of these societies and cultures" (Peterson 2004: 25). Westerners can then see the dominance of Western power as legitimate, even desirable in the case of what Mill called "culturally inferior peoples" (for the formulation by Mill, see chapter 2).

That is the road to aggressive Imposition. In earlier days, the position of principal superiority of white Europeans was a means to justify slavery and colonialism: inferior races were not capable of autonomously exercising their rights (Peterson 2004: 27). Therefore, to deprive them of rights that were otherwise considered universal was justified. Today's Imposition is less drastic, but it still involves an ideological element of "we know better than you do what is best for you" and a power element of "do whatever you wish, provided you do the right thing." It is this identity challenge ("we want you to abandon your identity and become like us"), combined with a power challenge ("do it our way or else …"), that is eminently suited to produce fierce resistance.

At the same time, when liberal values are considered as evolving principles linked to historical struggles in concrete social contexts, the road lies open to a position of radical relativism in which the very idea of universal values is rejected on the grounds that values and rights are connected to particular historical societies and their cultures (Donnelly 1993: 36). That is the Marxist view; values and moral beliefs are shaped by class structures in the context of historical struggles; consequently, they emerge from the concrete circumstances of contests between groups and are by no means universal.[8]

On that view, the idea of universal liberal values cannot be the basis for a common ground between different civilizations. Such a common ground, according to Robert Cox (2002), must emerge from "a mutual recognition of difference" and a "consensual understanding of basic human rights" (185). This is of course a direct rejection of externally imposed principles. Any local adoption of human rights must not be the result of imposition because "an externally imposed order would remain fragile, vulnerable to the charge of imperialism" (Cox 2002: 186).

---

8. According to Robert Cox (2002), "rights are not innate, they are the product of people's historical struggles which become enshrined in their common sense; and human nature is not uniform and universal, but is formed differently by different histories" (186).

But such a radical relativism cannot be a liberal position because it denies that people are entitled to rights simply by virtue of being human. The liberal position must insist that there are universal values. The rejection of radical relativism opens up two less extreme positions. One is *strong relativism,* which holds that values are principally determined by local conditions. In this case, the emphasis is on local values. "Universal" principles then "serve as a check on culturally specific values" (Donnelly 1993: 36). The accent, however, is on variation because local values come first and universal values second. In the case of *weak relativism,* by contrast, the emphasis is reversed because human rights principles are held to be "largely universal, subject only to secondary, cultural modifications" (Donnelly 1993: 36).

The dilemma facing the promotion of liberal values now stands in sharper relief. It is a core value for liberals to exercise Restraint, that is, to respect the values of other cultures and societies. It is also a core value for liberals to support universal (liberal) values for all; in that sense liberals must favor Imposition. In the best of worlds, societal progress will take care of the dilemma, because it will make sure that support for liberal values emerges from within, in the context of a process of modernization and secularization. But it was argued above that such changes are not forthcoming in many societies and may not emerge anytime soon, even if social change and modernization are taking place.

That introduces the question of what outsiders can do and the best ways of doing it. When radical relativism is rejected, the choice is between strong and weak relativism. In both cases, even with good intentions, such efforts are vulnerable to hostile interpretations from those on the receiving end. Any deviation from radical Restraint is liable to be seen as a policy of Imposition that involves both an identity challenge and a power challenge. In other words, the choice becomes a starker one between, on the one hand, doing nothing or very little while waiting for domestic changes to take the proper course, or, on the other hand, engaging in an activism that may be received as hostile Imposition.

Such activism is of course most visible in cases where the West is heavily present, as in Afghanistan, Bosnia, East Timor, and Iraq. In war-torn societies with a high degree of violent domestic conflict, outsiders will tend to take control of the democratization process. Their argument is that they know better what is good for the people and the country than the local conflicting parties. When Lord Paddy Ashdown took over as High Representative in Bosnia in 2002, he made the following statement: "I have concluded that there are two ways I can make my decisions. One is with a tape measure, measuring the precise equidistant position between three sides. The other is by doing what I think is right for the country as a whole. I prefer the second of these. So when I act, I shall seek to do so in defence of the interests of all the people of Bosnia and Herzegovina, putting their priorities first" (quoted from Chandler 2006: 480).

The problem when outsiders, even well-meaning ones, try to promote democracy (liberal values) by doing what they think is right is that domestic political processes are not allowed to operate. Although the technical trappings of democracy may be installed, they are devoid of political substance because all the key decisions are taken by outsiders. The situation is no different in Afghanistan and Iraq (see chapter 4). The occupation forces are not themselves held accountable to local groups; Iraqis complained with "increasing bitterness and anger" about the "corruption and abuse" by the CPA (Coalition Provisional Authority, the transitional government 2003–4) (Diamond 2005: 18). Afghans watched the United States make deals with northern (fundamentalist) warlords in their battle against the Taliban; when President Hamid Karzai then attempted to win the support of Islamic fundamentalists by signing a bill requiring "woman to obey their husband's sexual demands," he was quickly persuaded by the United States to correct the provisions of the law. The imposition of "good governance" by outsiders cannot help but contain an illiberal element because it restricts the influence of locally elected representatives (Chandler 2006: 480).

The identity game in such a situation is dominated by the roles of patrons (outsiders) and clients (insiders). The power game as seen from insiders' point of view is about getting as much as possible from the patrons in return for as little as possible, especially in the way of concessions that may endanger one's own position of power and influence. The power game as seen from outsiders' point of view is about ways to assuage international security threats, defuse domestic conflict, and, to the extent possible, support a more democratic polity. On either side, the promotion of liberal values is most frequently a secondary concern rather than a top priority.

Seen in this light, the conflict zones mentioned here are representative cases rather than outliers, because similar mechanisms are at work in other areas. We shall see in chapter 4 that external pressure for liberal economic reform in many developing countries became a power game in which local rulers attempted to secure new aid and loans while implementing as few policy reforms as possible. Chapter 5 explains how advanced liberal states are disciplining latecomers with neoliberal measures that tilt the playing field in favor of further economic upgrading of the highly developed countries and against the aspirations of the latecomers. The power game is one in which the latecomers attempt to preserve as much autonomy and policy space as possible while still being admitted to the global liberal economic order. Chapter 6 makes clear that there is no simple institutional path to a reformed liberal order; the liberal impulse toward universal institutions with equal rights for all is checked by a liberal impulse toward safeguarding liberal hegemony, if necessary by means of a concert of liberal democracies. At the same time, China and other nonliberal great powers play the institutional game to the extent that it is compatible with their core interests, but not in order to embrace liberal values in a larger sense.

Thus all the current efforts to establish a liberal world order amount to a power game played with a liberal vocabulary rather than to a gradual strengthening of liberal values on a global scale. Any major change in that situation would call upon outsiders to be less hypocritical and to support liberal values in practice and not just in theory; and it would call upon insiders to establish an agenda that gives real priority to the progress of liberal values. Such an agenda will be forthcoming only in cases where there are favorable domestic preconditions for the promotion of liberal democracy and liberal values in general. Thomas Carothers makes the point in a discussion of democracy promotion: the efforts from outsiders can only move a country more quickly in a direction in which it is already going. Even with the best of intentions, outsiders cannot "fundamentally reshape the balances of power, interests, historical legacies, and political traditions of the major political forces in recipient countries. They do not neutralize dug-in antidemocratic forces. They do not alter the political habits, mindsets and desires of entire populations. They do not create benign regional settings. They do not alter the basic economic level or direction of countries" (Carothers 1999: 305). In sum, the ambivalence of outsiders and the lack of forthcoming domestic preconditions should dampen any great expectations of rapid progress for liberal values on a global scale.

Conclusion

Liberal values fare better today than before in the world, helped by processes of modernization and democratization and by international cooperation. Still, the situation is problematic and raises questions to which liberals have no clear answers. The liberal belief in progress has been animated by too much idealist optimism. Progress may happen, but not in a smooth and automatic way. Nonidealist liberals persuasively emphasize the uncertainty of progress and the clashes of values that are bound to take place.

Any concrete assessment of the global progress of liberal values must confront a world where different trends point in dissimilar directions. What can be said with certainty is that there has been no great victory for liberal values. Liberal democracy has advanced, but in a fragile and uncertain way. There is no easy road to democratic consolidation. The society of states does endorse liberal values, but more in abstract principle than in practice. Modernization can lead to a stronger position for liberal values, but probably not anytime soon, and maybe not even at all.

In this uncertain situation, liberals face a dilemma: they cannot support a policy of radical Restraint; they must be committed to some form of activism that will frequently come across as hostile Imposition. And even if the defenders of liberal principles can overcome the ambivalences that raise suspicions of hypocrisy, favorable domestic preconditions remain decisive for the promotion of liberal values. Those preconditions are absent in many places. We remain in an uncertain order where the liberal message might not find many takers.

Kofi Annan (2003) recently found reason to ask: "Do we still have universal values?" His answer was: "Yes, we do—but we should not take them for granted. They need to be carefully thought through. They need to be defended—and strengthened" (6). At present, there appears to be a comprehensive lack of reflection on the appropriate response when efforts to promote liberal values provoke resistance and fundamentalist reactions. The standard reaction so far has been to reconfirm that liberal universal values will prevail in the end. But if that is not the case, not even in the medium or long run, the question of how to promote a firm commitment to common values that are also strongly rooted in local societies becomes acute.[9]

---

9. Hedley Bull (1995) talks about the need for "the preservation and extension of a cosmopolitan culture, embracing both common ideas and common values, and rooted in societies in general as well as in their elites" (305).

 CHAPTER 4

A Different Security Dilemma
Liberals Facing Weak and Failed States

This chapter will demonstrate how the difficulties for liberal states of responding appropriately to the challenges of weak and failed states are intimately connected to the tension between Liberal Restraint and Liberal Imposition. A policy of Restraint was embarked upon in the context of decolonization; a policy of Imposition has dominated the agenda in the new millennium. Neither the Liberalism of Restraint nor the Liberalism of Imposition promises to successfully confront the problems of weak and failed states, and there are no facile compromises between the two. Therefore, liberal democracies will continue to be, not merely uneasy and insecure about how best to confront the problem posed by weak and failed states, but also painted into a corner with few if any attractive options.

It was argued above (chapter 1) that the aggressive power balancing that was prompted by the traditional security dilemma and the imminence of violent conflict between sovereign states had been significantly mitigated, in some areas even transcended owing to the emergence of a liberal security community. Instead, the insecurity dilemma connected to weak states has appeared as a major item on the international agenda.

What is a weak state? Three major characteristics must be mentioned: First, the economy is defective. There is a lack of a coherent national economy, capable of sustaining a basic level of welfare for the population and of providing the resources for running an effective state. Defective economies often depend crucially on the world market, because they are mono-economies based on the export of one or a few primary goods. In sub-Saharan Africa, primary products account for 80–90 percent of total export. Furthermore, the economy is highly heterogeneous with elements of a modern sector, but also feudal or semifeudal structures in agriculture. In both urban and rural areas large parts of the population are outside of the formal sector, living in localized subsistence economies at very low standards.

The second major characteristic of weak states is that people in society do not make up a coherent national community. A national "community of citizens" was created at independence, but only in the formal sense of providing people with identity cards and passports. This was combined with some scattered attempts to launch nation-building projects that would develop a common idea of the state. But the real substance of citizenship—legal, political, and social rights—was not provided on a major scale by the new states. When the state does not deliver, or delivers only to a very limited extent, people turn elsewhere for the satisfaction of material and nonmaterial needs. In sub-Saharan Africa, they have primarily turned to the ethnic communities that are the focal points for a "moral economy" (Ndegwa 1997).

The lack of community is connected to the third characteristic of weak states: the absence of effective and responsive state institutions. In most cases, the new postindependence leaders were not actively interested in the creation of strong states; they feared that a strong state would be a potential threat to their firm grip on state power. But in contrast to the colonial elite, the new rulers were not insulated from society; they were closely connected to it by ties of clan, kinship, and ethnic affiliation. The network of clients had great expectations of benefits from the power over the state apparatus. This opened the way to clientelism, patronage, and nepotism (R. Jackson and Rosberg 1994).

The characteristics of weak statehood may be present in varying combinations; hence there are various attempts to measure the degree of weakness and sensitivity to complete breakdown or state failure.[1] State elites in weak states are strong in the sense that they do not face serious domestic or external threat. In the domestic realm, civil society is divided among many different groups, and it is unorganized with few possibilities of earnestly challenging the holders of state power. In the external realm the weak entities that were the newly independent, postcolonial states were left alone because borders were now considered sacrosanct. The UN, backed by the superpowers, provided these countries with a certified life insurance: no matter how bad

---

1. See for example the 2008 Index on State Weakness by S. Rice and Patrick (2008).

things might get, no matter how little development they might be capable of, the international community would continue to respect their newly won sovereignty and their right to formal independence (R. Jackson 1993).

Some intervention by the superpowers did take place during the Cold War, but the East-West confrontation also helped strengthen the new norms of the right of ex-colonies to sovereign statehood. The new states could take advantage of the fact that the global contenders were looking for allies around the world and were anxious not to see too many countries line up on the side of the opponent. Under these circumstances, state elites in weak states are powerful and unconstrained. At the same time, however, they remain vulnerable to rival groups, often including parts of the military that want to establish their own hold on state power (Goldsmith 2004). State elites often do not have the resources or the political will to accommodate rival groups; challenges are rather met by increasing repression, "not because it has a high probability of success but because the weakness of the state precludes its resort to less violent alternatives" (Mason and Krane, quoted in Job 1992: 29).

In sum, basing themselves on patron-client relationships, self-seeking state elites lacked legitimacy from the beginning and faced populations divided along ethnic, religious, and social lines. They created "captured states" that benefited the leading strongman and his selected groups of clients. The majority of the population was excluded from the system and faced a state that was rather an enemy and a mortal threat than a protector and a champion of development (Sørensen 2001).

This, then, is the general background for the insecurity dilemma in weak states. It emerges from the paradoxical situation that weak states are relatively free from serious external threat while simultaneously posing a serious security threat to major parts of their own populations. In a basic sense, anarchy is domesticized: there is an international system or relative order with fairly secure protection of the borders and territories of weak states, and there is a domestic realm with a high degree of insecurity and conflict. As seen from the perspective of the populations of weak states, this is an insecurity dilemma, because they cannot know what to expect from the state; furthermore, strategies of resistance and support may be counterproductive to achieving security. The government's primary task ideally should be to provide security for its population, but instead it makes up the greatest potential threat to people within its boundaries (Saideman et al. 2002: 106–7).

The human cost of weak and failed statehood has been extremely high. Three conflicts in Sudan, Ethiopia, and Mozambique each demanded the lives of somewhere between five hundred thousand and one million people; casualties in Angola, Rwanda, Sierra Leone, Liberia, and Uganda have also been very high. Violent conflict is no longer mainly interstate war; there was none such conflict between 2004 and 2008,[2] and since 1989 the annual number of interstate wars has been between zero and two. By contrast, there were 30 intrastate conflicts (or intrastate conflicts with external participation) in 2004; the annual number of such conflicts since 1989 has been between 27 and 53 (Harbom and Wallensteen 2009). The data confirm that violent conflict today takes place *within* weak and fragile states rather than *between* states.

The intensification of domestic disputes after the end of the Cold War led to "humanitarian intervention" in states where large groups of civilians were victims of violent conflict (G. Evans and Sahnoun 2001). After September 11, 2001, these problems took on new urgency, because leading Western policymakers found that "failed and dysfunctional states have become breeding grounds for civil wars, genocide and other atrocities, terrorism, famine and the spread of lethal diseases" (Delahunty and Yoo 2007). The U.S. National Security Strategy of 2002 explicitly identified "rogue states" that "brutalize their own people . . . display no regard for international law . . . are determined to acquire weapons of mass destruction . . . sponsor terrorism around the globe; and reject basic human values" (NSS 2002: 13–14). However, not all weak states are rogue states, and this raises the question of where to intervene and for what specific reasons—more on this below. Presently, it must be emphasized that from early on, dealing with both weak and rogue states contained an idealistic element of protecting people and promoting universal liberal values: "we will never forget that we are ultimately fighting for our democratic values and way of life. . . . Those values of freedom are right and true for every person in every society—and the duty of protecting these values against their enemies is the common calling of freedom-loving people across the globe and across the ages" (NSS 2002: 7, foreword).

So even if the empirical connection between state weakness and transnational security threats is underexplored (Patrick 2006), and even if further conceptual clarifications concerning "weak" or "fragile," "failed," and "rogue" states are in order (e.g., Dannreuther 2007), there is no doubt that the security problems connected with weak statehood today figure prominently on the agenda of consolidated Western democracies. The dilemma for liberal states is that they are incapable of defining durable solutions to these problems. They cannot fully embrace Restraint and they cannot fully embrace Imposition; nor do the possible compromises present a solid way forward.

---

2. When a conflict broke out between Djibouti and Eritrea; cf. Harbom and Wallensteen (2009).

The Road to Restraint: Abolition of Colonial Empires

The Liberalism of Restraint emphasizes respect for others, tolerance of diversity, and nonintervention, that is, leaving others alone, letting them decide their own path. The institution of sovereignty is a major element in the Liberalism of Restraint because it embraces nonintervention and upholds the autonomy of states to conduct their own affairs free from outside interference. Sovereignty became the dominant principle of political organization in Europe after the Peace of Westphalia in 1648. The peace brought about no momentous change (Krasner 2001; Teschke 2003); still it is justified to look at 1648 as a crucial point in the transition from feudal to modern authority. Within Europe, peaceful coexistence "was rooted in the beliefs that different cultures were equally valuable and should be give space to flourish" (Keene 2002: 98). Self-determination and nonintervention are basic principles of the system. This is the Liberalism of Restraint regime.

For a long period, sovereignty and thus membership in the society of states was a privilege of European countries. Non-European areas were not considered qualified for membership; they lacked the necessary level of civilization and religious (Christian) qualities. The white settlers that constructed the United States became early members of the system; Europeans and Americans agreed that beyond their own realm, there could be no room for a Restraint regime pursuing tolerance and nonintervention. What was needed was the promotion of civilization: "Europeans and Americans believed that they knew how other governments should be organized, and actively worked to restructure societies that they regarded as uncivilized so as to encourage economic progress and stamp out the barbarism, corruption, despotism and incompetence that they believed to be characteristic of most indigenous regimes" (Keene 2002: 99).[3] Sir Frederick Lugard asserted that "the African holds the position of a late-born child in the family of nations, and must as yet be schooled in the discipline of the nursery"; this was simply, according to M. F. Lindley, a part of the obligation that "the advanced peoples collectively owe to backward races in general" (both quotes from R. Jackson 1993: 71).

---

3. "Especially in North America, this was also connected with the idea that the whole continent was an uncultivated wilderness, which needed to be civilized through the establishment of properly organized settlements and through the provision of republican constitutions for the new states created thereby. In both cases, and again in contrast to the Westphalian system, statesmen, diplomats and international lawyers were quite prepared to entertain the possibility that violent actions and other interventions might have to be made in order to civilize savage peoples, or to prevent them from retarding the civilization of the wilderness that they insisted on treating as their homelands" (Keene 2002: 99).

This is the Liberalism of Imposition regime: we, the civilized peoples, need to go in and create the appropriate conditions for freedom to thrive.

In the age of empire, then, the tension between Restraint and Imposition was solved by applying one principle (Restraint) to civilized peoples in Europe and North America, and another principle (Imposition) to noncivilized peoples elsewhere. By the turn of the twentieth century, Europeans had fleshed out a "standard of civilization" containing the criteria that new members had to meet in order to qualify for membership in civilized international society (Gong 1984: 14–15). There were always borderline cases, of course; the standard had to be interpreted and applied. Latin American countries, which were considered offspring from the European civilization, had easier access to membership than African countries. Patterns of great power interests also mattered. In any case, the two systems, and the two principles, lived alongside each other until World War II.

Several factors helped create a new situation after the war. The ties between colonies and motherlands were weakened; several colonial dependencies provided troops to aid allied efforts and expected something in return once the job was done. The main colonial motherlands no longer controlled the international agenda, and the new great powers, the United States and the Soviet Union, were generally in favor of decolonization. In economic terms, the colonizers could be relieved of responsibility for the colonized while retaining ample opportunity to look after their own economic interests (Galbraith 1994). Finally, the norms concerning colonies changed dramatically: Before the war, the possession of colonies was considered legitimate and even necessary, given the backward condition of the colonized areas. After the war, colonialism came to be considered "an absolute wrong" (R. Jackson 1993: 48), even "a crime" (UN General Assembly Resolution 3103, quoted from R. Jackson 1993: 107).

With decolonization, standards of civilization could not be used to exclude states from membership in international society. Membership in the United Nations was open to "all peace-loving states" (United Nations 1945: article 4); the charter confirmed that the UN "is based on the principle of the sovereign equality of all its members" and that "nothing contained in the present Charter shall authorize the United Nations to intervene in matters which are essentially within the domestic jurisdiction of any state" (article 2). With the emphasis on sovereignty and nonintervention, the Liberalism of Restraint regime was extended to the newly independent countries; every state was given "the right freely to choose and develop its political, social, economic and cultural systems" (Special Committee report to UN General Assembly, cited in Goodrich et al. 1969: 40).

At the same time, the Liberalism of Imposition regime is not absent from the charter. The preamble reaffirms "faith in fundamental human rights, in the dignity and worth of the human person, in the equal rights of men and women." Article 1 defines the purpose of the UN as one of "promoting and encouraging respect for human rights and for fundamental freedoms for all without distinction as to race, sex, language or religion." In that way, the charter commits itself simultaneously to Restraint, that is, respect for sovereignty and nonintervention, and to Imposition, that is, promotion of the standard of civilization expressed in the principles of universal human rights. More recent UN documents share this dual commitment: the UN Millennium Declaration, adopted by the General Assembly in September 2000, reaffirms its support for "the sovereign equality of all states, respect for their territorial integrity and political independence... [and] non-interference in the internal affairs of states." It also reaffirms its support for the promotion of "certain fundamental values." These values include freedom: "men and women have the right to live their lives and raise their children in dignity, free from hunger and free from the fear of violence, oppression or injustice. Democratic and participatory governance based on the will of the people best assures these rights." They also include equality: "no individual and no nation must be denied the opportunity to benefit from development. The equal rights and opportunities of women and men must be assured" (United Nations 2000).

Thus there is a deep tension in international society, because it is based on an order that supports two different normative principles: on the one hand, respect for the sovereign independence of states, and on the other hand, the promotion of common, universal principles of civilization (Keene 2002: 143–44). Nonliberal regimes will not find it hard to emphasize the principle of Restraint, giving priority to sovereignty and nonintervention. Liberal regimes, by contrast, will support both Restraint and Imposition because they both express core liberal values. This creates a permanent predicament: how can liberal states reconcile principles that fundamentally contradict each other? In the context of decolonization, liberal states emphasized the principle of Restraint. The next section explains why this emphasis held no solution to the problem of weak and failed states.

Restraint in Practice: Weak Statehood Perpetuated

Hopes were high for rapid progress after independence: elites and popular groups had rallied around the common goal of getting rid of the colonizers. Once sovereignty was achieved, however, there was little left to create unity among groups in the population. At the same time, the elites heading the new states produced more political bads than political goods. What was the problem? Why could social, economic, and political development not get under way in a pattern repeating the European experience? First of all, the colonial legacy did not leave most countries well prepared for independence. Colonialism sets up a system of direct political control aimed at protecting the political and economic interests of the ruling power. The economic focus was on the export of primary commodities. Monocrop or monomineral economies served the needs of the motherlands. Production for local needs declined while the transport infrastructure was orientated toward export (Schraeder 2004). In political terms, colonialism did bring centralized governments, but they were small, authoritarian undertakings, often based on divide-and-rule, that would privilege some ethnic groups over others. Colonial rulers typically concentrated on maintaining a relatively strong set of repressive institutions, including military and police forces, whereas other parts of the state apparatus were clearly underdeveloped, including institutions having to do with welfare and economic development (Alavi and Shanin 1982).

The newly independent weak states were extremely conflict-prone because communal groups and elites would struggle over scarce resources, most importantly over control of the state apparatus (Gurr 1994). Seen from the comparative perspective of the European history of state making, this sounds like good news: "War makes states" is the well-known aphorism of Charles Tilly's (1985: 170) historical work on patterns of state formation in Europe. When war making is a vital ingredient in successful state making, comprehensive violent conflict should eventually pave the way for stronger (i.e., more effective and legitimate) states. That is indeed behind the recommendation of "Give War a Chance" by Edward Luttwak (1999). So why has war very rarely had positive effects on state making in the weak states of the third world? The answer is that the context and substance of violent conflict is qualitatively different in the two cases.

In Europe, geopolitical competition was intense, and states were "locked into an open-ended and ruthless competition" (Held 1995: 54), which forced state elites to create domestic order capable of resource extraction from societies that could support the military campaigns. States were forced to be effective at revenue collection in order to improve their financial basis. This also helped create new bonds between the state and civil society. Capitalists and bankers could relocate if they were offered unfavorable conditions, so states bargained with them in order to get access to the resources needed for war making. The process "gave the civilian groups enforceable claims on the

state" (Tilly 1990: 206). That is to say, compromises with the subject populations constrained the power of state elites and paved the way for rights of
citizenship. Citizenship in turn meant material benefits for the population.
Combined with the creation of domestic order and the promotion of capital
accumulation, these processes furthered the bonds of loyalty and legitimacy
between rulers and peoples.

In contrast, power holders in the newly independent states face no serious
external threat. Postcolonial states and regimes are protected from outside
threat by a norm of fixed borders created in the framework of decolonization
and strengthened during the Cold War.[4] Recolonization, annexation, or any
other format by which stronger states could take over weaker ones is out of
the question; sovereign, postcolonial statehood is guaranteed by the United
Nations. This obviously decreases the salience of power holders' long-term
considerations (i.e., to build a state that will last) and correspondingly increases the salience of short-term considerations (i.e., to get rich in a hurry).
With fixed borders, the need to create effective institutions in order to confront external threat or undertake territorial expansion is eliminated. The
mechanism that helps generate national identity and loyalty is taken away as
well. Weak statehood is now secure, and it might pave the way for processes
leading to even weaker or failed states.

It ought to be clear, then, that the conditions of state creation and
state building are fundamentally different in the context of decolonization
and in the European experience. Conceding sovereign independence to
colonies was the greatest transfer of political authority in world history.
Decolonization was primarily pushed by the international normative and
material changes recorded above; it was to a much smaller extent the result
of comprehensive domestic struggles. The new state elites confronted societies divided along ethnic, socioeconomic, and religious lines; no coherent national community existed. The elites presided over institutional and
administrative structures that were weak and ineffective. In this situation,
state elites quickly gave up on any attempt to provide public or collective goods. The state apparatus was instead turned into a source of personal power and enrichment. To the extent that the spoils of office were
shared, they went to groups of loyal followers in networks of patron–client
relationships.

---

4. As emphasized by Robert Jackson (1995), this practice of respecting existing borders "is
a fundamental normative change from the basis of state jurisdiction historically, which could be
determined by military force, by Machiavellian diplomacy, by commercial transaction, by dynastic
marriage, and by other such means" (66).

The extent to which sovereignty places political and economic benefits in the hands of state elites can hardly be overestimated.[5] Sovereignty confers legitimacy in the domestic as well as the international sphere; robbery and persecution take place in the official name of the state. Accused of plunder, a Congolese government spokesman retorted: "the Congolese government is the legitimate government of this country.... Whatever we do is legitimate" (quoted from Englebert and Hummel 2005: 414). Even when international society is critical of sovereign rulers, their legitimate right to rule is rarely questioned. Sovereignty provides domestic and international political power. In the domestic realm, the state defines the rules of the game, and even if the state is weak, formal regulation is pervasive. Identity cards, road tolls, authorizations, licenses, duties, and much more provide possibilities for control and revenue; no wonder that "the law is perceived as terrifying" (statement about Niger, quoted from Englebert 2009: 20).

In the international sphere, sovereignty offers formal membership in the society of states on an equal basis with every other state. It provides access to international institutions, including the UN system. Furthermore, the formal right of control of territory, government, and citizens is a valuable bargaining resource in international society. On the one hand, strong states cannot merely do what they want in the weak states. Intervention in other sovereign states cannot be conducted in complete ignorance of the rules of international society; such acts of intervention need justification. On the other hand, domestic rulers are empowered by sovereignty because outsiders are compelled to bargain with them. The CIA had to bargain with Mobutu when it wanted to operate in Zaire, for example; even the strongest state on earth could not merely ignore one of the weakest (Kelly 1993). The Cold War strengthened the hand of domestic rulers because they could play on the fact that the global competitors were looking for partners elsewhere in the world; they were at least anxious not to see too many countries line up on the side of the opponent (David 1991; Clapham 1998).

Sovereignty opens the door to vast economic gain. State authority can be marketed and sold in both domestic and international tenders. In the mid-seventies, for example, Zaire's President Mobutu gave a German firm control over 150,000 square kilometers of Shaba Province in exchange for rents (Young and Turner 1985: 387). An elite network of Zimbabwean and

---

5. For recent analyses, see Englebert and Hummel (2005); Englebert (2009); Atzili (2006/7); Leonard and Straus (2003); Dannreuther (2007); Eriksen (2005). For general analyses of weak statehood, see R. Jackson (1993); Bayart (1993); Bratton and van de Walle (1997); Chabal and Daloz (1999); Sandbrook (1985).

Congolese state and military groups practiced "asset stripping," a process where assets were moved out of the state mining sector into the control of private companies. The transaction concerned "at least US$5 billion of assets" and there was "no compensation or benefit for the state treasury of the Democratic Republic of Congo" (Englebert and Hummel 2005: 413). Since the possibilities for economic gain are frequently larger in dealing with the outside world, weak states tend to focus on external rather than internal mobilization of resources (Eriksen 2005). Development aid is a major source; by the mid-nineties, "the average African country received the equivalent of 12.3 percent of its GDP in ODA (Official Development Assistance), an international transfer that is unprecedented in historical terms" (van de Walle 2001: 8).[6] In 2003, ODA had reached a staggering 18.6 percent of GDP; by comparison, the Marshall aid at its peak amounted to 2.5 percent of the GDP of Germany and France. Foreign investment and loans are the other main sources of funds where state elites can offer access to raw materials and primary commodities in return.

Secure existence behind fixed borders, combined with a reliance by state elites on external sources for economic gain, helps create a situation where there is little interest in strengthening the state. Furthermore, domestic control over raw materials does not necessarily depend on an effective state (Eriksen 2005). Zaire (now the Democratic Republic of Congo), for example, is rich in natural resources: copper, zinc, cobalt, and diamonds. Mobutu took private control of many of these assets, sometimes licensing them to foreign companies, sometimes leaving them to be exploited by strongmen in his own network. He actively avoided consolidating state power, not least out of fear that bureaucracies might acquire interests and powers of their own (Reno 2000: 1). The state became what William Reno calls a "shadow state": it was maintained as a disguise for what were really private forms of wealth accumulation and political management. The state was a necessary façade because it provided access to domestic control, international support, and foreign aid.

Guaranteed sovereignty behind fixed borders and economic gain via external connections also have consequences for insurgent groups struggling against incumbent regimes. They will rarely seek secession, because that road is closed; nor will they often turn to civilians for economic and other support, because international legitimacy does not depend on such support. It is rather connected to de facto control of the capital city "from where access

---

6. Excluding South Africa and Nigeria.

to a seat at the United Nations provides all the protections of sovereignty" (Weinstein 2007: 71).

In sum, colonialism came into terminal disrepute after World War II and was replaced by a new international norm of the right to independence, to formal sovereignty, for previous colonies. This is the Liberalism of Restraint in practice: even weak countries have a right to independence, to chart their own course, decide their own fate. Decolonization tied liberal states to a policy of Restraint; they had to respect the principle of sovereignty for weak states. This naturally severely limits what outsiders can do in weak states; everything must go through negotiation with the dominant insiders, the state elites that are part of the problem rather than part of the solution. They know they do not face mortal danger because neocolonial takeovers are out of the question. Therefore, state elites can be self-seeking predators without fear that rising domestic economic and political chaos will cost them the ultimate price: termination of the state. The Liberalism of Restraint gave sovereign freedom to weak states, but that same move perpetuated underdevelopment and domestic insecurity for the populations.

The Road to Imposition: Increasing External Pressure

Liberal states knew about these problems from early on and have attempted various ways of increasing the pressure on weak state elites. During the 1980s, the focus was on market strategies, that is, economic reforms and liberalization; during the 1990s, emphasis was on democratization and good governance; today, the accent is on the strengthening of civil society. None of these strategies have yielded impressive results.

The market strategy was a response to a severe debt crisis prompted by increasing energy prices and interest rates for weak states in the late 1970s. As a condition for provision of new loans, liberal states together with the World Bank and the IMF demanded reforms intended to make weak states less statist and more market-oriented. These Structural Adjustment Programs (SAPs) were generally in trouble a decade later, as the World Bank itself admitted (World Bank 1994; Callaghy 1991). The programs themselves were not flawless (Schatz 1994), but the main problem was the gatekeepers, the weak state elites. The adjustment programs were often formally accepted, but implementation was not pursued to any serious degree. Regimes were frequently able to carry out the measures in ways that transferred the cost away from the state elites and their clients (Clapham 1996).

By the early 1990s, focus shifted toward reform of the state itself. Instead of doing away with the state, it was now admitted that efficient and democratic states are indispensable for economic and social development (World Bank 1997). That led to new demands for democratization and good governance. The promotion of democracy is probably the area where outsiders face the most severe problems in dealing with weak states. Democracy means self-determination, rule by representatives of the people free from outside interference. How can outsiders influence, even control, the democratic process without risking the charge of being seen as undemocratic? The intervention forces are not subject to local democratic control; nobody guards the guardians (Coyne 2006a). To escape charges of imperial control, outsiders are compelled to quickly help set up free and fair elections and to help empower people in civil society. But in many weak states the democratic political process is viewed with suspicion because politics is understood as a zero-sum game where winners get all and losers get nothing. In the case of Somalia, for example, there have been thirteen failed foreign-led attempts at creating national reconciliation since 1991. All efforts to create responsive central government have led to more rather than less conflict (Coyne 2006b; Menkhaus 2004). Faced with such problems, outsiders will naturally attempt either to stay in control of the political process (not a very democratic solution) or to get out in a hurry and recognize the limited possibilities that outsiders have for creating effective and democratic institutions of government; neither option promotes democracy in a sustainable way.

Undeniably, there has been some democratic progress in weak states, but in a significant number of cases, incumbents have managed to remain in power through a combination of often repressive divide-and-rule tactics and the use of violence against political opponents. At the same time, rulers play the democratic game just sufficiently to "pass themselves off as democrats" (Carothers 1997). Democratic institutions are more a façade to satisfy current international democratic norms than indications of substantial political change (Joseph 1998).

The current emphasis on strengthening civil society as part of a program of decentralization and poverty reduction must confront the same problem as the market and the democratization strategies: external forces can accomplish very little on their own; they need domestic allies. The terms under which alliances with domestic groups can be established are always subject to substantial influence by the strongest and most resourceful group in society, the incumbent state elites. Instead of producing political goods for the population such as economic welfare and political freedoms, the reforms recorded here have often led to more violent conflict. When the Cold War ended, humanitarian intervention aiming at mitigating violent conflict became another way for liberal states to confront the problems in weak states.

The End of the Cold War, 9/11, and a New Security Environment

The bipolar confrontation that was the Cold War ended when one of the contenders was demolished; the immediate consequences for weak states were not clear. On the one hand, as UK foreign secretary Jack Straw asserted, "the East and the West no longer needed to maintain extensive spheres of influence through financial and other forms of assistance to states whose support they wanted. So the bargain between the major powers and their client states unraveled" (quoted from Bilgin and Morton 2004: 174). Such a development would turn weak states into a "pole of indifference" (Wolfers quoted from R. Jackson 1993: 88) and thus arguably accelerate state failure. On the other hand, the fall of communism left the Western model of liberal democracy and market economy without any major contenders. As recorded above, a broader and more global effort to advance democracy became a central element on the agenda of both the United States and other Western democracies (Carothers 1999: 40).

The democratic openings in weak states were often accompanied by sharply increasing violent domestic conflict. In societies with frail institutions and low levels of trust and mutual acceptance among contending groups of the elite and of the population, democratization can easily lead to sharper confrontations because political pluralism means better possibilities for formulating demands and voicing disagreements. In the most serious cases, such conflicts have involved genocide and state collapse. By 1993, there were forty-seven armed conflicts in the world; all conflicts were domestic, most all of them within weak states. The level of casualties was extremely high in Ethiopia, Mozambique, Sudan, Angola, Uganda, Somalia, Liberia, Sierra Leone, and Rwanda (Copson 1994). Such human cost had to attract the attention of international society. The liberal view of human rights as a universal value had gained ground after the end of the Cold War. At the same time, UN Security Council initiatives were no longer completely blocked by the East/West conflict.

This led to attempts by liberal states to intervene in order to bring conflicts to a halt and protect civilians. Not all cases of violent domestic conflict led to this kind of humanitarian intervention, but some did, including Rwanda, Haiti, Somalia, Liberia, Bosnia, East Timor, and Serbia/Kosovo. Former attempts to influence developments in weak states were negotiated with the respective governments. Humanitarian intervention is a more direct version of liberal Imposition in that it can take place without the consent of the affected governments.

It was clear from early on that many countries would be skeptical about setting aside the sovereignty principle of nonintervention. Most liberal states, by contrast, pressed for a change of international norms that would provide a stronger basis for humanitarian intervention. At the behest of UN General Secretary Kofi Annan the Commission on Intervention and State Sovereignty was established in the fall of 2000, and one year later, the commission—chaired by Gareth Evans and Mohamed Sahnoun—issued a report titled "The Responsibility to Protect." It endorsed two basic principles:

A. State sovereignty implies responsibility, and the primary responsibility for the protection of its people lies with the state itself.
B. Where a population is suffering serious harm, as a result of internal war, insurgency, repression or state failure, and the state in question is unwilling or unable to halt or avert it, the principle of non-intervention yields to the international responsibility to protect (G. Evans and Sahnoun 2001: XI).

International society's willingness to embrace such principles probably culminated by the late 1990s; the responsibility to protect was eventually acknowledged at the UN World Summit in 2005. But the final document from that meeting claims that this is a responsibility of "each individual State," while the international community should merely "encourage and help States to exercise this responsibility" (quoted from Jentleson 2007: 285).

With bipolarity replaced by unipolarity, the views of the United States on humanitarian intervention became of primary importance. The George W. Bush administration came into office critical of the Somalia and other humanitarian operations undertaken during the Clinton presidency. There should be no further cases of "the 82nd airborne escorting kids to kindergarten" (quoted from Jentleson 2007: 278); focus was to be on places more closely tied to national security interests. The 9/11 attack helped reemphasize the priority of national security in the eyes of the administration but it also changed the attitude toward involvement in weak states. The 2002 U.S. National Security Strategy pledges to "extend the benefits of freedom across the globe. We will actively work to bring the hope of democracy, free markets, and free trade to every corner of the world. The events of September 11, 2001, taught us that weak states, like Afghanistan, can pose as great a danger to our national interests as strong states. Poverty does not make poor people into terrorists and murderers. Yet poverty, weak institutions, and corruption can make weak states vulnerable to terrorist networks and drug cartels within their borders" (NSS 2002: 2).

In other words, the humanitarian impulse toward intervention was supplemented by a national security impulse toward intervention. Some commentators hoped that this would "stiffen humanitarianism with the iron fist of national security" (Farer 2003: 88–89). But national security concerns and humanitarian concerns far from always overlap; the security factor has not helped amplify the humanitarian factor (Jentleson 2007: 284). The intervention in Iraq demonstrated the profound disagreement among liberal states concerning the appropriate motives for action. Humanitarian concerns are still in play, but only "selectivity on the basis of 'national interests' of the interveners" (Bellamy 2004: 145).

In sum, the policy of Imposition has been much strengthened since the Cold War in that humanitarian and/or security concerns may lead to intervention, including intervention by force, in weak states. But Imposition has not completely replaced Restraint: First, intervention remains highly selective, undertaken in some cases but not in other cases, even if humanitarian (Sudan, Burma) and/or security (Iran, Pakistan) concerns would seem to point in that direction. Second, when intervention is eventually undertaken by the use of significant force, the purpose is not an old-fashioned takeover of the country in question. The purpose is rather to replace a weak state by a strong state by promoting state building, democratization, and economic development. Such ambitions profoundly empower locals, because they are key players in the construction of stronger statehood. The following section demonstrates why it is extremely difficult for outsiders under these circumstances to push a transformation from weak to strong statehood.

Limits to Imposition I: The Nature of Involvement

Some weak or failed states will be singled out for intervention; others will not. The most important elements in making that choice are power and interest. Great powers play a special role in that context. On the one hand, intervention cannot be undertaken in the great powers themselves even if there may be reasons for doing so, be it in Chechnya or Tibet. On the other hand, given the level of resources needed to carry out intervention, such undertakings rely on the willingness of the great powers to shoulder most of the burden; the autonomous capacity of international society (the UN system) is strongly limited. That is to say, perceived national interest among the great powers weighs heavily in deciding where to intervene.

The next important issue is timing. There is a risk that intervention will be delayed so much that substantial parts of the population in the weak state have already been exposed to serious violent conflict. Even if early warning systems are in place, international society is almost always slow to react, especially in cases of humanitarian crisis. That is because intervention involves material and potential human cost for those undertaking it. Humanitarian crises that have not caught the attention of Western public opinion are rarely realistic candidates for external intervention (Jakobsen 1996). Conflict prevention would appear an easier task than postconflict reconstruction, yet intervention almost always has to deal with the latter.

The final and most important factor is the volume of intervention in terms of troops, money, and time (Dobbins et al. 2003). The American Defense Science Board (DSB) estimates that "ambitious goals for transforming a society in a conflictual environment" will require "20 troops per 1,000 inhabitants... working for five to eight years" (quoted from Logan and Preble 2006: 17). On this calculation, Iraq would require more than 500,000 troops; Afghanistan would need close to 600,000 troops; current deployments (in early 2010) are much lower; the troop-to-population ratio in Afghanistan is about 0.5 soldiers per 1,000 inhabitants. In economic terms, the seven largest peacekeeping operations supported by the UN in the 1990s cost more than \$230 billion. A current estimate of the costs of the Iraq war runs from \$60 billion to a staggering \$1 trillion (Stiglitz and Bilmes 2008). In other words, even very resourceful great powers face limitations in their ability to commit manpower and money to intervention.

Intervention today is not a replay of colonial takeover. Even so, there is widespread suspicion in weak states that intervention will be abused to pursue more narrow Western political goals (Ayoob 2004). In this situation, outsiders are under pressure to get out in a hurry, "to declare the mission complete, restore (formal) domestic sovereignty, and fully disengage" (Belloni 2007: 106). This leads to what has been called "imperialism in a hurry" (Ignatieff 2003). States that are formally independent and where even a modicum of formal democracy has been restored cannot stay under foreign occupation for a long period of time. Being in a hurry leads to the emphasis on shorter-term projects that are geared toward quick changes rather than on the creation of long-term conditions for improved state capacities.

In the best of worlds, intervening states can work on improving these problems by preparing the missions better (Fraser 2007). But this is not merely a problem of better planning. Intervening states have little or no control at all over the most awkward problem: domestic conditions in weak states.

Limits to Imposition II: Domestic Conditions in Weak States

When the aim of intervention is not takeover but the creation of a self-sustaining state that is effective, democratic, and capable of economic development, then local conditions in the subject society become crucial. The long-term undertaking of state building must be carried out by locals; outsiders cannot do it for them. Externally imposed institutions will have little legitimacy and sustainability unless they carry support by major groups in domestic society. This is one area where there is universal consensus in the scholarly literature: state institutions "cannot simply be imposed by external actors, but need to grow out of indigenous realities."[7] It follows that state-building projects crucially depend on prior conditions in the subject society. Successful interventions, such as the post–World War II reconstructions in Germany and Japan, have been able to build upon local groups and institutions (Brownlee 2007: 339–40).

The difficulties that external forces face begin immediately upon entering. Weak states cherish their entitlement to formal sovereignty and independence; they are most often ex-colonies with populations divided along ethnic, linguistic, sociocultural and other lines. Sovereignty behind internationally recognized borders is of supreme importance in this situation and gives a crucial framework to the community within a weak state. In that situation, outsiders must be viewed with concern as to what can be their real intentions. Robert Dahl diagnosed the problem already in 1971:

> the end of formal colonialism means that the outside power today must move into a nominally independent country where nationalism is probably strong and the boomerang effect [of mass disdain for the occupier] is likely to be powerful. A substantial proportion of political activists are likely to favour a hegemonic regime of some sort. Public contestation, which may allow deadly enemies to enhance their following, will seem to be a luxury at best, at worst downright pernicious.... Thus the outside power is drawn into massive coercion. (200)

The U.S. intervention in Iraq, for example, was viewed with resentment and suspicion from the beginning. Lacking support and legitimacy, outside actors face great difficulties in promoting positive change. In the absence of

---

7. Papagianni (2007: 254); see also Lyons (2004); Zartmann (1995); Talentino (2007); Eriksen (2005); Gizelis and Kosek (2005); Englebert and Tull (2008).

such change, international forces "become a source of resentment" (Talentino 2007: 162). Aversion is present in Afghanistan too; in Bosnia and Kosovo prolonged international presence has created a "broken promises" logic where local support has dwindled because of the inability of international forces to stem corruption and push political and economic change. Because international forces remain in control, they are blamed for all the ills of the country (Talentino 2007).

International forces thus tend to confront a skeptic population from early on. In particular, any state-building effort requires the support of local elites. At the same time, substantial groups among local elites will often be "spoilers" because an effective and responsive state is a threat to their self-seeking orientation toward power and wealth. Contending elite groups and their supporters must be pacified and neutralized while at the same time included in the process of state building (Eizenstaat et al. 2005: 138). This is easier said than done. The proposals for UN trusteeship (Helman and Ratner 1992), for international control of some governmental functions in a "shared sovereignty" arrangement (Krasner 2004), for counterinsurgency and long-term involvement (Fearon and Laitin 2004), or for putting politics on hold while the appropriate institutions are created (Mansfield and Snyder 2005; Paris 2004) do not speak to the problem of how to create support for state institutions from local elites or the larger population (Papagianni 2007: 256).

In Iraq, new institutions in a more democratic setting were not created by negotiations and compromises between contending elites. A narrow elite supported by the United States guided the transition; rival groups were offered minimum consultations. The new institutions were erected and elections were held, but "consensus on the sharing of economic and political power within one state was still missing" (Papagianni 2007: 268). Instead of consensus, increasing tensions and conflict led toward a civil war (Fearon 2007).

Violence is substantially down in Iraq, but this is owing to the division of territories into zones of influence by Sunni and Shia militias. Political agreement between the factions is not in sight; therefore, progress is fragile and easily reversible. This is not to say that an agreement securing a political solution with long-term stability is always impossible; rather, such solutions emerge from indigenous political processes managed by domestic groups, and the role of external actors in this process is necessarily a limited one: "You can lead a horse to water, but you can't make it drink" (Elklit 1999).

The recognition that outsiders can play only a secondary role and that the efforts of domestic groups are decisive takes us back to the problems of the Liberalism of Restraint. In weak states, domestic actors frequently have little interest in strengthening the state. They want it to remain weak for reasons connected to their narrow, self-seeking interests. First, patrimonial states offer material rewards in return for political support; state elites therefore need to control the distribution of state positions, licenses, regulations, access to property, and money. An effective state would prevent such control and thus impede the reproduction of client networks. Second, the funds at the disposal of state elites often consist of raw material rents and external funds (aid, military assistance) combined with revenues from smuggling and other illicit activities. That considerably lowers the state's interest in pushing economic growth and strengthening revenue collection (Eriksen 2005: 400).

Should reform-oriented leaders come to power in weak states, they are rarely able to accomplish much on their own; they need support from strong groups in society. The problem is that the social forces most often dominating weak states are not greatly interested in reform. State bureaucrats benefit from a patrimonial system; reform would threaten their power over scarce resources. Industrialists are a potential ally for the creation of an effective state, but they are usually few in number and also linked to the patrimonial system. Rural elites are not necessarily strong forces for reform either; they wish to preserve privileges for agriculture and to limit surplus transfers out of that sector. Cases such as Botswana, where rural elites supported effective state building (Acemoglu et al. 2003), are the exception rather than the rule.

In Iraq, the primary challenge is the accommodation of Sunnis, Shias, and Kurds within the framework of a single state. Previously, these groups were held together by coercion, first in the context of British colonialism, then by a series of strongmen of which Saddam Hussein was the last. Under present conditions, the country is held together by U.S. troops; a democratic future for Iraq must be based on a community driven by consent rather than by coercion. Again, this points to the decisive role of insiders. It is up to the Iraqis to create the new basis of consensus; if they fail, the whole project of state building will be in jeopardy (Ottaway 2005: 2).

The above considerations demonstrate some of the major difficulties involved when outsiders attempt to pursue state building in weak states. A strong state is both capable of efficient regulation and control and responsive to groups in civil society; it is a democratic state that is ultimately under control of the citizens. There are strong limits on how much outsiders can do in setting up a strong state because major aspects of state building are tied to domestic conditions and cannot be easily changed in the short and medium run. So the problems run deeper than mere organizational design and management; one commentator points to the "necessity of dismantling both those socio-political structures that have been preserved since the days before colonialism and those that were appropriated during colonial rule before effective political and economic institutions could be developed" (Rocha Menocal 2004: 775).

One analysis has formulated the question of state building as one of "getting to Denmark" in the sense that Denmark has effective and responsive state institutions (Woolcock and Pritchett 2002); it is not possible to get to Denmark by sending in a team of experts to supervise state reform. Effective and responsive institutions cannot be imported or copied from the outside; they have to build on local conditions, including local cultural and socio-structural factors (Fukuyama 2004).

The above reflections have indicated why such a process of locally embedded state building is problematic and often unlikely to take place in weak states: First, major groups among local elites are frequently spoilers because their self-seeking interests are threatened by a process of state building. Second, since the economic surplus does not derive primarily from revenue collection, there is little or no incentive to strengthen administrative capacity. Third, the creation of a democratic basis for legitimacy is impeded by the lack of support from citizens and groups who fear that democracy is a zero-sum game of politics between winners and losers where they will end up on the losing side. Fourth, citizens are further disillusioned by the holding of elections that are accompanied by serious democratic deficits and poor institutional performance. Fifth, in many weak states the core democratic precondition of national unity is lacking; major groups in the population are not ready to stay together in a democratic setting but would rather have autonomy or even independence.

Outsiders cannot easily—or at all—manipulate the underlying conditions that must impede state building in weak states; they seem to be at the mercy of local institutions and traditions. The recommendation that focus should shift toward "the evolution of endogenous mechanisms for governance" (Coyne 2006b: 350) is understandable because effective institutions of government cannot be imposed from the outside. But, once again, this puts the state-building process at the mercy of domestic groups that are far from always interested in the creation of stronger and more democratic states.

The Decisiveness of Domestic Conditions

Even when arriving in force with sufficient military power to win the day, outsiders quickly find themselves deeply dependent on insiders to bring about state building. There will always be limits to the number of interventions that outsiders are ready to undertake, and when they do go into action it is always with an eye to quickly disengaging and going home. When commitments are made to stay for a longer period, intervening forces swiftly learn that effective change needs the support and commitment of insiders.

Therefore, democratization, better governance, and socioeconomic development in weak states primarily depend on the presence of favorable domestic preconditions. A core element is the willingness of state elites to move in the right direction; there must be a local demand for reform. The big difference between previous successes of state building involving outsiders and today's problems with such projects is not that outsiders were previously more clever in their efforts than they are today; it is that domestic preconditions were dramatically different. Germany and Japan were not weak states; they had previous experiences of well-organized (and in the case of Germany even democratic) statehood to build on. They could reach back to that earlier experience; it was not the occupation forces that rebuilt statehood and led the way in constructing democracy, it was the locals. The occupation forces—being sufficient in number—contributed in the sense that they created the security environment in which such a process was possible.

Therefore, both Germany and Japan confirm the claim of the limited role of outsiders. Early U.S. plans for postwar Japan were focused on economic and military "deconstruction" of the country. The U.S. policy guidelines set out in 1945 stipulated that "the existing economic basis of Japan's military strength must be destroyed and not permitted to revive" (quoted from Samuels 1994: 131). The Cold War imposed new priorities: Japan was going to be "industrially revived" and made "internally stable" (records of George F. Kennan's Policy Planning Staff, quoted from Schaller 1997: 16). The most controversial element in U.S. policy was to seek rearmament of the country. After the outbreak of the war in Korea, the U.S. aim was for a Japanese army of at least 300,000. But the Japanese government firmly resisted the U.S. proposals for rearmament. The old system had been a thoroughly militarized society; the population resolutely opposed the reconstruction of a strong army. The government's strategy was to concede no more than was sufficient to ward off U.S. pressure, and by 1951 Japan had created a "National Police Reserve" of 110,000 men. Japan successfully withstood U.S. demands for remilitarization and developed a "trading state" national identity as a nation that focused on economic development instead of political-military power (T. Berger 1996: 338).

In the case of West Germany, domestic political forces responded to the new Cold War context by seeking to integrate the country as much as possible—in political, economic, and military terms—into Western Europe and the Western alliance. West Germany entered NATO in 1955, and the United States had pushed for a West German contribution to the defense of

Europe since the outbreak of the Korean War. The rebuilding of an army
followed a pattern similar to that of the rebuilding of the country; the West
German military capability was firmly embedded in a Western alliance, and
in contrast to earlier arrangements, the armed forces were integrated in civil
society through conscription and through the concept of *innere Führung* (internal leadership), emphasizing a democratic ethos and civil rights in the
army. It was a "non-nuclear, non-aggressive" approach to defense (T. Berger
1996: 338). In sum, the United States devised new plans for Germany and
Japan in the context of the Cold War. But they depended on the support
of insiders and could be successful only to the extent that domestic political
forces supported their ideas. The domestic forces had different ideas about
the future of their countries; they prevailed, even when the countries were
occupied and deeply dependent on the Western alliance.

Taiwan is sometimes mentioned as a case of successful state building of a
developing country led by outsiders. But again, Taiwan rather demonstrates
the importance of domestic preconditions. When Jiang Kaishek took over
in Taiwan, having lost the struggle for power against Mao, it was feared that
the Guomindang would be as oppressive, inept, reactionary, and corrupt as
it had been during the last years on the mainland, and there were early signs
that this would indeed be the case (Gold 1986: 51). Yet the regime instead
helped create an effective state that headed a rapid process of development.
The United States had a big hand in this, guaranteeing Taiwan against communist invasion and pushing economic reform. But conditions having to
do with the regime itself were decisive. First, during 1948–49 the status of
Taiwan changed in the Guomindang scheme, from the role of a resource base
bolstering the struggle on the mainland to a last bastion from which retaking
the mainland would be a long-term rather than an immediate venture. In late
1948, an exodus began that would eventually total some 1.3 million people
and increase the island's population to about 7.5 million. Second, Jiang Kaishek emerged from the utter humiliation of defeat by the communists with
the realization that for his movement to survive with any hope of going back
to the mainland, a solid basis had to be built on Taiwan: "the party had to
be fundamentally cleansed and the people of Taiwan given an incentive to
support it" (Gold 1986: 57). An additional factor in Taiwan's success (also relevant for South Korea) is that the precolonial era and the period of Japanese
colonialism had left behind a sound basis for development (Kohli 2004).

When domestic conditions are decisive, it becomes relevant to speculate
about the actual extent and character of weak statehood in today's world. Not
many countries contain the good basis for state building that characterized
Taiwan, not to mention Germany and Japan. They are not all predestined

for disaster, of course; some might succeed because domestic preconditions are more propitious than elsewhere. For outsiders, this points in the direction of intervening in places where domestic preconditions are more favorable to development (Jenkins and Plowden 2006: 170), but such decisions may conflict with other concerns related to humanitarian or security issues.

A Different Kind of Sovereignty?

Against this background, there has been some search for more radical options, especially proposals for evading the "slavish devotion to the sovereignty of existing states" (Herbst 1997: 182). They include changing the rules of secession, making the formation of new states easier; the decertification of states by the international community, so that highly ineffective states would "no longer be considered as sovereign" (Herbst 1996–97: 142); circumventing sovereignty by giving aid to regions instead of states, thereby making a connection to precolonial conceptions (in Africa) of overlapping jurisdictions; and "sharing sovereignty" between domestic rulers and representatives of international society (Krasner 2004).

These are interesting proposals because they go to the heart of what was diagnosed as the core problem above: the empowerment that sovereignty provides to the elites controlling weak states. They also face practical difficulties because international society is a strong supporter of the status quo, especially when it comes to supporting the inviolability of sovereign borders. New states are admitted to the club only when two conditions are met: First, they can point to previously existing jurisdictions. Second, all states affected by the independence of new states consent to it (R. Jackson 1994). This has been the principle behind the formation of new independent states for some time, including the states that came out of the former Soviet Union.[8] States that have collapsed completely still retain formal international recognition, as in the case of, for example, Somalia, Sudan, and Sierra Leone.

Would more willingness by international society to embark on a manipulation of sovereignty effectively confront the problem of weak statehood? Unfortunately, that is not clear. To see why, let me focus on secession. It is possible that secession will improve the prospects for viable statehood in some cases, Somaliland and Kosovo, for example. But secession may also create more problems than it solves: in the former Soviet Union and in ex-Yugoslavia, secession has been accompanied by massive acts of so-called eth-

---

8. A few possible exceptions are discussed in R. Jackson (1994).

nic cleansing (Bennett 1995). In sub-Saharan Africa, the human cost could be even higher. Where there are many ethnic groups, the logic of secession, says William Zartmann (1995), threatens "an infinite regress of self-determination" (268). That is to say, there are no facile criteria for where to stop secession, beyond the consensus that Africa cannot contain seven hundred or more states. This is the secession dilemma: the old borders are holding together groups that fight against each other because they cannot agree on forming a political community; the result is insecurity and underdevelopment. Splitting them up appears to create more problems than it solves. Damned if you do and damned if you don't.

Even these brief reflections demonstrate how difficult it is to manipulate sovereignty in a way that avoids excessive human cost and leads to the creation of more effective states with capacities for delivering security and other political goods to their citizens. This is not to say that state building and development can never happen in weak states. But in many cases it will not happen, because appropriate domestic and international preconditions for development are not present and cannot easily be produced. In other words, domestic and popular insecurity will continue to characterize a large number of weak states. The measures taken by liberal states are bound to be constrained in such a way that they are not capable of effectively addressing the problem.

Conclusion: The Liberal Dilemma in Dealing With Weak States

After World War II, weak states became free in the sense that they were accepted as full members of the international society of sovereign states. This was a Liberalism of Restraint regime emphasizing sovereignty and nonintervention, the right of weak states to chart their own course, to freely choose and develop their political, social, economic, and cultural systems. The problem was that many weak states were comprehensively unable to get any kind of development under way. The typical weak state is fundamentally different from the successful modern and postmodern states in the OECD-world. It has a history of external domination combined with a domestic scene controlled by self-seeking elites not particularly interested in general development to the benefit of their populations. The greatest asset of these elites is formal sovereignty because it empowers them with respect to both outsiders and insiders. In particular, they are the gatekeepers that have to be bargained with in order for outsiders to gain access to and influence development inside weak states. The Liberalism of Restraint respected the power and control of domestic forces; the latter often exploited that position to pursue self-seeking policies of economic and political gain.

Liberal states were aware of the problem from early on. Since the 1980s, they have turned toward Imposition in the attempt to create conditions that would help discipline weak state elites. But neither the market strategy nor the democratization or "civil society" strategies have significantly improved state capacity or the situation for the people in weak states. The end of the Cold War and 9/11 ushered in an even stronger emphasis on a Liberalism of Imposition, including intervention by force, in weak states. But since the purpose of intervention is not takeover but the promotion of state building, democracy, and general development, the increased activism of outsiders does not leave insiders powerless. On the contrary: when outsiders want them to do certain things such as create democracy and more effective statehood, they continue to be the rent-seeking gatekeepers of any such initiative.

It is clear that a Liberalism of Restraint does not solve the problem of weak states. It cannot promote basic liberal goals of liberty, welfare, security, and order in a sufficiently effective way. A Liberalism of Restraint has been at work in international society, at least to some extent, for the last five decades. But problems of utmost severity persist in weak states: 11 million children die each year of malnutrition and preventable diseases, stark inequalities of income endure, more than 1 billion people subsist on less than one dollar per day, and some 800 million people are undernourished. Blatant abuses of basic human rights continue to take place in many countries, not merely in authoritarian systems, but also in restricted and frail democracies.

State elites need to be disciplined, that is, to be constrained by domestic or external forces pushing them toward developmental (i.e., liberal) objectives, or they will become overly self-serving, pursuing their own narrow interests and not delivering public or collective goods to a sufficient degree. In the history of European state formation, there were two solutions to this problem, one realist and one liberal. The realist solution focuses on external threat and the anarchic self-help international system. State elites are compelled to provide for domestic order, because without it, the state will be disabled and powerless against external enemies. This was a crucial factor in European state formation; elites sought to create such domestic order and civility that the state—and thus the regime—would be able to face external threat. It was a core element in North American, Japanese, and Chinese state formation as well (Sørensen 1996). But the mechanism does not work for fragile state formation, and we have seen why: the external threat of extermination of the state is absent owing to the new norm of the right to survival of even the weakest entities.

The liberal solution focuses on constitutional government, that is, democratic institutions that provide checks on the power of rulers. Ideally, democracy assures that predatory state elites will not remain in power and that elites in power are subjected to the rule of law. But democracy is no quick fix; it took up to several hundred years to establish consolidated democracy in the OECD-world. It is extremely difficult to graft democracy on fragile states lacking the proper institutions and a level of trust and mutual acceptance among contending group of the elite as well as of the general population. There have been elections and other democratic elements in the fragile states reviewed above, but they remain far away from consolidated democracies. At the same time, early processes of democratization mean better possibilities for formulating demands and getting conflicts out in the open; this can easily lead to sharper confrontations and conflicts that can threaten to undermine frail democratic openings.

So none of these approaches work well in the case of weak states. But other attempts at disciplining weak state elites by turning toward increased Imposition have not worked well either. There is an outer limit to Imposition: it cannot involve recolonization or conquest. Any attempt at Imposition rests on a consensus about the continued right to existence of the weak state on the basis of formal sovereignty. That means, as the cases of Afghanistan and Iraq have demonstrated, that even vastly superior military power can face serious obstacles and limitations.

There are also inner limits to Imposition, as was demonstrated above. Large-scale intervention must always be selective, as the costs in blood and treasure will reduce domestic support for a Liberalism of Imposition. A further barrier to a Liberalism of Imposition is the potential loss of legitimacy. If the avowed promotion of human rights and democracy is carried out in a way that can be perceived as power-hungry militarism seeking control of oil and other resources, the country in charge will not be relied on as a true force for liberal values (Nozzel 2004). The coercive "power over" of Imposition is much less effective in the long run than the cooperative "power through." This is behind the emphasis by many liberals on soft power, that is, "the ability to set the political agenda in a way that shapes the preferences of others" (Nye 2002: 9). Soft power requires legitimacy, and a distinct Liberalism of Imposition may squander the moral authority of liberal states (Ikenberry 2004: 20).

In sum, the liberal dilemma is that neither Restraint nor Imposition is effective in addressing the severe problems in weak states. Are there viable alternatives? One optimistic way of approaching weak states is to reconfirm a liberal belief in progress; that is to say, the problem will eventually take care of itself over time because weak states will follow in the footsteps of the now developed countries and develop politically, economically, and otherwise. That is the liberal modernization view: less-developed countries see a picture of their own future when they look at more developed countries. But the view is misleading because it misinterprets both the past and the future. In the past, weak states have experienced trajectories that are radically different from the typical path taken by the developed West. Fragile states emerge from a mixture of domestic and international conditions that are fundamentally unlike anything experienced by the successful states in the West. As regards the future, it is not predetermined of course. There is no guarantee, nor is it even very likely, that weak states will follow in the footsteps of the consolidated and successful ones. Just as their historical experiences are different from those of the successful states, their futures will most likely be different as well. History, alas, has no built-in law ensuring that progress and modernity await everyone. The trajectory of most weak states over the last five decades provides no basis for a firm belief in progress.

Furthermore, there is little reason to believe that modifications in the aid strategies by liberal states will make a significant difference. Fifty years of development politics has introduced a large number of different strategies: industrialization and infrastructure development in the fifties and sixties, basic human needs in the seventies, liberal market reforms in the eighties, good governance and democratization in the nineties, strengthening of civil society and the informal sector in recent years, to mention a few of the most popular aid strategies. Current Chinese aid for Africa has gone back to basics in that it has taken up the emphasis from the fifties and sixties on infrastructure and industry. Each new trend has its own advantages and drawbacks; none of them have made a developmental breakthrough in weak states.

There are many defenders of the status quo as the sovereign border is convenient for state elites on both sides of it: seen from the outside, it helps contain desperate problems of security and development; seen from the inside, it helps provide resources and autonomy to incumbents. But seen from the people in weak states it often provides insecurity rather than security. Despite good intentions, dramatic change for the better in this regard is not likely.

In effect, there can be no clear blueprint for liberal countries dealing with weak states. Their own state interests and willingness to do something will vary from case to case. The precise preconditions and the attitudes of local elites and major groups in the states they are dealing with will vary as well. The impulse toward humanitarian intervention is much weaker today than it was in the 1990s, as evidenced by the hesitations of the international community in the cases of Burma and Sudan. The impulse toward intervention for security reasons is probably weaker too, because of the misfortunes of the Iraq and Afghanistan interventions. A clear and consistent Liberalism of Restraint will not win the day because liberal states will always feel obliged to do something about humanitarian and other conditions in weak states that are seen as unacceptable. Nor will a clear and consistent Liberalism of Imposition win the day because liberal states know that they can do only so much and that the chances of short- and medium-term success are slim indeed. Weak and failed states will continue to pose a problem that liberal democracies can meet only with awkward and ineffective compromises; therefore, such states will continue to work against any aspiration for a stable liberal world order.

 CHAPTER 5

Free Markets for All

The Difficulties of Maintaining a Stable Liberal World Economy

We now turn to the economic dimension of liberal world order. A stable global economy based on liberal principles of free markets and private property is a cornerstone of liberal world order. Some will see the economy as the easy part of the liberal project; there is, after all, almost universal support today for a liberal-capitalist free market arrangement. Even classic, diehard opponents of a liberal economy, such as North Korea and Cuba, are slowly moving in that direction. But the economy directly affects the well-being of citizens around the world, including people (and voters) in liberal states. Therefore, economic issues are easily transformed into topics of political contestation: less-satisfied individuals and groups will seek to change or modify the rules of the economic game in their favor. On the one hand, then, liberal states support the universal principles of "an open, equitable, rule-based, predictable, non-discriminatory and multilateral trading and financial system" (United Nations 2000: 4). On the other hand, liberal states frequently seek to preserve, and even expand, special economic arrangements that support domestic groups and often protect them from the vagaries of international competition.

The following section specifies major dimensions of the relationship between politics and economics, that is, between states and markets. I will examine the meaning of Liberal Imposition and Liberal Restraint in the economic sphere. Restraint dominated in the first decades following

World War II: the Bretton Woods system of embedded liberalism was, in the terminology of this book, a Liberalism of Restraint system as it combined open markets with domestic autonomy in economic policymaking. It was a successful system for the Western countries. I will, however, argue that it cannot be restored under the current conditions in the globalized economy.

A Liberalism of Imposition system has taken the driver's seat since the 1980s, under the heading of "Washington Consensus" principles. But these principles cannot sustain a stable global economy because they do not sufficiently address major problems in weak and modernizing countries. For latecomers, there is less room for developmental choice today, and full participation in neoliberal economic globalization is the recommended, if not mandatory, option. At the same time, leading liberal states themselves uphold significant nonliberal elements of protectionism. These states have long practiced double standards: advocating neoliberal principles to others that they do not abide by themselves, not now and not in their earlier phases of development.

Finally, instead of delivering transnational goods, the liberal world economy is increasingly producing transnational bads, including financial crisis, environmental problems, and illegitimate transactions involving people, drugs, and money. So three major problems obstruct the establishment of a stable liberal world economy:

1. Construction of an appropriate state-market matrix: Liberal states have imposed neoliberal principles on the rest of the world, but they have not worked well, and the establishment of a Restraint order with higher flexibility in the adaptation of liberal principles is not likely.
2. Lack of leadership: There is no strong coalition of liberal states today ready to take the lead in consistent economic policymaking with universal appeal; even in a time of serious crisis, hegemonic management is absent.
3. The problem of transnational bads in the liberal world economy: There are no coherent strategies for confronting transnational bads.

The three sets of problems hang together, of course; hegemonic leadership requires hegemonic power, but the economic leadership of liberal states is increasingly challenged in a world where rising economic powers do not necessarily support liberal values. Economic disaster is probably not in the cards; rather a simmering crisis exacerbated by the current downturn of the world economy.

States and Markets: Restraint and Imposition

Since the end of the Cold War, the expansion of market-based economic relations across borders has entered a new and more intense phase, often labeled economic globalization. For the first time ever, there is an international market for goods, money, and finance with a truly global reach (Held et al. 1999; Dicken 2003); a large number of countries that had planned economies have transformed into market economies and are becoming integrated in the global market. This recent process of economic globalization is not a pure market phenomenon: a significant enabling condition of current globalization consists of changes in political regulation in the direction of a more market-friendly state-market matrix that helps market-based economic activity to expand.

It follows that the globalization pressures faced by single countries are not purely economic but political and expressed through the policies of the dominant coalitions in such organizations as the International Monetary Fund, the World Bank, and the World Trade Organization. Economic globalization adds a new dimension to the state-market interplay because different national modes of that relationship are opened up to each other. That raises the issue anew of the proper mode of regulation for that larger context, including the basic question about the extent to which markets should be integrated. In the global context, political power is decentralized or fragmented in that it is unevenly distributed among sovereign states. But at its core, the global topic is a replication of the national one: a struggle between different political and social coalitions that want to move in different directions. Some groups claim that they want an unfettered market while others claim that they want a market regulated according to certain sociopolitical objectives. In spite of this, the former frequently aim to preserve certain elements of protectionism, while the latter also seek to achieve the benefits that free market dynamics can create.

It is clear that any agreement among liberal states about free markets must always be accompanied by potential disagreement about who gets what, that is, about relative and absolute advantages for countries and groups flowing from any specific state-market matrix. Therefore, strong leadership in the making of a stable liberal economic order with potential benefits for all participants emerges only under special circumstances. Such was the case after World War II: the United States (and the democratic West) faced a serious security challenge from the Soviet Union, and Germany and Japan had to be rebuilt into solid members of the community of democracies. The democracies in Western Europe faced significant economic difficulties as well, and the United States was by far the strongest economy in the world. Security interests, national economic interests, and a concern for the Western democratic community came together in motivating the United States to create a Western economic order. They also provided great incentives for Western democracies to successfully manage their collaboration and avoid serious splits and divisions among them.

Today, these conditions are no longer present. There is not a common security challenge that gives the United States a clear role as security provider for the Western alliance. The liberal economic order is now a global system with a great many different stakeholders who do not easily agree on the precise setup of the economic order. The economic superiority of the United States—and also of the entire community of Western democracies—is much less pronounced than earlier. Principal support for a liberal free market system still exists, but each participating state in that system is much more conscious of its national economic interests than previously.

Restraint and Imposition Since World War II

The principal postures of the Liberalism of Restraint and the Liberalism of Imposition can now be defined in relationship to the international economy. Both positions agree on the fundamental advantages of an economy based on free markets and private property, but they have markedly different positions regarding the freedom of single states to decide on the makeup of the state-market relationship. The Liberalism of Restraint, on the one hand, is pluralist: it seeks to leave very substantial political-economic decision power in the hands of individual states; they should comprehensively participate in international economic exchange at all levels, but they should also be given maximum freedom to construct their own preferred version of the state-market relationship, be it social democratic, Catholic conservative, or neoliberal. The Liberalism of Imposition, on the other hand, is universalistic: it aims at imposing a certain set of market-economic principles in all countries. These principles are drawn primarily from the neoliberal understanding of the state-market relationship, and that means they include liberalization of investment inflows and interest rates, competitive exchange rates, fiscal discipline, deregulation, and tax reform (Williamson 1990).

When the international framework for economic exchange had to be reconstituted after World War II, great emphasis was put on the preservation of domestic policy autonomy. Under the joint leadership of the United States and Britain, the Bretton Woods conference in 1944 set out that new framework. The dollar was tied to gold at a fixed rate of $35 per ounce, and other states pegged their currencies to the dollar. But it was not a return to the discipline of the gold standard: On the one hand, countries could adjust the value of their currencies when they encountered a "fundamental disequilibrium." On the other hand, they were also given the right of enforcing capital controls. Finally, currency convertibility was not introduced until 1958. Under these conditions, countries were given a free hand domestically to pursue appropriate macroeconomic planning and decide the optimum interest rate; in other words, liberal openness was combined with domestic autonomy in a system of "embedded liberalism" (Ruggie 1982). In the terminology of this book, it was a Liberalism of Restraint system.

A similar development took place in the area of trade. The United States government initially sponsored the establishment of the International Trade Organization (ITO), which should seek to provide the widest possible freedom of movement for goods and services, but Europeans were not ready to let go of preferential trade agreements and subsidy systems. The support for some protectionism was also strong in the U.S. Congress. The less ambitious GATT (General Agreement on Tariffs and Trade) system came to be the vehicle for tariff reductions and free trade, but special national support arrangements in agriculture and elsewhere were allowed to continue (Spero and Hart 1997).

On one level, the Liberalism of Restraint system worked very well for the United States, Europe, and Japan: trade barriers were reduced, economic interdependence for mutual benefit increased dramatically, short- and long-term liquidity was made available, and the European and Japanese economies quickly recovered from the war. On another level, however, it is clear that the system depended on the benevolent management of the United States, including a willingness to forgo short-term national interest for the sake of the larger arrangement. First, the United States provided liquidity for the system by promoting a huge outflow of dollars; the Marshall Plan and U.S. military expenditures in NATO countries were important elements in this. Second, the United States accepted Japanese and European trade restrictions while encouraging exports from these countries to the United States. Finally, the United States supported a range of measures to increase the competitiveness of Europe and Japan (Mastanduno 2008).

In the longer term, these initially successful policies contained their own built-in problems. In order to provide sufficient international liquidity, the United States needed to run a balance-of-payments deficit; but doing so on a more or less permanent basis would inevitably undermine confidence in the dollar's convertibility into gold. That would lead to runs on the dollar where speculators converted their dollars into gold; a first occasion of this occurred already in the fall of 1960.[1] During the 1960s, large military expenses caused by the Vietnam War contributed to inflationary pressures and an overvalued dollar. By 1971, the United States showed a trade deficit for the first time in the twentieth century.

At that point, President Nixon announced a new policy that reflected immediate U.S. priorities: the dollar would no longer be convertible into gold and a 10 percent surcharge would be imposed on dutiable imports. Two major pillars of the Bretton Woods system were thus removed: the dollar convertibility into gold and fixed exchange rates. Instead, the major world currencies now floated, with management left to market forces and occasional interventions by central banks. It made the system markedly more unstable, but it also increased flexibility. The continued economic strength of the United States kept confidence in the dollar at a high level, while floating exchange rates removed the need for adjustment through trade restrictions and capital controls, thereby enabling rapid growth of financial and commodity flows. But it was also a volatile system of "casino capitalism" (Strange 1986), with ordinary producers and consumers exposed to dramatic currency fluctuations brought about by speculators seeking short-term gain. Capital controls were abolished by the United States already in 1974 and by Britain in 1979; the other advanced capitalist countries followed suit in the 1980s. In a short period of time, private actors massively entered the field of international finance, and they quickly began to develop financial derivatives (futures, forwards, options, swaps) that boosted the level of activity. Foreign exchange trading had a daily size of $15 billion in 1973; by the late 1990s that figure was $1,500 billion, and world financial flows exceeded trade flows by a factor of at least 30 to 1.

The 1970s was a period of economic slowdown exacerbated by two rounds of sharply rising oil prices. The advanced liberal countries increasingly became subject to a combination of stagnation and inflation. When Ronald Reagan became president in 1981 he initiated a program of neo-liberal "supply-side" economics that involved tax cuts for the wealthy and deregulation of the economy. With decreasing inflation the dollar appreciated; high interest rates attracted very large inflows of capital, in spite of the twin deficits of the U.S. trade and balance of payments on the one hand and the federal budget on the other hand. During the Reagan presidency, the

<hr>

1. Diagnosed by the U.S. economist Robert Triffin, this became known as the Triffin dilemma: the international economy needs dollars for liquidity and reserves, but this undermines U.S. domestic economic stability and leads to large current account deficits. Triffin argued that this would eventually put pressure on the dollar and undermine its position as a reserve currency (Campanella 2010).

United States would move from being the world's largest creditor to being the world's largest debtor nation. Regardless of some initial attempts, the leading liberal states were unwilling to control the large financial fluctuations through a more tightly managed system. Taking that road would have sharply decreased their macroeconomic policy autonomy, and they were not inclined to accept that. As a consequence, "the period since 1976 has been one of muddling through, characterized as much by national and regional management as by multilateral management.... Despite the growth of interdependence, national governments have been either unwilling or unable to adjust national economic policies to international economic needs" (Spero and Hart 1997: 30).

The large amounts of capital coming into the United States, attracted by low inflation and high interest rates, contributed to problems elsewhere in the system. Many developing countries had borrowed heavily during the 1970s, when inflation was high and real rates of interest were low, even negative. Now these countries faced sharply rising real interest rates, frequently combined with expensive oil imports. Mexico declared its inability to service its debt in 1982, and a large number of countries soon faced similar problems.

The 1980s, then, was a decade of debt rescheduling where the Bretton Woods financial institutions, the World Bank, and the IMF played a central role. Pushed primarily by the United States under Reagan and Britain under Thatcher, but also by other advanced industrialized countries, these institutions took the lead in advocating a policy of structural adjustment in the Third World. The new policy followed the principles of what would be termed the "Washington Consensus" (Williamson 1990). It was strongly felt that government failures were a more serious problem than market failures; consequently, the policy of structural adjustment aimed at liberalizing economic exchange. Regulations should help set economic flows free by removing the heavy, and distorting, hand of direct state intervention. In concrete terms that meant (a) lifting trade restrictions and currency regulations; (b) instituting public sector cutbacks, fiscal discipline, and tax reform; (c) removing industrial and agricultural protectionism, privatizing state enterprises, and supporting the establishment of private enterprises (Taylor 1997: 148–49).

The Washington Consensus represented a turn to a Liberalism of Imposition system. At its core is a common set of neoliberal principles believed to be appropriate for promoting economic growth and social welfare in any economy. But the endorsement of these principles by leading liberal states took place in a highly selective manner. The neoliberal principles were imposed on less developed and developing countries with major external imbalances; they were highly indebted and/or ran large balance-of-payments deficits. Neoliberal imposition was therefore a disciplining instrument aimed at correcting the external imbalances of these countries so that they would be able to meet their international obligations. Julius Nyerere (1980) of Tanzania stated the issue in no uncertain terms:

> The IMF has an ideology of social and economic development which it is trying to impose on poor countries irrespective of their own clearly stated policies. And when we reject IMF conditions, we hear the threatening whisper: "Without accepting our conditions, you will not get our money and you will get no other money.". . . When did the IMF become an International Ministry of Finance? When did nations agree to surrender to it their power of decision-making?

There was initially no external imposition of neoliberal economic principles on the liberal states themselves; they continued to freely organize their state-market matrices as they saw fit. Since the 1970s, then, global liberal economic order is to a much larger extent than earlier a field of contestation, where countries and groups of countries attempt to influence the regulatory framework in a way that best suits their interests.

The promotion of neoliberal principles by leading liberal states took place at a point in time where various groups of countries in the world were moving in different directions. The developing countries, who had stood together in the 1970s in demanding a "New Economic World Order" from the rich countries, were now increasingly differentiated into separate groups: very weak and poor states, many of which were in sub-Saharan Africa; newly industrializing countries (or "emerging markets") in Southeast Asia, parts of Latin America, and most recently also in Eastern Europe; oil producers in the Middle East; highly indebted countries; less indebted countries; and so on.

It would soon be clear that the neoliberal principles contained in the economic Liberalism of Imposition were not an adequate answer to the challenges faced by these different groups of states. At the same time, a return to the previous Liberalism of Restraint system is not feasible because the old preconditions are now absent: on the one hand, the economic system is now so integrated across borders that some substantial coordination of policies is required; on the other hand, the United States is less willing and able to supply the benevolent management of earlier days. The following section demonstrates the flaws of the Liberalism of Imposition system in relation to various groups of countries. Since a clear-cut Liberalism of Restraint is not feasible either, the global economy will remain a serious challenge in the quest for a stable liberal world order.

One Size does not Fit all: Economic Liberal Imposition in the Developing World

In the economic realm, Liberal Imposition is about imposing the principles contained in the Washington Consensus. John Williamson coined the term "Washington Consensus" in 1990; it was meant as specific advice to a number of Latin American countries in order to promote macroeconomic discipline, a market economy, and openness to the world with respect to trade and investment. In that sense, he said in 2002, the term is "motherhood and apple pie and not worth debating" (Williamson 2002: 4). But the consensus took on a life of its own. It became a set of neoliberal principles with universal application, and on that basis a series of measures focused on fiscal discipline, privatization, and economic openness were promoted around the world by the international financial institutions (IMF and the World Bank), backed by the leading liberal states. In many cases, the measures did have some positive effects like promoting growth and macroeconomic stability, but it was soon clear that there were also considerable negative effects (Taylor 1997). In the weak and poor states, attempts to increase exports had to rely on one or a few primary products; they accounted for more than 90 per cent of total export production in sub-Saharan Africa in the 1990s. These were goods for which long-term global demand was shrinking in an increasingly technology-intensive world economy.

Nor was it easy for weak states to attract great amounts of foreign direct investment (FDI). These countries had never been able to create coherent national economies. They were disjointed amalgamations of traditional agriculture, an informal petty urban sector, and some fragments of modern industry. Political institutions were inefficient and corrupt, frequently run by self-serving elites offering what state services there were to the highest bidder. FDI was not very interested in coming into these countries in the first place because of the lack of stability and attractive conditions of operation; by the turn of the century less than 2 per cent of total FDI (World Bank 2000: 38) went to sub-Saharan Africa.

In the domestic realm of weak states, a dramatic slimming down of the public sector had negative consequences for employment and welfare. Public sector workers were either laid off or had their pay frozen. Cutting back government spending in education, health, and other areas of basic infrastructure together with increasing prices for food and other basic necessities meant falling social standards for those already in need. These short- and medium-term consequences were indicative of a larger problem that Liberal Imposition did not address: weak states were in need of more rather than less state capacity in order to promote long-term development. Trevor Manuel, South African minister of finance, pointed to the predicament in 2003: "The problem in Africa is that most states are weak and limited, not that states try to do everything.... Most states need to expand, not contract, their public sector—and dramatically improve its efficiency in delivering quality public services. This demands institutional capacity, especially in the areas of regulation, service delivery, and social spending.... Technical capacity needs to be combined with transparency and representation in public institutions" (19).

In other words, capable states are needed to set up the rules that enable the market to function properly. But to the extent that weak states have actually set up and enforced rules governing the market, these regulations have often been counterproductive for long-term growth and welfare. Instead, they have benefited leaders and their select groups of clients. For many rulers, the game became one of extracting as much as they could in new aid and loans while offering as little as possible in actually implemented policy reform; "a perfectly understandable attitude for African rulers, who were anxious to get their hands on the money, but whose long-established practices and possibly political survival were threatened by the conditions which accompanied it" (Clapham 1996: 177).

In sum, the economic Liberalism of Imposition did not sufficiently aim at addressing the major problems impeding long-term economic development in weak states: the need for stronger institutional capacities combined with more transparency and accountability. Nor did neoliberal principles adequately address underlying problems connected with human capital creation and technical and social infrastructure, especially related to the large informal sectors in weak states. Macroeconomic discipline, a market economy, and openness to the world might be economic motherhood and apple pie, but dressed up in a narrow framework of neoliberal economics they were not well suited to address the economic development problems of weak states (Toye 2003).

In furthering the transition from planned economies to market economies in Eastern Europe, including Russia, Liberal Imposition economics was no great success either. The Washington Consensus prescribed a "shock therapy" (World Bank 1996) aimed at quickly installing the institutional and regulatory framework of a market economy (Stiglitz 2001: 153). The reformers "underplayed the importance of social, organizational and informational capital; they underestimated the impediments to the creation of new enterprises; and perhaps most importantly, they paid too little attention to the issues of corporate governance" (Stiglitz 2001: 158; Woodruff 1999). The challenges of the transition to a market economy cannot be reduced to technicalities concerning regulations and institutions: a well-functioning market depends on a well-functioning state, and a well-functioning state depends on a well-functioning civil society. So a market economy entails a new economic order (market building), a new political order (state building), and a new basis for social order (civil society building). Harmonizing these three interrelated transformations is highly complex: on the one hand, they depend on each other; on the other hand, market actors, state actors, and groups in civil society have interests of their own that are not necessarily conducive to a smooth process of transition. In short, Liberal Imposition economics does not have a comprehensive answer to the challenges of transition from plan to market.

We turn to the emerging markets in Latin America and Southeast Asia. One should expect the neoliberal economic principles to work better here as these countries have much stronger domestic economies and substantially higher capacities for designing and implementing policies. Adopting the principles of openness in trade and finance combined with "sound money," meaning a stable exchange rate, should mean that "capital flowed into a country that was following the right path" (Krugman 1995: 38). True enough, money poured into these countries during the first half of the 1990s. From a very low level in the 1980s, private capital flows to developing countries reached a staggering $130 billion in 1993 and $236 billion in 1996 (the abundance of available capital is explored in Wade 1998). The bulk of the money "went to countries that had done poorly in previous years, but whose new commitment to Washington consensus policies was believed to ensure a dramatic turn-around" (Krugman 1995: 40). They included many Latin American countries plus Thailand, Malaysia, the Philippines, and a few others. But already by 1994 investors were fleeing from Mexico, and a few years later the crisis hit in Asia; what went wrong?

First, expectations were probably too high. Abandoning protectionism and embracing free trade might support faster growth, but the precise magnitude of that growth is hotly contested. A World Bank study from 1987 concluded that open economies had faster economic growth, but the results of this type of analysis are far from clear because of the conceptual and empirical problems involved (Edwards 1993). Furthermore, stable exchange rates curbed inflation and increased international confidence, but they also led to overvalued currencies, decreasing ability for export sectors to compete, and a boom in cheap imports.

Second, the capital coming into these emerging markets was more short term than earlier. In what was known as carry-trade, financial institutions borrowed in yen and dollars and invested in short-term notes in Southeast

Asian countries that were paying much higher interest rates. "There was less and less compulsion on the part of lenders, borrowers, or governments to improve financial supervision or control bank asset quality" (Wade 1998: 1539). The system could function only to the extent that countries receiving large capital inflows could maintain a stable exchange rate. Capital abundance fueled domestic prices at a time when inflation in the United States and Japan was on a much lower level. With currencies pegged to the dollar in order to create stability, real exchange rates (the ratio of prices in dollars in emerging markets compared with those in the United States and Japan) increased dramatically. The Mexican peso revalued by 28 percent in 1994; in Southeast Asia, inflationary pressures were exacerbated by a Chinese devaluation of the yuan in 1994 that further enhanced China's relative capacity to compete. In Thailand, inflation and the availability of capital led to speculation in real estate. Property prices went up more than 40 percent per year in Bangkok in the early 1990s.

This could not go on; a crisis of confidence seemed unavoidable. In Mexico, it came when the government attempted to boost economic growth; the loss of credibility meant that investors "became unwilling to hold peso assets unless offered very high interest rates; and the necessity of paying these high rates, together with the depressing effect of high rates on the economy, increased the pressure on the government to abandon the fixed exchange rate—which made investors even less willing to hold pesos" (Krugman 1995: 42). In Thailand, the property market bubble burst and slowed down economic growth; again, the prospect of devaluation made investors unwilling to hold the local currency, baths. By July 1997 the Thai central bank had to give up defending the currency, letting it float, and sink. Higher real interest rates and cutbacks in domestic demand led to a massive contraction in economic activity.

In sum, Liberal Imposition economics was not an effective way forward for emerging markets. Economic openness and the desire for sound money eventually led to enormous capital outflows rather than inflows, and a large number of local companies could be bought up by outsiders at fire-sale prices. This opens the question about the appropriate framework of regulation for international finance, an issue that reappeared in 2008 when a real estate bubble in the United States sparked a financial crisis in the global economy. The economics editor of *Financial Times*, Martin Wolf, made the following comment during the crisis a decade ago:

> It is impossible to pretend that the traditional case for capital markets liberalization remains unscathed. Either far greater stability than at

present is injected into the international monetary system as a whole or the unavoidably fragile emerging countries must protect themselves from the virus of short-term lending.... After the crisis, the question can no longer be whether these flows should be regulated in some way. It can only be how. (Quoted from Wade 1998: 1550)

A similar argument about the need for regulation is frequently voiced in context of the 2008 financial crisis. Overall, then, one size does not fit all: Liberal imposition economics has serious flaws in dealing with the challenges of different types of developing and transition economies. The problems point in the direction of returning to a strategy based on a Liberalism of Restraint, allowing much more space for adapting general liberal principles to the particular situations in different states. However, such adaptation may also involve deviations from strictly liberal economic principles, and the leading liberal states have not been able to agree on how to go about doing that. The liberal strategy as regards the developing world is spearheaded by the World Bank. Most of the critique mentioned here has been recognized by the bank (World Bank 2005); the current emphasis is on "the need for humility, for policy diversity, for selective and modest reforms, and for experimentation" (Rodrik 2006: 3). However, "there is little evidence that operational work at the Bank has internalized these lessons to any significant extent" (Rodrik 2006: 7); therefore, neoliberal imposition policies, with their recognized flaws, continue to dominate in the process of actual policy implementation.[2]

Do as I Say, not as I do: Rhetoric and Reality in the Promotion of Neoliberal Standards

Neoliberal standards are not being imposed on developing and transition economies because they represent the development experience of the advanced liberal states themselves. The now developed countries did not rely on trade and investment liberalization, privatization, and deregulation during core phases of their development trajectories (Chang 2002). They instead

---

2. At the same time, the Commission on Growth and Development, supported by the World Bank, issued a report in 2008 that further emphasized a movement away from the Washington Consensus in that it advocated pragmatism and gradualism in economic policy (Commission on Growth and Development 2008). Dani Rodrik (2008) summarized the commission's results as follows: "Yes, successful economies have many things in common: they all engage in the global economy, maintain macroeconomic stability, stimulate saving and investment, provide market-oriented incentives, and are reasonably well governed. It is useful to keep an eye on these commonalities, because they frame the conduct of appropriate economic policies. Saying that context matters does not mean that anything goes. But there is no universal rulebook—different countries achieve these ends differently."

used interventionist policies related to support of domestic industries, regulation of trade and foreign investment, and promotion of national capacities in technology and research. Britain became the first industrially advanced country; it did so by vigorously pursuing infant industry protection, subsidizing exports, and building "high and long-lasting tariff barriers" (Bairoch 1993: 46). The repeal of the Corn Laws in 1846 did represent a significant turn toward free trade, but this happened at a point where British economic supremacy was so well established that free trade would be to British advantage. Economic openness and deregulation are fair weather principles: they work well in economies that are already well established and ready to face the international competition that such principles must imply.

Nor was the United States for a considerable period any champion of economic openness. On the contrary, it should be viewed as "the mother country and bastion of modern protectionism" (Bairoch 1993: 30). Alexander Hamilton, one of the founding fathers of the United States, was a strong proponent of mercantilism in the form of protectionist policies aimed at promoting domestic industry in the United States. It was only after World War II, when the United States was established as the industrial powerhouse of the world, that it liberalized trade, acting according to fair weather principles. There has always been substantial political support, in the United States, for the mercantilist view that economic activity is and should be subordinated to the primary goal of promoting a strong state.

A German economist, Friedrich List, developed a theory of "productive power" in the 1840s. It stressed that the ability to produce is more important than the result of producing. In other words, the prosperity of a state depends not primarily on its store of wealth but on the extent to which it has developed its powers of production: "A nation capable of developing a manufacturing power, if it makes use of the system of protection, thus acts quite in the same spirit as the landed proprietor did who by the sacrifice of some material wealth allowed some of his children to learn a production trade" (List 1966: 145). These mercantilist principles were much more dominant as guidelines for the now developed countries than were Ricardian and Smithian recommendations of comparative advantage and economic openness. List remarked that the secret of the "cosmopolitical doctrine of Adam Smith" lies in the fact that the country that has advanced by mercantilist means now "*kicks away the ladder*" (296) for latecomers, denying them similar advance by imposing principles of free trade on them.

The argument is not that protectionism and import substitution are always so much better for developing nations than free trade; on several occasions, protectionism has gone too far and led to inefficiency and lack of innovation.

But import replacement remains a relevant part of a larger industrial strategy "to nurture the capabilities of domestic firms and raise the rate of domestic investment in the context of a private enterprise, market-based economy" (Wade 2003: 634). Import replacement and export development can go together, as the Southeast Asian "tiger economies" have demonstrated.

Imposing neoliberal principles narrows strategic options in economic development, and that also violates another lesson from the experience of the now developed countries (NDCs): their history demonstrates "a considerable degree of diversity...in terms of their policy-mix, suggesting that there is no 'one-size-fits-all' *model* for industrial development" (Chang 2003: 27). Sequencing—the notion that some policies are relevant for certain phases of a country's development but not for others—is part of this diversity. Both the NDCs and the successful late developers in Asia made extensive use of sequencing.

The narrowing of development options in the current international system proceeds in ways other than the ones described above. Current international regulations of intellectual property rights (TRIPS), of investment measures (TRIMS), and of trade in services (GATS) can be seen as a contemporary way of kicking away the ladder by constraining national development strategies for latecomers. Trade-Related Aspects of International Property Rights (TRIPS) introduce standards for intellectual property protection. Developed countries are net producers of patentable knowledge; developing countries are net consumers. TRIPS make it more expensive and more difficult for latecomers to get access to advanced technology. The United States in its time, and later Japan, Taiwan, and South Korea, made ample use of duplication in their early phases of development. TRIPS, by contrast, "[raise] significant development obstacles for many countries that the earlier developers did not face" (Wade 2003: 626).

Trade-Related Investment Measures (TRIMS) prevent host countries from demanding performance requirements from foreign investors. Such requirements may include locally produced inputs, export targets, or joint venturing with local firms; they are important elements in guaranteeing that foreign investment will contribute to domestic industrial upgrading. Successful late industrialized countries, including Taiwan, South Korea, China, India, and Brazil, have all made extensive use of these performance requirements (Amsden and Chu 2003). The General Agreement on Trade in Services (GATS) stipulates market liberalization in services (e.g., health care, sanitation, education, banking, insurance). Governments are not allowed to protect their service industries from foreign competition. Again, this puts developing countries in a worse position than previously successful developers.

In sum, the three agreements are much more favorable to the advanced countries than they are to latecomers. They put serious limitations on the rights of developing countries to implement policies aimed at growth and technological improvement of domestic industries (Wade 2003: 630). The advanced liberal states, by contrast, continued to make use of protective measures, even in recent times. The Multi Fiber Agreement (MFA), operating between 1974 and 2005, protected labor-intensive textile industries in the North from more competitive imports from developing countries. Tariffs and quotas continue to protect textile and apparel markets in the advanced economies. Agriculture is another area where the developed world offers a high level of subsidies to its own producers.

The United States has supported the establishment of a stronger WTO whose role is to promote free trade principles. As a consequence, the United States itself has had to comply with WTO measures promoting openness (Chorev 2005). At the same time, the United States and other advanced liberal states have found new ways of domestic promotion of advanced, knowledge-intensive undertakings. The WTO playing field, it turns out, is not level: according to Linda Weiss (2005b),

> the measures now *prohibited* under the WTO are those of *diminishing importance* to a relatively *advanced* level of development, which depends increasingly on knowledge-intensive technologies. Second, the measures *permitted*—or at least not explicitly prohibited—are *advanced country friendly:* they enable the industrialized state to align its national growth goals with significant support for industry, technology, and export. (724)

High-tech capabilities and innovative technologies are the core areas of interest for the advanced countries. Even under the new global rules of economic openness, there is ample room for advanced countries' public efforts to promote these areas through public-private partnerships, the development of information infrastructures, environmental upgrading, technology diffusion and other means. Such "strategic activism" (L. Weiss 2005b: 731) in combination with a substantially more restricted development space for the latecomers shows that the new rules appear to have served "more generally as an *upgrading device* for the *developed* economies" (L. Weiss 2005b: 725).

One important element of strategic activism that is of increasing importance is government procurement (GP), that is, public purchase of goods and services from the private sector. A recent study of the United States demonstrates that the effort to promote openness and nondiscrimination abroad is combined with an emphasis on "Buy American" at home. The United

States, according to one recent study, actively seeks to protect the home market from foreign penetration. The Buy American principle is a key element in this: "government procurement has moved on from being an important mechanism for nurturing national champions to become a major instrument of trade policy" (L. Weiss and Thurbon 2006: 713, 719).

In sum, there is a gap between the advanced liberal countries' rhetorical support for neoliberal principles of economic openness and free trade and the development experience of these countries, which in practice relied very much on mercantilist principles of state activism and intervention in support of domestic industry promotion. Today, such principles carry little weight in the liberal economic world order; here, the emphasis is on market access and full participation in economic globalization. There are not many serious debates on development strategies and state-market frameworks specifically tailored to meet development needs in countries at dissimilar levels facing a variety of challenges.

At the same time, the neoliberal rhetoric on the part of the advanced liberal states is combined with substantial policies that tilt the playing field in favor of further economic upgrading of the highly developed countries and against the development aspirations of the latecomers. The unequal development prospects that result from this situation could perhaps be seen as a manageable problem in a period where the world economy was expanding to the benefit of most states, a group of weak states being the exception to the rule. But in a prospective period of severe recession the question is whether this unbalanced framework is sufficient to sustain a stable liberal economic order. We now know that more troubled times for the liberal world economy have already begun.

Fall 2008: Financial Crisis and Impending Recession

A financial crisis is "a disturbance to financial markets that disrupts the market's capacity to allocate capital—financial intermediation and hence investment come to a halt" (Portes 1998: 1). Most financial crises emerge and disappear without being much noticed; they are part of the rhythm of capitalist development. Big financial crises are relatively rare; they simultaneously involve "foreign exchange market disturbances, debt defaults (sovereign or private), and banking system failures" (Portes 1998: 1). It was a general international crisis of this kind that engulfed the advanced liberal states and much of the rest of the world in the fall of 2008.

The crisis began with a burst housing bubble in the United States. That led to extensive mortgage defaults, and as a consequence, financial institutions had to incur heavy losses. Lack of capital forced them to decrease investment and tighten credit. With substantial reductions in demand, asset prices declined, leading to further losses. Banks lost trust, not only in borrowers, but in each other. In effect, money markets effectively shut down; "the only things anyone wants to buy right now are Treasury bills and bottled water" (Krugman 2008a).

How could it come to that? A comprehensive crisis rarely has a single cause, and the present one is no exception. Two sets of circumstances, each of them complex in itself, have pushed it. First, the U.S. Federal Reserve has kept short-term interest rates at a low level for a long period of time; during that period, the government-sponsored credit agencies, Fannie Mae and Freddie Mac, extended loans to new groups of less credit-worthy homeowners, stimulated by political initiatives to increase homeownership. China and other fast-growing economies were highly willing to invest in American securities as part of a strategy to hold down their own exchange rates; capital flowed into the United States in spite of the meager returns on securities. Low interest rates and capital abundance pushed up real estate prices in the United States. The Federal Reserve was highly successful in avoiding the threat of recession when the dot.com bubble burst around 2000, but it soon became clear that the recovery was based on replacing the technology bubble with a housing bubble.

Second, the comprehensive financial crisis marks the culmination of a long period of development where financial markets have become increasingly more complex, offering a number of products the real value of which it is frequently complicated to ascertain. The system of floating currencies began in the 1970s and quickly led to new ways of hedging the exchange-rate risk; the currency futures market began operation in Chicago in 1972. As recorded above, capital controls were soon lifted, and a host of new private players in the financial market stimulated further innovation. Any transaction involves separate types of risk; each major component of risk was now identified and traded separately. Option contracts, futures contracts, swaps (issuing bonds in one currency and swapping them for another), credit default swaps (insurance against default), portfolio insurance (stock-index futures protecting from future falls in portfolio values), and securitization (bundling loans into packages that are then sold to investors) were the major products. According to the *Economist* (2008), "these asset-backed securities became ever more complex. Securitization eventually gave rise to collateralized debt obligations, sophisticated instruments that bundled together packages of different bonds and then sliced them into tranches according to investors' appetite for risk. The opacity of these products has caused no end of trouble in the past 18 months."

Banks and other financial institutions were growing extraordinarily fast on the basis of these new instruments. Expansion became much less dependent on ordinary deposits from customers. But the entire operation was predicated on open markets, and when mortgage owners defaulted and that assumption no longer applied, the overly extended financial institutions immediately faced mortal danger. Solvency and liquidity problems of this magnitude could not be handled by the private players in the marketplace. Even if the financial system today acts as a real-time, twenty-four-hour integrated organism where exchange rates and interest rates are determined in the context of the global market, there was no cooperating political center, no common global or even Western institution of financial governance that could adequately respond to the crisis. The financial system is deeply integrated on a global scale, but regulation and control remains almost purely national. It was thus left to national governments, beginning with the United States where the crisis broke, to work out responses to the crisis and to coordinate those responses with other national governments to the extent that they deemed necessary and expedient; "at moments of confidence-withering crises, who would ultimately be responsible for bailing out financial institutions confronting the prospect of collapse? . . . Lender-of-last-resort facilities remain under the exclusive purview of individual states themselves" (Pauly 2005: 188).

Therefore, the national reactions came country by country: Germany set up a EUR 500 billon stabilization fund, France pledged EUR 360 billion, the Netherlands EUR 200 billion, and the United States would invest $250 billion in its banks and has extended guarantees for new bank debt as part of a larger rescue package. Almost all of the advanced liberal countries have proposed similar measures. Will they solve the problem? The system currently appears to be unfrozen, but the question remains whether the measures taken are sufficient to stop the credit crunch. On the one hand, neither consumers nor companies are likely to begin large-scale lending, and banks will themselves be holding back in order to meet new demands for capital ratios. On the other hand, the *Economist* speculated already in 2008 that the rescue package itself had come at a cost and "investor's nerves are shot. . . . Concern about banks' creditworthiness may yet morph into worry about sovereign risk as the full cost of the various bail-outs becomes clearer."

And so it happened; the enormous financial commitments by countries seeking to mitigate the economic crisis put their financial stability under immense strain, thus risking a sovereign-debt crisis. It began with Greece in late 2009 when investors suddenly and without warning dumped their Greek bonds and drove their market value into a free fall. Weaker versions of the crisis emerged in Portugal, Spain, Ireland, and other countries in Europe that were under similar financial stress. A comprehensive disorder now threatened the entire eurozone, and the European Central Bank had to mount a rescue operation in the spring of 2010. Together with severe public austerity measures in the most affected countries, the operation managed to restore a relative calm to financial markets, but the risk of a meltdown in Europe's financial system has not gone away.

Because of the dollar's status as a reserve currency, the United States does not face a similar sovereign-debt crisis. But the Chinese Central Bank governor, Zhou Xiaochuan, has recently suggested that a dollar-based international monetary system is inherently unstable. "Issuing countries of reserve currencies are constantly confronted with the dilemma between achieving their domestic monetary policy goals and meeting other countries' demand for reserve currencies," he wrote. "They may either fail to adequately meet the demand of a growing global economy for liquidity as they try to ease inflation pressures at home, or create excess liquidity in the global markets by overly stimulating domestic demand" (quoted from Steil 2010). In other words, we have a return of the Triffin dilemma mentioned earlier. China wants the debtor to bear the burden of adjustment. The United States is not enthusiastic about a tighter monetary and fiscal policy under current conditions. Taking that road would also aggravate the threat of a global economic slump.

One alternative for China, which it already pursues with Brazil and Russia, is trading without dollars. But the only way to do this is to balance trade bilaterally, and this would involve trade discrimination and so turn against the multilateral trading system that has been built up since the 1950s: "In those days, it was a dollar shortage that destroyed multilateral trading. Tomorrow it may be a dollar glut that does it. There is no escaping the Triffin dilemma" (Steil 2010).

In sum, the financial and economic crisis may re-erupt at any point. The crisis has, over a very short period of time, led to a level of state involvement in the advanced liberal economies—including the United States—that nobody could have expected or foreseen, even a short while ago. The advanced liberal states themselves have become living proof that the state-market relationship must develop and change over time in order to meet new challenges and new conditions. They are now in uncharted territory where densely integrated economies are combined with political frameworks that are overwhelmingly national and accustomed to put national economic priorities over international ones. Neither liberal economic theory nor liberal economic politics provides good guidelines and answers to the problems raised by this situation.

Conclusion

An international economic order based on liberal principles cannot create itself. It must be supported by a political framework of appropriate regulation
that allows the free market economy to function. This introduces the issue
of what sort of state-market matrix is appropriate for the liberal economy:
How much room should there be for market forces versus how much for
state intervention and control? What is the proper framework in more detailed terms? The principle of domestic policy autonomy underpinned the
reconstitution of the liberal economic system after World War II; it was a
Liberalism of Restraint system that lasted until the early 1970s. The ascen-
sion of Ronald Reagan in the Unites States and Margaret Thatcher in Britain
helped usher in a Liberalism of Imposition system in the 1980s. The aim was
to set market forces free in the developing world by lifting trade restrictions
and currency regulations, cutting back the public sector, and ending industrial and agricultural protectionism.

Since then, global general support for a liberal state-market arrangement
based on private property and free market exchange has increased. Processes of economic globalization have amplified the level of interdependence
among many nations. But the neoliberal principles in the economic Liberalism of Imposition did not represent a coherent answer to the problems faced
by different groups of countries. In the weak states, economic liberalization
did not have the desired effects, and the neoliberal measures did not address
core issues of insufficient state capacity and infrastructure. Nor did they give
a sufficient answer to the complex challenges of transition from planned to
market economies. In the emerging markets of Latin America and Southeast Asia, the rapid influx of short-term capital ended in capital flight and
economic crisis.

The advanced liberal states had not themselves relied on neoliberal principles in their own processes of development. They instead turned to mercantilist policies of support for domestic industry and regulation of trade
and foreign investment. Only when their domestic industries were robustly
competitive did they begin to support economic openness and free trade.
The current imposition of neoliberal standards on latecomers kicks away the
ladder as they are denied certain ways forward. This disadvantage is exacerbated by rules and measures that tilt the economic system in favor of the
developed countries; TRIPS, TRIMS, and GATS constrain the development
options of latecomers, forcing them in a neoliberal direction. At the same
time, the current system leaves space for new inventions in strategic activism
for the advanced countries.

The current financial crisis has opened an even larger gap between advanced liberal countries' rhetorical support of neoliberal imposition economics and their actual deeds. Deregulation of the financial system led to solvency and liquidity imbalances that could not be absorbed by market adjustments. Nor was there any multilateral institutional framework among liberal states ready to face the problems; they had to be handled through national reactions by means of country-specific rescue packages.

In the liberal tradition, an open international market economy based on free trade was always a force for cooperation, progress, and peace. The removal of economic barriers to establish equal trade was a central element in Woodrow Wilson's peace program. The Liberal International Manifesto from 1997 also emphasizes its support for free trade, an open economy, and resistance to protectionism. The notion that progress is promoted by free men pursuing peaceful economic intercourse not interrupted by governments is a core belief in the liberal tradition (chapter 2).

The actual trajectory of liberal economic development has not corresponded to the liberal vision. There is broader support for a liberal state-market arrangement than ever before, but progress is very unevenly distributed; some groups benefit more than others. The advanced liberal states attempt to bend the rules, supporting a system where the playing field is tilted to the advantage of the advanced states and to the disadvantage of the latecomers. The system imposes constraints on latecomers not faced by the advanced states; in this basic sense the system is not liberal. Strong reactions from the disadvantaged may yet intensify the contestation over liberal economic order.

Even with such inequalities, the system can potentially provide benefits for all participants; the question is whether they will be sufficient to uphold and develop a stable global economy based on liberal principles. There are three major reasons to believe that they will not. First, it has become increasingly difficult to formulate an appropriate state-market matrix, a set of substantial liberal economic principles that can be fully supported by the vast majority of countries. Countries at different levels require dissimilar answers to their economic development problems, depending on the specific challenges they face. There is not a one-size-fits-all Imposition model that all can embrace. At one extreme, the successful development strategy currently pursued by China combines elements of capitalism and a market economy with authoritarian government, political control, and a quite substantial role for the state in the regulation of economic development. It is not a version of development that owes much to the liberal idea of free men pursuing peaceful economic intercourse uninterrupted by government. As for the weak countries, liberal economic principles alone will not solve their problems;

they need much more effective and responsive statehood, and there is no straightforward path to that as indicated in the previous chapter.

The second reason is the lack of leadership. The largest difference between now and the postwar period of a successful Liberalism of Restraint is the lack of a leading country or group of countries, able and willing to take responsibility and go in front. Liberal states on both sides of the Atlantic are looking inward, focusing on their own problems.[3] The International Civil Society, a global organization of NGOs, recently complained that instead of repairing the global economy, G20 leaders had "injected 1.1 trillion dollars into many of the same institutions whose economic, finance, and trade policies exacerbated the speed, scale and impact of the crisis. Reforms have been superficial, and any shifts to the current economic paradigm still seem temporary, rather than long term" (International Civil Society 2010). Focusing on trade, Ian Campbell made the following statement already in 2004:

> the world no longer has a leader in economic policymaking. Nowhere is that lack of leadership more evident than in trade. The failure of the ministerial summit meeting of the WTO in Cancun, Mexico in September was prepared by the prior positions adopted by the main players: the United States, the European Union and developing countries. The positions of all were characterized by hypocrisy. Perhaps the greatest hypocrisy, however, was that of the United States, which preaches the merits of free trade more strongly than almost any other country and yet spends tens of billions of dollars to prevent its own markets from being free and has taken fresh measures in recent years to discriminate against other countries' producers.... Developing countries that depend utterly on agriculture are forced to compete with a U.S. agricultural sector that is hugely subsidized. Yet the United States constantly urges countries to open their own markets and allow freer access to U.S. goods and services.... What the United States and the European Union bring to trade meetings at present is not a willingness to do what is right but a determination not to give anything away. (111–12)

Finally, on the issue of transnational bads, the indicators of economic downturn and crisis are presently stronger than they have been at any point since the 1930s. A complete breakdown of liberal economic order will probably not take place, if the early reactions are valid indicators of what is going

---

3. President Obama spent seven minutes out of seventy-one on issues outside U.S. borders in his 2010 State of the Union address. The EU has just come out of a long process of adopting the Lisbon treaty and is presently preoccupied with the economic stability of its southern European members.

to come. But in a period of severe crisis, countries will be less willing to forgo what they see as core national economic interests. This is no less true for finance than it is for trade, or any other major economic domain. At the same time, a period of severe crisis can spark more profound institutional change, as happened after World War II. The current economic crisis, however, does not appear to be leading to initiatives for major reform; emphasis is on minor adjustments aimed at restoring confidence in existing markets.

Liberal states appear comprehensively unready, unable, and unwilling to construct a stable economic order based on liberal principles. The financial and economic crisis has been met with piecemeal reform aimed at national challenges in single countries; it can break out again at any time. Instead of exercising leadership in economic policymaking, liberal states focus on their own short- and medium-term troubles. And it is not at all clear what the principles of a reformed order should be—neoliberal Imposition will not do, and a return to classical Restraint is not feasible. Today's globalized world economy will continue to pose serious difficulties for any hope of a stable liberal world order.

CHAPTER 6

Institutions and Liberal World Order

Institutions, international as well as domestic, play a significant role in any liberal order. Institutions were defined in chapter 2 as sets of rules, formal and informal, that states and other actors play by. According to liberals, a rule-based order is much to be preferred to the alternative, an order without rules. That is because even powerful actors such as great powers would face very high costs if they were to use only force in order to influence events (Keohane 1998). Furthermore, a purely power-based order is thin and shaky because it lacks legitimacy, the lawfulness that follows from being authorized by institutional consent. Institutions enhance transparency, predictability, and credible compliance; they provide information and opportunities to negotiate and thus reduce the costs of making and reinforcing agreements.

For these reasons liberals support a rule-based order, and as was briefly mentioned in chapter 2, there has indeed been a sharp quantitative rise in the number of IGOs and INGOs, especially during the latter half of the twentieth century. Increasing numbers of organizations are, of course, only part of the story; international agreements have also grown thicker and more complex. The NAFTA agreement runs some 26,000 pages; the *acquis communitaire,* which new EU members must accept, totals more than 85,000 pages. Furthermore, rules are increasingly about behind-the-border issues, that is, they are less about regulating barriers to entry and exit and more about positive regulation related to citizens' behavior in a variety of different areas (Hurrell 2006: 60).

We have seen that liberal theories of IR generally emphasize mutually beneficial cooperation and progress. Institutions fundamentally improve the ability of states and other actors to cooperate. It would appear that the general developments since World War II have confirmed liberal expectations about stronger cooperation and increase of institutionalization. At the same time, beneath the optimistic surface of these changes are tensions concerning power, legitimacy, and, eventually, the concrete substance of liberal values. They point to a somewhat more problematic role for international institutions in the liberal view of world order, and they ultimately call into question whether there are appropriate conditions for such an order in the present international system.

The central liberal dilemma when it comes to international institutions was identified in chapter 2. Liberal states support a pluralist approach to international institutions; a universal community of liberal as well as nonliberal countries is the appropriate framework for global cooperation and the promotion of liberal values. But liberal states also favor a nonpluralist approach to international institutions: only a strong concert of liberal democracies can take the lead and create a better, that is, more liberal, world order. The universal, pluralist approach is the Liberalism of Restraint attitude toward international institutions. The nonpluralist, selective approach is the Liberalism of Imposition, which wants to put liberal states in the driver's seat in order to define rules and principles for others; if necessary the hegemonic liberal power can go it alone with the support of a "coalition of the willing."

The unique conditions after the end of World War II led to the establishment of a universal Restraint order centered on the UN system combined with a distinct liberal order centered on West-West cooperation within the framework of NATO and other transatlantic institutions. Universal cooperation succeeded in containing the confrontation between East and West so that it remained a cold rather than a hot war. Within that framework liberal cooperation across the Atlantic successfully intensified. The European liberal states welcomed U.S. leadership because it provided both security and economic benefits; it was an "empire by invitation" (Lundestad 1986).

The preconditions for that order were removed with the end of the Cold War. The United States was now a unipolar power, but it was also more concerned with its own economic and security priorities. The United States sought to create a Liberal Imposition order with universal reach, where it defined the rules for others. It was a bid for dominance that other great powers would not agree to, and it quickly became clear that unilateral Imposition could not be the basis for a transformed liberal order. But there is no road back to the earlier Restraint order because the preconditions are now different. The road forward to a stable and effective order confronts obstacles of leadership, legitimacy, and institutional setup. The major aspects of this dilemma are illuminated in the following sections.

Power and Institutions I: Liberal Hegemony is Necessary—and Dangerous

The liberal approach, whether pluralist or nonpluralist, is reflected in the attitude toward power and institutions: On the one hand, a preponderant liberal power, a hegemon, is needed to set up and run a liberal order. On the other hand, liberals worry about hegemony because, as Lea Brilmayer (1994) notes, it is antiliberal in the sense of being "quintessentially autocratic" (61). Judith Shklar (1989) takes that liberal worry one step further; liberals must primarily fear the exercise of arbitrary power by states and other types of collectivities, or by individuals: "the assumption, amply justified by every page of political history, is that some agents of government will behave lawlessly and brutally in big or small ways most of the time unless they are prevented from doing so" (28). As regards the international realm, liberals and realists are in agreement on this point; "I distrust hegemonic power, whoever may wield it," Kenneth Waltz (1986) says, "because it is so easily misused" (341).

So liberal power is needed and hegemonic power can be abused: liberal hegemony is necessary and dangerous. Liberal theory has an uneasy relationship with power, for good reasons: in the terminology of this book, why would a hegemonic power not be excessively Impositionist, even imperialist, when it is in a situation where it is capable of exercising arbitrary power? And if it does demonstrate a substantial measure of Restraint, how will it be able to create order in a situation where many different interests are in play? I aim to show that the United States did indeed create an effective liberal Restraint order after World War II, but because of changed circumstances, especially in the underlying patterns of power, the conditions for creating a reformed liberal order may not be present today. Unilateral and Impositionist U.S. leadership has been rejected, while the conditions for creating a reformed liberal Restraint order are absent.

To repeat, liberal scholars overwhelmingly tend to agree with realists and Marxists as concerns the relationship between power and international institutions; it requires a hegemon, a dominant military and economic power, to create and develop an international liberal order, because in the absence of such a power, liberal rules cannot be enforced around the world: "with a sole hegemonic power, the rules of the game can be established and enforced. Lesser countries have little choice but to go along. Without hegemonic power, conflict is the order of the day" (Moffitt 1987:576). This argument was first developed in the field of international political economy, where it specifically concerned the development of an effective liberal international economic order (Kindleberger 1973; Gilpin 1987). But it has been extended to cover the larger framework of liberal international or world order set up mainly by the United States (Ikenberry 2001; Deudney and Ikenberry 1999).

There have been two periods in which leading liberal powers sought to create liberal international orders: the Pax Britannica of the nineteenth century and the Pax Americana in the twentieth century, after World War II. Since the British order unfolded in a predominantly nonliberal environment, it is really only the U.S. postwar order that can provide us with information about the relationship between power and international institutions in a world with a large number of liberal states.

The theory of hegemonic order has led to a large debate about the extent and quality of power resources (military, economic, and otherwise) that the leading state needs in order to perform the role of hegemon (Keohane 1984; Nye 1990). That debate need not concern us at the present time. There is no doubt that the United States was overwhelmingly powerful after World War II: the country controlled almost half of the world's economic production, and that was combined with dominance in military, technological, and other resources, even if the Soviet Union quickly became a military rival (Krasner 1982).

It was this unique position that the United States could rely on when taking the lead in the postwar construction of order. The task did not follow a clear blueprint from the beginning; the project had to be changed and modified, especially owing to deteriorating relations with the Soviet Union and the demands of the European allies. There were also several competing U.S. visions of order in the early years after the war (Trachtenberg 1999; Ikenberry 2001).

Two major elements stood out in the new order (Ikenberry 1996). On the one hand, the containment arrangement provided security for the Western world against the Soviet threat. Balance of power, nuclear deterrence, and political/ideological competition characterized the relationship between the two blocs. NATO, the institutional core on the Western side, was, in the words of Lord Ismay, created to "keep the Russians out, the Germans down, and the Americans in." Put differently, the organization not merely helped balance the Soviet Union but also performed two significant intra-alliance tasks: securing the U.S. commitment to allies in a domestic political context where there was weariness of such obligations and reassuring European allies against fears of an uncontrolled rise of Germany.

On the other hand, the new order aimed at intensified Western economic and political cooperation, working toward liberal goals of economic openness and political democracy. The Bretton Woods institutions, the World Bank, and the International Monetary Fund "were important because they served as a basis for building broader coalitions around a relatively open and managed order" (Ikenberry 2001: 190). In the context of bipolarity and containment, the Bretton Woods institutions quickly abandoned global ambitions and became core elements in a Western order that also included the U.S. dollar as reserve currency and the U.S. home market as a source of economic growth.

The postwar order was a huge success. Even if nuclear deterrence led to situations of potential disaster such as the 1962 Cuban missile crisis, a system of superpower management restrained competition between the blocs until the Soviet system eventually proved unviable and broke down. The Western economic order saw the reconstruction of Japan and Germany, a new era of close cooperation in Europe, and an unprecedented period of economic growth and welfare progress in the OECD-world. There were elements of crisis in the economic order in the 1970s, and because the huge U.S. economic lead was disappearing, the United States adopted protectionist measures to support its own economy (see chapter 5). According to some observers, the United States was becoming a "predatory hegemon" (John Conybeare, quoted from Gilpin 1987). But the system did not break down. On the one hand, the relative economic decline of the United States was often exaggerated (Strange 1987); on the other hand, once a set of international institutions have been set up, they have a staying power of their own, and they are able to sustain cooperation even in circumstances of hegemonic distress (Keohane 1984).

It would appear at first that the end of the Cold War merely concerned one of the two major elements in the postwar order: the bipolar containment arrangement. The other major element, the liberal economic and political order, was untouched. If anything, the liberal order stood to gain from the end of superpower rivalry; it could now grow from a limited order inside the bipolar system to a global liberal order encompassing the entire system (Ikenberry 1996). The notion of the end of history expressed that aspiration in no uncertain terms. But the two decades since the end of the Cold War have not confirmed that liberal optimism; the end of bipolarity changed the constellation of power in ways that also had a negative influence on the stability of the liberal order.

First, bipolarity was replaced by unipolarity; never before in modern history had a single superpower dominated the world in this way, "unchecked by any rival and with decisive reach in every corner of the globe" (Krauthammer 2004). In the previous bipolar system, the United States had worked under an incentive to provide stability and security to the Western world. "America needed allies and allies needed America. This provided the basis for bargains—and it created incentives for cooperation in areas outside of national security" (Ikenberry 2009: 79). In a situation of unchecked unipolar power, by contrast, the hegemon faces no severe international constraint; it can basically do whatever it wants. This is potentially bad news for international institutions because unchecked power has less incentive to institutionalize itself. Instead, it may be tempted to choose between two other options. One is isolationism: "hoard that power and retreat" (Krauthammer 2004). Such a retreat will of course weaken international institutions because they are not firmly supported by the leading power. If isolationism is doing too little, the other option is to do too much, to embark on expansionist policies, making hegemonic influence felt everywhere. International institutions are then weakened because they are sidestepped. Some combination of those extremes is of course also possible. Liberals and realists agree that any such policies, in the absence of serious external constraint, will be determined by patterns of domestic preferences (Moravcsik 1997; Krasner 1992).[1] I return to the issue of domestic U.S. politics and its implications for world order below; the liberal predicament in this regard is of course that liberal governments might not necessarily pursue liberal policies.

During the first term of the George W. Bush presidency, the United States did indeed initiate a "new unilateralism" in its foreign policy. This was surely amplified by the terrorist attacks of September 11, 2001, but it began sometime before that. The Clinton administration had supported "assertive multilateralism," but it ended up stressing assertion rather than multilateralism: the United States was to be able to engage in war alone, and it backed away from commitments to UN peacekeeping efforts. By June 2001, Charles Krauthammer could claim that the United States had embarked on a foreign policy that "seeks to strengthen American power and unashamedly deploy it on behalf of *self-defined* global ends." The president confirmed these intentions in a West Point commencement address: "America has, and intends to keep, military strengths beyond challenges—thereby making the destabilizing

---

1. Constructivists persuasively argue that dominant ideas also play a role; see Monten (2005, 2007).

arms races of other periods pointless, and limiting rivalries to trade and other pursuits of peace" (G. W. Bush 2002).

Second, unilateralism was combined with a high-profile U.S. activism in the wake of 9/11. The National Security Strategy (NSS) of 2002 vows to "defend liberty and justice because these principles are right and true for people everywhere" (NSS 2002). It is also emphasized that the United States must be unconstrained in responding to threats, including preemptive use of force—the wars in Afghanistan and Iraq followed. A further aspect of unilateralism is the retreat from international institutions and agreements: the abolishment of the 1972 Anti-Ballistic Missile Treaty with the Soviet Union, the rejection of the Kyoto Protocol on global warming, of the Biological Weapons Convention, and of the International Criminal Court. Finally, there was still formal commitment to an open, liberal economic order, but as shown in chapter 5, actual U.S. policies embarked on a more mercantilist path "classically associated with the idea of Japan Inc." (L. Weiss 2005a: 1). The United States time and again rejected WTO demands in favor of measures that have eroded other states' exports (Mowle and Sacko 2007: 3).

In sum, the unipolar power requested the rest of the world to subject itself to an order that left the United States entirely unconstrained while requiring commitments to rules and regulations from everybody else. The arrangement licensed the United States to set aside sovereignty and intervene according to principles set forth by the United States itself. Other states were to play by a different set of rules that respected sovereignty and international commitments. This is a Liberalism of Imposition order amounting to a "neoimperial vision in which the United States arrogates to itself the global role of setting standards, determining threats, and meting out justice" (Ikenberry 2002b: 44).

Imposition was not a coherent and stable recipe for a post–Cold War liberal world order. Several close liberal U.S. allies (Germany, France) would not accept it, nor would other great powers such as China, Russia, and India. One might indeed ask why there was no stronger reaction against this bid for unilateral dominance. Several answers suggest themselves: first, active power balancing is a very costly undertaking given the huge lead of the United States, especially in the military field; second, liberal allies in Europe and elsewhere may be critical of a neo-imperial strategy, but they do not perceive U.S. impositionist activism as a direct threat; third, in this situation many states have chosen softer forms of balancing where they "strengthen and refine their hedging strategy" (Wivel 2008: 303), perhaps preparing for a more autonomous role in the future (T. Paul et al. 2004; Ikenberry et al. 2009).

Meanwhile, the impositionist, neo-imperial impulse in the U.S. foreign posture has become much less pronounced. Even if unipolarity remains in place, the United States is militarily fatigued owing to the campaigns in Iraq and Afghanistan. It has proven difficult to translate military hegemony to dominance on the ground under adverse conditions; according to Barry Posen (2003),

> the closer U.S. military forces get to enemy-held territory, the more competitive the enemy will be. This arises from a combination of political, physical, and technological facts...U.S. command of the commons provides an impressive foundation for selective engagement. It is not adequate for a policy of primacy [that is, a nationalist, unilateralist version of hegemony]. (20, 42)

Furthermore, the financial crisis, erupting in full in 2008, has laid bare weaknesses in the U.S. free market model and has emphasized the increasing economic importance of modernizing states, especially China. While the real U.S. economy remains strong, some substantial adjustment is required to correct present imbalances, and this will require the full attention of the U.S. political system. Finally, military and economic problems and the turn away from international institutions have weakened the soft power resources of the United States—soft power can be defined as "getting others to want what you want...the ability to set the political agenda in a way that shapes the preferences of others" (Nye 2002: 9).

The Barack Obama administration has gone to work on these problems in a way that promises more Restraint in the form of cooperative multilateralism rather than Imposition. This will surely lead away from the dangers involved in liberal order making through excessive Imposition. But is it possible to create a stable liberal Restraint order under the new circumstances of the post–Cold War world? A major factor here is the foreign policies of leading liberal states. The next section comments on the domestic sources of foreign policy in the leading liberal state and explains why they need not always lead to liberal policies.

Domestic Sources of Liberal Policy

A stable, rule-based liberal international order is dependent not merely on international institutions; it has a domestic institutional foundation as well. For many liberals the domestic aspect is the more important one because it fundamentally decides the nature of the state. John Locke argued that states exist to underwrite the liberty of their citizens and thus enable them to live their lives and pursue their happiness without undue interference from other people. Liberals see the state as a constitutional entity that establishes and enforces the rule of law that respects the rights of citizens to life, liberty, and property. Such constitutional states would also respect each other and would deal with each other in accordance with norms of mutual toleration. Jeremy Bentham believed that it was in the rational interests of constitutional states to adhere to international law in their foreign policies (Rosenblum 1978: 101). Immanuel Kant thought that a world of such constitutional and mutually respectful states could eventually establish "perpetual peace" in the world (Gallie 1978: 8–36).

There are two major problems when these views are applied to current liberal policies: First, there are a great many nonliberal states in the present international system. Cooperation with them is difficult because when "non-liberal governments are in a state of aggression with their own people, their foreign relations become for liberal governments deeply suspect. In short, fellow liberals benefit from a presumption of amity; non-liberals suffer from a presumption of enmity" (Doyle 1986: 1161). Second, the policy preferences emerging from a process of democratic deliberation[2] may not necessarily be liberal: instead of openness, prevailing groups can request protectionism; instead of peaceful cooperation, they can request conflict; instead of equal rights for all, they can request unequal treatment.

There is a large debate about the relationship between the democratic public and foreign policymaking that cannot be taken up here (see Sørensen 2008: 136–52). It is sufficient in the present context to endorse the view by recent liberal theory that "state behavior reflects various patterns of state preferences" (Moravcsik 1997: 520). State preferences emerge from deliberations among social and political groups in society. Whether such preferences, for example concerning global order, eventually prevail in the international system still depends on a later process of interaction between states and other actors. But to begin with, the patterns of preferences emerge from a primarily domestic process of deliberation.

The question is whether domestic preferences in leading liberal states, especially in the United States, are supportive of a policy of liberal internationalism—defined as the employment of U.S. power toward international cooperation with the aim of establishing and maintaining a liberal economic and political order. In the postwar liberal order, "the United States would

---

2. "In a democracy, the national interest is simply what citizens, after proper deliberation, say it is" (Nye 2002: 139).

project its military strength to preserve stability, but it would seek to exercise its leadership through multilateral partnership rather than unilateral initiative. It was the coupling of U.S. power and international partnership that gave the nation's foreign policy such a distinctive character in the decades following World War II" (Kupchan and Trubowitz 2007: 8). This was the stable liberal Restraint order mentioned in the previous section.

Charles A. Kupchan and Peter L. Trubowitz argue that the basis for the liberal compact is eroding in the United States. First, the absence of a Cold War threat from the Soviet Union has loosened political discipline and increased the appeal of unilateralism. Senate minority leader Tom Daschle wrote in 1996: "The Cold War exerted a powerful hold on America, and it forced the parties to work together to advance American interests through bipartisan internationalism.... The tragedy is that such cooperation increasingly seems an artifact of the past" (4–5). Second, bipartisanship is weakened for domestic reasons as well: regional divisions are stronger, with the South as the Republican party's main regional power base, and coalitions cutting across party and regional divides are increasingly difficult to establish. Uneven globalization has exacerbated regional tensions and disparities. Support for free trade "now depends on the backing of congressional delegations from Red states in the South and Mountain West" (Kupchan and Trubowitz 2007: 33). Generational change is a factor as well: the World War II generation is retiring, and the new members of Congress are not socialized toward bipartisan compromise. In sum, the United States "long embraced the liberal internationalist compact between military power and institutionalized partnership, but this compact has now come undone" (Kupchan and Trubowitz 2007: 39).[3]

This leaves no easy path to a stable liberal Restraint order (Tepperman 2004). The analysis summarized above foresees a period of continued partisan quarrel reminiscent of the pre–World War II era of "domestic stalemate, inconstancy, and detachment" (Kupchan and Trubowitz 2007: 4). It argues in favor of a "selective withdrawal" that leaves larger geopolitical responsibilities to others, including the EU and rising great powers such as China and India, as well as regional organizations. But the substantial message of the analysis is that domestic conditions in the United States presently do not provide a supportive foundation for a stable liberal Restraint order. A clear project for a liberal order with solid bipartisan backing will probably not

---

3. There is by now a comprehensive debate about the extent to which domestic support for the liberal compact has eroded (Chaudoin et al. 2010; Busby and Monten 2008; Wiarda and Skelly 2006). The major point in the present context is that domestic support for a liberal compact can never be taken for granted.

emerge from the domestic political process anytime soon. Policies will be more tentative, based on alliances that are more fragile. As emphasized by Craig Murphy already in 2000, even if the United States is the last remaining superpower, "it is also a 'normal' state, one that pursues its self-interest in all of its international relations; it is not like the early Cold-War era hegemon ready to sacrifice its short-term interests in order to create and defend 'The Free World'" (19).

Power and Institutions II: What Kind of Institutional Order Follows from a Goal of Liberal Restraint?

This section will further explain why the road to a stable liberal Restraint order with global reach is blocked or severely hindered in various respects. The first problem concerns the need for liberal power behind a liberal order. Who will set up and run a reformed liberal order? The obvious candidate is the United States, but the previous section argued that domestic support and to some extent capabilities are missing for a new Grand Strategy initiative. It is important not to misread the historical record in this respect. The United States was always a hesitant constructor of order: "The United States has not been wed in any principled way to multilateralism, or to any other particular institutional approach. To be sure, in many instances U.S. officials initiated and nurtured multilateral institutions. But just as significantly, they have resorted to unilateralism and promoted bilateral, minilateral, and *ad hoc* institutional arrangements. The baseline U.S. approach to international institutions has been pragmatic rather than principled... [involving] a tendency to focus on what works in terms of U.S. domestic and foreign policy interests" (Mastanduno 2005: 318, 331).

The EU has adopted a Common Foreign and Security Policy (European Union 2010), but it is in no position to replace or even rival the United States in terms of political coherence and resources of power.[4] Nor is Japan, although the country has moved away from its previous international role as "global civilian power" toward an emerging role as "global ordinary power with Japanese characteristics" (Inoguchi and Bacon 2005: 126–27). The latter role involves a greater support for the use of force, but solely for defensive purposes; the relationship to the United States remains vital for Japan.

The stalemate in establishing a reformed global liberal order can be traced to the disagreements among liberal great powers as concerns the reform of

---

4. For an in-depth analysis of "Euro-paralysis," see Zielonka (1998).

international institutions and the relative emphasis on different types of institutions. A reform of the United Nations has been on the agenda almost since the establishment of that organization (T. Weiss and Young 2005). The debate contains three major items: (a) The Security Council reflects the distribution of power at the end of World War II, especially as regards the five permanent members. Great powers that are nonpermanent members (India, Japan, Germany, Brazil) and many countries in the South are critical of this situation. (b) In an era of economic globalization, the UN does not have an economic body with sufficient ability to address issues of inequality, welfare, and economic growth. This is a core issue for many countries in the South. (c) Administrative reform of the UN in order to eliminate inefficiency and excess bureaucracy is a major issue for many countries in the North.

There is no agreement among the leading liberal states in the G7 (United States, Japan, Germany, United Kingdom, France, Italy, and Canada) concerning these proposals for UN reform. Canada and Italy are most open toward changes, but they also value their special relationship with the United States. Any changes in the Security Council toward a better reflection of the current global distribution of power will reduce the influence of the United Kingdom and France; Japan is preoccupied with economic crisis and with regional order; the U.S. Congress wants to increase transparency and accountability of the UN, but will not accede to any reform that curtails U.S. power or autonomy within the organization. In sum, there is no consensus among major liberal powers with regard to reform of the UN system (Murphy 2000).

Another major issue concerns the type of multilateral institutionalism that is pursued by liberal states: is it universal in scope, encompassing all sovereign states, or is it selective, aiming primarily at states that are liberal democracies? Recall the proposition quoted above: liberal states are much more comfortable cooperating with other liberal states than with nonliberal states. With the end of the Cold War and with the rapid progress of economic globalization, there is an increased demand for cooperation that is universal rather than selective. Liberal states continue to cooperate most intensely in liberal forums such as NATO, the OECD, and the EU, but the changed circumstances have raised the issue anew. This is a further aspect of the liberal ambiguity emphasized earlier: liberal states support a pluralist as well as a nonpluralist approach to international institutions.

The response liberal states have come up with reflects this ambiguity. The report of the Princeton Project, which puts forward the principles of a reformed liberal world order, emphasizes that the United Nations needs to be reformed, but it also proposes an alternative liberal body, a global

"Concert of Democracies," "dedicated to the principles of underpinning liberal democracy, both as a vehicle to spur and support the reform of the United Nations and other global institutions and as a possible alternative to them" (Princeton Project 2006: 25). So on the one hand, a liberal posture supports universal organizations; on the other hand, it supports a selective organization of liberal states as a possible alternative.

It is easy to see why the idea of a concert or a league of democracies would sound immediately appealing to the liberal states; they can work toward the promotion of common interests without the difficulties of objections and resistance from nondemocratic states. They have military and economic resources that could be put to effective use in the pursuit of liberal ends, perhaps especially in cases where the UN Security Council would be blocked by Russian or Chinese opposition. But there are also significant potential problems: First, who would be members of a democratic league? A "Community of Democracies" was established in 2000, comprising more than 120 members; it has adopted a general declaration in favor of worldwide democracy promotion and not much else. According to one proposal, an organization with more restricted membership following higher democratic standards would include about 60 countries (Daalder and Lindsay 2007). Second, should such an organization become effective, there is a risk of antagonizing major nondemocracies, including China, Russia, and a number of Middle Eastern countries. Decisions by a group of democracies are highly legitimate in the sense that they emerge from systems with domestic democratic legitimacy, but they would of course not be seen as legitimate by nondemocracies in the larger society of states. Most democracies in Europe are strong supporters of the UN and would be skeptical of a league of democracies with the potential to undermine it. Third, such a league might not be able to overcome current disagreements among democracies in security affairs (the Afghanistan and Iraq operations) or economic issues (the Doha round of trade talks). Finally, the world may not be headed for the end of history anytime soon; nondemocracy may persist, and a league might even help sustain that situation. According to Charles Kupchan (2008),

> state-led, authoritarian capitalism has at least as much appeal in many quarters of the globe as the democratic alternative. . . . If a new global order is to emerge, Washington and Brussels will have to adjust to the preferences of rising autocracies, just as Beijing and Moscow have had to adjust to the West. Fashioning a peaceful order for the twenty-first century will require navigating a two-way street; the West cannot just make a take-it-or-leave-it offer. If the liberal democracies fail to

understand that the coming world will be both multipolar and politically divisive, they will be heading down a dead-end. (92)

In sum, there is no clear institutional choice. Charles Kupchan wants to reform the UN Security Council rather than sidestep it with a league of democracies, but it was argued above that this road may be blocked as well. Liberal democracies are not at all in agreement about the institutional setup of a future liberal world order, and they tend to utilize the current institutional framework according to their relative abilities to exert maximum influence. According to Lloyd Gruber (2005), power politics "has been fuelling much of the international cooperation and institution-building we have recently been seeing across Europe, North America, and the developing world" (128). That leaves no clear institutional path to a reformed liberal Restraint order.

Nondemocratic States in a Liberal Restraint Order: The Case of China

As indicated above, a reformed liberal Restraint order will be compelled to seek to integrate what Kupchan calls "rising autocracies," including the great powers of Russia and China. Both scholars and politicians agree on this view: then U.S. deputy secretary of state Robert Zoellick talked in 2005 about "taking our policy beyond opening doors to China's membership into the international system. We need to urge China to become a responsible stakeholder in that system" (quoted from Drezner 2007: 18). Daniel Deudney and John Ikenberry (2009) emphasize the need for a successful foreign policy to "integrate, rather than exclude, autocratic and rising great powers" (90). The financial crisis has added new urgency to the U.S. aspirations of integrating China into international society (Clinton 2009). That raises the issue of what kind of players emerging great powers are going to be and how they will affect the liberal order. The following remarks will focus on China.

China greatly emphasizes sovereignty and the norm of nonintervention. China's history of foreign dominance is an important reason for this view. The official Chinese historical memory is of "one hundred years of suffering and humiliation" at the hands of Japan and the Western powers. China's international isolation during the Cold War, especially after the separation from the Soviet Union, further strengthened the idea of a hostile and extremely competitive international environment. China's economic opening to the world in the context of domestic reforms initiated a new period of Chinese participation in international society. Post-Mao China has joined a very large number of international regimes and organizations, some of which China previously criticized as parts of an American hegemony. In particular, China has become a member of the World Trade Organization. In November 2000, President Jiang Zemin declared that a nation's participation in economic globalization is an "objective requirement" for economic development. He went on to argue that globalization has a beneficial impact on international relations, in that "closer economic and technological ties between nations and regions" make up a "positive factor to promote world peace and stability" (quoted from Garrett 2001: 409).

One should not assume that this amounts to an embrace of liberal values. China sees integration into a liberal order as necessary for the promotion of national greatness and power; such integration is not at all connected to a liberalism emphasizing individual freedom and rights. In China, "the prior necessity has been for a programme of nation-building, in which the value of individual liberties is assessed in terms of their compatibility with the task of achieving freedom for the state as an actor in international society" (Hughes 2002: 198). Put differently, China embraces capitalism but emphatically rejects individual liberty and democracy because they threaten fragmentation and chaos. Singapore is the role model, not Taiwan. In Singapore's case, "capitalism is lauded, but liberal democracy is seen to be a block to economic development.... Party dictatorship continues to be legitimized in terms of maintaining integrity and the strength of the Chinese state" (Hughes 2002: 203).

What does this mean for liberal world order? The answer depends much on an evaluation of the long-term prospects for development in the "rising autocracies." The optimistic liberal view is that economic and social modernization will, eventually, be followed by liberal changes in the political sphere as well. The basic reason for this is that there are "deep contradictions between authoritarian political systems and capitalist economic systems... and the resolution of these contradictions is likely to lead to political liberalization" (Deudney and Ikenberry 2009: 83; Inglehart and Welzel 2009). Higher levels of education, the emergence of a diversity of interests, the need for a rule of law, for confronting corruption and inequality, for better accountability and flows of information, all point in that direction. The skeptic view is that after more than thirty years of market-oriented reform, there continue to be few indications of a more open political system; furthermore, authoritarianism might be quite compatible with capitalism and may "represent a viable alternative path to modernity" (Gat 2007).

Modernization does contain impulses toward political liberalization, but in China's case there are reasons to believe they may be too muted or progress too slowly to have any relevance in the foreseeable future. In particular, three factors indicate that any firm liberal progress will come slowly. First, the middle classes that have emerged from the rapid economic growth in China (and in Russia) are not particularly democratic; they prefer techno-cratic authoritarian rule to democracy, which they fear will bring chaos and conflict (Chen 2003). Second, the development of the rule of law in China is confined to the regulation of economic activity; it has not spread to civil and political rights (Pei 2005). Third, there is a civil society in China, but it is under state control and surveillance (Brook and Frohlich 1997; Andersen 2009; Human Rights Watch 2010). One forecast made by Francis Fukuyama (1992) almost two decades ago—and not in line with any end-of-history optimism—appears rather compelling today: "If Asians become convinced that their success was due more to their own faith than to borrowed cultures, if economic growth in American and Europe falters relative to that in the Far East, if Western societies continue to experience the progressive break-down of basic social institutions like the family, and if they themselves treat Asia with distrust or hostility, then a systematic illiberal and non-democratic alternative combining technocratic economic rationalism with paternalistic authoritarianism may gain ground in the Far East" (43).

These developments will most probably not lead to the return of ag-gressive power balancing in a raw anarchy with risk of imminent war (pace Kagan 2007). There is every reason to believe that China will continue its policy of economic openness and political participation in international in-stitutions (as will Russia), but China will surely also continue to be a less en-thusiastic member of international society, viewing international politics as a struggle for position, power, and relative advantage (Lampton 2008; Ross and Feng 2008).[5] Leading liberal states, headed by the United States, will want to accommodate China. Any support for human rights in China or for Tibetan secession or self-rule or for other liberal developments will take second place to the strategic issues of the partnership; "our pressing on those issues can't interfere with the global economic crisis, the global climate change crisis and the security crisis. It is essential that the United States and China have a positive, cooperative relationship," Hillary Clinton told reporters in February 2009 (Clinton 2009).

In other words, a reformed liberal Restraint order will be compelled to include nondemocratic great powers as major stakeholders in the system. The latter will emphasize traditional values of sovereignty, nonintervention, and

---

5. Anne Applebaum (2010) recently diagnosed that "Chinese military, territorial, and diplomatic aggression is rising."

fundamental differences of national interest. In such an order there will be no common value foundation that includes freedom, democracy, and human rights. That will further discourage any developments toward a universal compact of "Responsibility to Protect" (chapter 4) to look after human rights. China's current activism in Africa goes in a different direction: it is ready to support full-blown dictatorships insofar as the bargains meet Chinese national interests by providing access to raw materials, energy, and agricultural products (Malone 2008).

There is a further tension in the inclusion of nondemocratic states in a reformed liberal order. The development of economic globalization leads to intensified interdependence. That increases the demand for regulation across borders. Instead of negative regulation (i.e., regulations that prohibit states from taking certain measures), there is an emphasis on positive regulation (i.e., regulations that require states to take certain measures). Furthermore, focus is increasingly on behind-the-border issues (i.e., regulations that concern not tariffs or quotas but product standards, investment regulations, competition policies, transparency measures, etc.). According to Michael Zürn (2002), economic globalization tends to change the character of international institutions; "increasingly, their aim is to regulate not only the action of state actors but also those of societal actors, and not only at the border, but also behind-the-border issues. In doing so, positive regulations have gained importance relative to negative regulations. The extent and the objects of international governance no longer easily match the notion of a sovereign state in the Westphalian system" (247). But it is exactly this traditional notion of sovereignty and nonintervention that China wants to emphasize.

Power and Institutions III: The Issue of Legitimacy

Legitimacy was briefly defined above as the lawfulness that follows from being authorized by institutional consent; this is a narrow definition of legitimacy that is not sufficient to cover the problems raised by that concept. This section argues that the concrete understanding of legitimacy is tied to the larger debate about whether policies are sufficiently legitimate or not. I aim to show why the Liberalism of Imposition order could not be sustained on the grounds of legitimacy; a Liberalism of Restraint order, by contrast, would at first sight appear to have great legitimacy, but I will demonstrate why that is not necessarily the case either.

It was clear that the unilateralist Liberalism of Imposition order promoted during large parts of the George W. Bush administrations could not be legitimate in the sense defined above because a major element of it was the sidestepping of international institutions in the unashamed pursuit of national ends. The lack of legitimacy follows from the way in which decisions are made: others are not consulted, no compromises are made. This aspect of legitimacy can be seen as "input legitimacy." It emerges from the procedure by which decisions are reached rather than from the results these decisions produce (Schimmelfennig 1996).

Some supporters of the new strategy appeared not to be concerned with legitimacy at all. As William Kristol put it, "if people want to say we are an imperial power, fine" (quoted from Nye 2003: 65). But this was not the preponderant view. Most politicians and scholars made a different claim about the legitimacy of an Imposition order. The reasoning was as follows: During the Cold War, U.S. foreign policy was basically supported by European and Asian allies because even if it was sometimes questionable, it was understood to serve the larger purpose of defending the free world against the Soviet Union and international communism. Legitimacy, then, rested on the promotion of policies deemed to serve not merely the interest of the United States, "but also the common interest of the liberal democratic world" (Kagan 2003: 71). This aspect of legitimacy is "output legitimacy"; it rests on the achievement of desired ends through the actions taken. This logic can be applied to the case of Iraq: if liberal democracy is fostered and the United States is seen to have undertaken the war "not only for its own interests but also in the interests of others, then the question of legitimacy will be settled largely in America's favor" (Kagan 2003:71). Output legitimacy, in other words, hinges on the capacity to solve problems that are seen as real and serious for the stakeholders in the liberal order: "the higher this capacity, the more legitimate the system" (Schimmelfennig 1996: 2).

But as it turned out, this claim to output legitimacy failed to convince much of the world, including like-minded, liberal states. Lack of enthusiasm for the way in which the United States conducted post–Cold War foreign affairs began sometime before 2001. Already in 1999, Samuel Huntington argued that the United States had become a "lonely superpower" (35–49). Erik Voeten (2004) has demonstrated empirically how "the preference gap between the United States and the rest of the world widened considerably and at a constant rate between 1991 and 2001... [leading to a] common shift away from the United States" (747). In sum, the unilateral Imposition order lacked input legitimacy from the beginning and eventually could not claim significant output legitimacy either. As we saw above, the Obama administration has turned toward a higher emphasis on Restraint. That leads to the next issue: the possible claims to legitimacy of a liberal Restraint order.

Let me begin with the problem of input legitimacy of a liberal Restraint order. First, how much is enough? Clearly the idea is that decisions in such an order are not made by the most powerful state alone; they are made in consultation with the other relevant stakeholders in the system. In other words, the hegemon gets support because it practices self-restraint in a process of institutional co-binding. These are the core terms in the characterization by John Ikenberry of the liberal Restraint order established after World War II. Co-binding is the attempt "to tie one another down by locking each other into institutions that mutually constrain one another" (Deudney and Ikenberry 1999: 182). Self-restraint is the acceptance by the leading state of "limits on the exercise of its own hegemonic power" (Ikenberry 2001: 199).

But is it possible for institutions to both project and limit state power, to be "mechanisms of hegemonic self-restraint and tools of hegemonic power" (Schweller 2001: 163)? Realists reject that possibility: they emphatically argue that institutional arrangements created after World War II did not work to constrain U.S. power; the institutions were used as instruments of hegemonic foreign policy "to project and enhance the unilateral exercise of American power" (Schweller 2001: 177). In the current post–Cold War world, realists and liberals agree that there will be many situations in which "the United States must take the lead by itself as it did in Afghanistan" (Nye 2003: 70). There will be many instances in the area of security, economics, and the environment where common interests are not sufficient to pave the way for compromises. When the hegemon takes the lead by itself, the input legitimacy of a Restraint order is questionable.

In the old liberal Restraint order of the post–World War II period, the crisis potential of such situations was muted by the fact that this was a community of democracies with common values and a common enemy. In a reformed Restraint order with universal aspirations the same mechanism no longer applies. Is it then sufficient that the leading liberal power, or group of powers, goes through the motions of multilateral consultation before it takes the lead? On the one hand, realists say no: "the more the United States exerts itself to maintain its hegemonic status, the more others will work to undermine it. In the end...assertive multilateral schemes...will not fool anyone" (Schweller 2001: 185). Liberals, on the other hand, are more hopeful. They rest their optimism on the assumption that there is a sufficient amount of common interest among democratic and nondemocratic states—irrespective of great power discrepancies—in upholding a common institutional order. That, however, remains to be seen; the input legitimacy foundation of a reformed liberal Restraint order is on shakier ground than it was earlier.

The second point concerning input legitimacy concerns the degree of commitment by the hegemon, or put differently, how much self-restraint and co-binding will the United States actually be able to deliver? The hesitant U.S. commitment to multilateralism was noted earlier. Writing in 2005, Richard Betts argues that even if U.S. Democrats talk about soft power and multilateralism, they are just as insistent as the Republicans in wanting to "use U.S. power to shape the world in the American image" (6). If this "symbolic" rather than "substantive" multilateralism (Betts 2005: 14) is pursued by future administrations as well, the question is whether it will be sufficient to produce a stable liberal Restraint order. When the leading power is not seriously committed, the commitment by others may diminish also: "When a powerful and influential state like the United States is seen to treat its legal obligations as a matter of convenience or of national interest alone, other states will see this as a justification to relax or withdraw from their own commitments" (Deller et al. 2003: 27).

Beneath this question of commitment to international institutions is a larger liberal issue concerning the appropriate context for liberal democracy. So far, democracy has developed only in independent states. Many theorists of democracy have argued that the sovereign nation-state is a necessary precondition for democracy. The independent nation-state makes up the framework for a community of people that build democracy, and without such a well-defined community democracy is not possible in the first place (Rustow 1970). In the international context, there is no obvious *demos;* that is to say, there is no well-defined political or moral community outside of the national context. That is the reasoning behind Will Kymlicka's (1999) statement: "the only forum within which genuine democracy occurs is within national boundaries" (124).

There are additional problems associated with democracy outside the nation-state context. Governance across borders is not based on a distinct constitutional framework, and therefore core decision makers are not subject to sufficient democratic accountability and control. Decisions are made behind closed doors, frequently by high-ranking bureaucrats without a clear democratic mandate. Robert Dahl (1999) argues that the real democratization of international organizations is a next to impossible task, and he proposes to retain decision making within democratically elected national governments. Marc Plattner (2005) argues that this view of national democratic primacy is deeply ingrained in the U.S. constitutional order: "Americans believe in universal principles but hold that their implementation should be the business of democratically elected and accountable governments" (86). There are different views on this "democratic dilemma" in the liberal tradition that cannot all be discussed here (Sørensen 2004: 67–79); the point in the present context is that the underlying liberal dilemma concerning national democracy versus international cooperation further complicates the road toward a stable liberal Restraint order.

When we turn to the issue of the output legitimacy of a reformed liberal Restraint order, the dilemma just mentioned might be mitigated somewhat. A more effective governance across borders means that global processes of development are brought under political control; seen from the individual state, this means increasing the scope of democracy. That *national* political procedures within a single country are highly democratic is not so reassuring when—because of intense interconnectedness—economic, social, and other significant developments in that country are determined or highly influenced by external forces over which the national polity has little or no control. Increasing the country's influence over such vital external forces is a democratic gain, not a loss. Because of multilateral involvement, the political system is better capable of regulating the forces that shape people's lives, and that in turn creates output legitimacy because the political system is more effective than before.

Yet this aspect of international cooperation has failed to convince large groups in Europe and in the United States, both among political elites and in particular among the populations at large. As indicated earlier, the issue emerges at a time when the demand for more intense cooperation is increasing because globalization creates a larger need for regulation. But large groups see international institutions as increasingly intrusive, and that underlines the democratic deficit that they embody. "The more intrusive these international institutions become, the more justified and intense the demands will be for their democratization" (Zürn 2004: 286). In the United States, however, another possible reaction is to retreat from international institutions and turn to a more isolationist posture (Betts 2005). Should that happen, the effectiveness of international institutions will decrease and so will their output legitimacy.

This section has looked at the issue of legitimacy in relation to a reformed liberal order. A unilateralist Liberalism of Imposition order lacked both input and output legitimacy. Current emphasis is on a higher degree of Restraint, but such an order has legitimacy problems as well. First, is there sufficient common interest among the major stakeholders to uphold such an order? Second, will the United States be willing to restrain and bind itself to a reformed order beyond a thin commitment of symbolic multilateralism? Third, the underlying liberal dilemma of national democracy versus international cooperation remains unresolved. Finally, effective international cooperation potentially creates output legitimacy, but large popular groups remain skeptical, and that may lead to a retreat from international institutions. In sum, there is no secure legitimacy basis for a reformed Liberalism of Restraint order.

Transnational and Transgovernmental Relations: a New Centerpiece of Liberal World Order?

Some liberals argue that transnational and transgovernmental relations and networks can compensate for many of the problems reviewed above and create a more solid basis for liberal order. This section discusses why this might not be the case.

Liberals take a positive view of individuals and private groups, regarding them as the principal drivers of progress and cooperation. That raises the question whether transnational and transgovernmental relations or networks can be considered core elements in an emerging liberal world order and thereby perhaps lessen the pressure and demands on liberal governments. If a new order based on such relations is on the rise, the problems discussed above that confront liberal governments would appear to be mitigated or even overcome. As indicated earlier (chapter 2), processes of modernization have led to the expansion of transnational and transgovernmental relations. Many liberals find that a significant change is taking place. In earlier days, national *governments* ruled within well-defined territorial borders. Today, politics is increasingly taking the shape of international or global *governance,* a term that refers to activities everywhere—local, national, regional, global—involving regulation and control. Governance is thus an international, transgovernmental, and transnational activity that includes not only governments or units of government and traditional international organizations but also nongovernmental organizations and other nonstate actors (Zürn 1998: 169–71).

The quantitative rise of IGOs and INGOs has indeed been accompanied by an expansion of transgovernmental and transnational relations. The former signify that states are connected with each other at many different levels; external relations are no longer the sole responsibility of the ministry of foreign affairs and the head of state. Ministries and other units of government (such as regulatory agencies, courts, and executives) are connected with their counterparts in other countries in a dense web of policy networks. Transgovernmental activity is especially developed among national regulators, the officials responsible for corporate supervision, environmental standards, antitrust policies, and so on. According to one observer, "transgovernmental activity is rapidly becoming the most widespread and effective mode of international governance" (Slaughter 1997: 185; 2004).

As explained in chapter 2, transnational relations are cross-border relations between individuals, groups, and organizations from civil society (nonstate actors). There is great diversity among INGOs; on the one hand, many of them are critical of governments and international organizations. Whether it concerns issues of trade policy, the environment, disarmament, or human rights, they "keep saying things governments do not want to hear" (Ingram 1995: 5). On the other hand, INGOs increasingly work alongside governments and international organizations in a number of areas, including, for example, development aid, environmental protection, and health care. Wolfgang Reinicke (2000) argues that governance is increasingly managed by global public policy networks; that is, "loose alliances of government agencies, international organizations, corporations, and elements of civil society such as nongovernmental organizations, professional associations, or religious groups that join together to achieve what none can accomplish on its own" (44). A study by the World Bank has identified fifty such networks in a variety of areas, such as crime, fisheries, public health, agricultural research, environment, and water resources.

But is this flurry of transgovernmental and transnational activity sufficient to make up the new basis for a world order, and if yes, would it be a liberal order? There are several reasons for suggesting that these relations, important as they are, cannot be the new centerpiece of a liberal world order. A major problem concerns the general nature of transnational relations. Liberals tend to paint a much too optimistic picture of their substance and potential. It was underlined previously (chapter 2) that transnational relations involve not only transnational goods but also a significant number of transnational bads such as crime, drugs, terror, pollution, and economic crisis. To the extent that this is the case, the transnational networks do not contribute to effective governance; rather, they constitute problems that need to be brought under supervision and control.

Furthermore, the optimistic liberal view of transnational relations is accompanied by a similarly optimistic view of cross-border civil society relationships. Civil society networks do not uniformly seek the strengthening of liberal democratic governance from below. They exhibit great variation, as evidenced, for example, by the growing Islamic transnationalism that draws on a long tradition of Islamic transnational networks; the progress of globalization has "given a greater intensity and reality to transnationalized Islam and stimulated pan-Islamic visions and values" (Hurrell 2006: 103). This points to a more general tendency: globalization stimulates the general growth, not merely of supporters of that process, but also of skeptics or resistance movements that seek alternative directions or even a reversal of the development toward intensified interdependence. A recent study identified four different positions on globalization: Supporters, Regressives, Reformers, and Rejectionists (Kaldor et al. 2003: 6). They illustrate that transnational relationships are multifaceted and complex and that they represent contestation and conflict in relation to global developments as much as order and regulation.

This is not to deny the role of transgovernmental and transnational networks in the formulation, diffusion, and implementation of a variety of norms, rules, and regulations, covering a range of issues "from banking supervision to securities regulation, to antitrust regulations, and health policy" (Hurrell 2006: 98). But it would be misleading to see them as an emerging alternative system of global governance. First, such networks are thoroughly dominated by individuals and groups from the advanced liberal states in the OECD-world (Slaughter 2004: 228–29). This might change with the increasing involvement in globalization by modernizing states such as Brazil, India, China, and Russia, but such a development will also most likely increase contestation and conflict in the networks.

Second, there is a tendency to overemphasize the relative autonomy especially of transnational networks (e.g., Rosenau 1990, 1992) in relation to states; perhaps this tendency follows from the liberal principle of prioritizing individuals and groups before states. But it is most often the actions of sovereign states that enable the networks to play their role in the first place: the networks would amount to very little if they did not enjoy the support of states. It is frequently the states that provide most of their funding; it is states that invite them into the UN system, the World Bank, and elsewhere, in order to consult them. And NGOs, like most other civil associations, do indeed spend most of their time attempting to influence states and their policies. They may be of growing importance, but they lack the power to lead, to formulate and oversee global political, economic, and security priorities.

All this confirms the central role of states. The distinctive role of states is emphasized every time a crisis appears. When terrorism strikes, states are called upon to provide security, order, and justice. The central role of states is not confined to security-related issues, the traditional core area of state responsibility, but also concerns economic emergencies, such as the financial crisis erupting in 2008, or environmental issues, such as the regulatory framework for combating global warming. However, all this being said, the fact that political decisions are increasingly made by networks involving many different types of actors should not be ignored. But the networks discussed here are not in and of themselves a possible autonomous source of a liberal world order.

Conclusion

International institutions are central elements in a liberal order, but liberal states have always been torn between a pluralist and a nonpluralist approach to international institutions. Liberals acknowledge that a liberal hegemon is needed to provide a stable power basis for liberal institutions. But liberal hegemony is also dangerous because hegemonic power can be abused. The United States was a successful liberal hegemon after World War II. On the one hand, it had sufficient power and purpose to establish a new order; on the other hand, bipolarity created a constraint that prevented hegemonic abuse of power. The end of the Cold War put an end to that delicate balance: there were no longer constraints on the hegemon. This led toward a liberal Imposition order that was rejected by allies and other great powers.

The current central question, then, concerns the prospects for a reformed, stable liberal Restraint order with universal reach. There are several reasons to believe that no easy path to such an order exists. First, domestic changes in the United States (and other leading liberal countries) may have eroded the support for liberal internationalism. Second, major universal institutions are in need of serious overhaul, and there is no agreement among major liberal powers about institutional choice. Third, the incorporation of rising nonliberal great powers such as China in a reformed order is necessary, but it will weaken rather than strengthen a common value foundation of liberal order. Furthermore, there are several reasons to believe that there is no secure legitimacy basis for a reformed Liberalism of Restraint order. Finally, transgovernmental and transnational networks are increasingly important, but they are not alternative sources of a reformed order.

It is not a situation of chaos, insecurity, and potential war. There is a strong liberal security community, and rising nonliberal powers seek participation in the global liberal economic and political system rather than violent confrontation. But it is not a well-functioning and stable system. One observer speaks of an "authority crisis in today's liberal order. . . . How to establish legitimate authority for concerted international action on behalf of the global community—and do so when the old norms of order are eroding—is the great challenge to liberal international order" (Ikenberry 2009: 80).

As indicated above, in an increasingly interdependent world there is a rising demand for sophisticated regulation of behind-the-border issues. This happens at a time when international institutions are less able to supply such regulation because they are confronted with skeptical new players that contest their authority and limit their room to maneuver and because states stress national interests and traditional values of sovereignty and nonintervention.

In sum, the liberal Imposition order proposed by the George W. Bush administrations in the United States was no success, and there is no simple road to a reformed Restraint order. The transatlantic liberal order established after World War II had some specific characteristics that made it extraordinarily robust: First of all, it rested on a basis of support for common liberal values of political and civil liberties. Further, it included great powers (Germany and Japan) who imposed constraints on themselves; an important part of this was to forgo the acquisition of nuclear weapons. Finally, it locked the liberal states into a common security arrangement led by the United States, which underpinned the entire edifice (Deudney and Ikenberry 1999). None of these characteristics can easily be part of a reformed, universal liberal Restraint. The common foundation of liberal core values is missing; the new, rising great powers will not impose constraints on themselves; and there is no straightforward basis for a common security arrangement. To repeat, chaos and war are not in the cards; we will probably see the emergence of a more loosely constructed patchwork order. Whether that will be enough to satisfy the demands for regulation remains an open question.

Conclusion

Prospects for Liberal World Order

Fifteen years ago, in 1996, one observer of Eastern Europe confirmed the rising popularity of liberal democracy: "to live under autocracy, or even to *be* an autocrat, seems backward, uncivilized, distasteful, not quite *comme il faut*—in a word, 'uncool'" (Nadia 1996: 15). In 2007, a mere eleven years later, *Time Magazine* celebrated Vladimir Putin as "Person of the Year"; a man with "steely confidence and strength," he had allegedly moved Russia away from the "rudderless mess" that prevailed under Boris Yeltsin toward order, stability, and economic prosperity. In the following year, 2008, the WorldPublicOpinion survey, managed by the University of Maryland, registered a whopping 93 percent public Chinese support for leader Hu Jintao; there was strong Russian support for Vladimir Putin as well. "The fact is," said one commentator, "that the poll found most of the world now seems to have more confidence in undemocratic than democratic leaders. The war of ideas may not be over... but at this point, the West clearly isn't winning the battle for influence" (AsianOffbeat 2008).

Liberal values, practices, and institutions are on the defensive; the profound optimism of the post–Cold War 1990s is a thing of the past, and the present is dominated by economic crisis, frail and wilting democracies that cannot consolidate, ineffective and only partly legitimate international institutions in need of serious overhaul, new security threats, and a flagging support for liberal values. All of this is true, but as a portrait of liberalism's standing in the world today it is also partly misleading. That is because the current problems facing the liberal world order must be seen against the background of profound and unprecedented liberal progress since the mid-twentieth century. Many more countries are more democratic, there is a network of international institutions based on liberal doctrines, nearly all countries are capitalist market economies, and there is no serious ideological rival to liberal principles. Current difficulties should not overlook this improved situation for liberal order.

The popular uprisings in the Middle East in early 2011 have revived the hope for democratization in a part of the world long dominated by dictators. In countries where a majority of the population is under thirty years of age, coalitions of young people from all layers of society and middle classes frustrated by deteriorating living conditions quickly toppled autocrats who had ruled for decades.

What the final outcome of the mobilizations will be is unclear. These are countries where the armed forces have long played a significant political role, and without their tacit and open support the movements could not have succeeded. At the time of this writing, regime change has not taken place. In Egypt, for example, Hosni Mubarak has stepped down but the country continues to be ruled by the military. The formation of a new regime is a long-term process, and there will certainly be variation among the countries because their preconditions are dissimilar. Some form of liberalized authoritarianism is more likely than full-blown democracy: it may be in the form of more discrete military rule (e.g., in Egypt); some form of tribal rule (e.g., in Libya), or perhaps more liberalized regimes with a strong role for Islamic parties.

What is clear, however, is that these transformations do *not* mean that the West is winning "the battle for influence" in the Middle East (Kleinwächter and Krämer 2011). Strong support for Arabian autocrats over many years, the misfortunes in Iraq and Afghanistan, and the inability to move Israel toward dialogue with the Palestinians have not been helpful. New leaders will be skeptical toward the United States and Europe. China, by contrast, represents a model of a strong state, economic growth, and basic welfare that will appeal to many Middle Eastern leaders. Both the United States and the European Union must therefore revise their policies toward the region. They will remain subject to the liberal dilemmas analyzed in this book, and any support for democracy will be balanced against strategic and other interests that may point in a different direction.

It was in view of liberal progress in the world rather than liberal crisis that a number of more pessimistic scenarios for current world order were rejected in the opening chapter of this book, even if it was conceded that they also contain relevant insights. We are not in a back-to-the-future order, engulfed by aggressive power balancing; postmodern states are engaged in a security community, and international society's great respect for existing borders further reduces the relevance of the classical security dilemma. Weak states are a serious problem, but we are not on the road to a "coming anarchy" with general breakdown of established states. International terror is an important challenge, but not a new, existential menace. Finally, in a globalized world, identity issues sometimes involving conflict are of increasing significance, yet they do not amount to a world order defined by a "clash of civilizations."

But liberal progress must not be exaggerated either. A major problem of order, I have argued, is related to tensions in liberalism. I have identified a liberal dilemma related to the core liberal concept of freedom: it involves the choice between Restraint, nonintervention, tolerance, and empathy on the one hand, and Imposition, intervention, and activist promotion of universal liberal principles on the other hand. The Liberalism of Restraint and Liberalism of Imposition dilemma was analyzed in relation to the four areas that liberals understand to be the core elements of liberal world order: (a) the prospect of universal support for liberal values, that is, the ideological basis for a liberal world order; (b) the advance of liberal democracy, with a focus on the weak and failed states considered to be the major current security problem and source of violent conflict; (c) the development of a liberal market economy on a world scale, the material basis for a liberal order; and (d) the strengthening of international institutions, a cornerstone in the liberal vision of international cooperation and peace. Each of these areas disclosed the tension between Imposition and Restraint, as briefly summarized in the following sections.

Weak States as a Challenge to Liberal World Order

There is a tension in liberal thought between the overarching goal of freedom and the institution of the sovereign state. On the one hand, sovereign government is needed in order to protect and defend the fundamental rights of human beings, including the right to property. On the other hand, John Locke (1965) was perfectly aware that state elites are "but Men" (314), that is to say, mere mortals who will act as "self-centered power-seekers" (Nelson 1982: 174) if given the opportunity. Locke's solution was constitutional government, meaning government with limited powers resting on a popular mandate, what we would call liberal democracy. In the liberal tradition, then, there is a precarious balance between the need for a strong state that protects and enables freedom and the need for a not too strong state that ensures that state elites will not abuse their power and undermine freedom.

Weak states are free in the sense that colonialism and empire have been replaced by sovereignty and constitutional independence. Sovereignty means recognition as an equal player in the international system on a par with any other state, as basically reflected in the equal membership of the United Nations (one member state, one vote); it also means that weak states have the right to look after their own affairs according to the principle of nonintervention. But weak statehood has manifestly not led to constitutional government in the form of liberal democracy. On the contrary, it has empowered state elites to be self-seeking predators in the extreme.

Therefore, the required liberal balance between strong and less strong statehood does not exist in weak states. Individual freedom for citizens is challenged in every way by the lack of public services, poor administration, and corruption. Instead of security, weak states are the most dangerous source of insecurity for their citizens. What, if anything, should consolidated liberal democracies do about this situation? One liberal maxim requires them to respect sovereignty; another liberal maxim requires them to intervene, that is, to come to the rescue of fellow human beings.

A Liberalism of Restraint has the consequence of leaving self-interested elites alone, free to pursue narrow aims of enrichment and power accumulation. A Liberalism of Imposition, by contrast, leads toward interventionism, which must always be selective and compelled to produce short-term results. And even when outsiders arrive with great force, they quickly find themselves dependent on insiders, that is, dependent on the willingness of local elites to move in the right direction. Restraint brings one set of problems; Imposition brings another. The uneasy compromise between the two must vary over time in relation to the current willingness of liberal states to act, and in relation to the concrete nature of the problems in weak states. Note that replacing a "U.S." Imposition approach with a "European" Restraint approach does not promise to solve the problem.

It is relevant to emphasize that this is not merely a practical issue of policy choice. It is a dilemma that goes to the heart of liberal thinking, because the precarious balance that Locke requires between states that are simultaneously strong and not too strong does not exist in weak states and shows no promise of emerging in many places. The tension reappears in foundational documents for international society, such as the UN Charter, the Human Rights Charter, and the Millennium Declaration, because these texts promise to respect sovereignty and nonintervention while they also require states to provide their citizens with the basic liberal values of freedom, order, security, and welfare. On today's balance, the principle of sovereignty and nonintervention continues to dominate, while the principle of intervention continues to be the exception that has to be justified in each particular case (cf. R. Jackson 2000: 375).

Free Markets and Liberal World Order

Liberals support a market economy based on private enterprise, but liberals also support democracy. There is a tension between the inequality produced by a private-enterprise-based liberal society and the equality required by democracy. As John Stuart Mill recognized, the laissez-faire economy may produce inequalities of income, wealth, and power that impede the democratic process based on equality of citizens. Rousseau, like Mill, argued that socioeconomic inequality would prevent citizens from obtaining equal political rights; in other words, political democracy cannot exist in the presence of steep socioeconomic inequality (cf. Sørensen 2008: 6–10). More recently, Robert Dahl (1985) has argued that modern corporate capitalism tends "to produce inequalities in social and economic resources so great as to bring about severe violations of political equality and hence of the democratic process" (60).

In sum, there is a tension between equality and inequality, both domestically and in the international sphere. The domestic aspect of this tension has been a subject of debate in liberal states for a long period. In the international sphere, liberal states have committed themselves to "equality and equity at the global level" in the Millennium Declaration. However, the economic strategies promoted by liberal states have led to inequality. Liberal states have for some time emphasized the principles of private enterprise and free trade, from Wilson's fourteen-point program to the 1997 Liberal International Manifesto (see chapter 2). Since the end of the Cold War, liberal states have followed an impositionist path; they have promoted a neoliberal model of "structural adjustment" that places primary confidence in self-regulating, efficient markets and seeks to minimize the role of state intervention and regulation. But neoliberal Imposition does not address the fundamental economic problems of weak states, which concern stronger institutional capacities combined with more transparency and accountability. Nor is it fully adequate for the transitional economies and the modernizers in South Asia and Latin America. At the same time, the advanced liberal states themselves did not employ neoliberal principles when they were in the early phase of development and sought to catch up with a competitor that had taken the lead. They have made substantial use of protective measures, both now and in the past. Stephen Walt (2005) makes the point in relation to the United States: "U.S. leaders routinely invoke the principle of free trade and condemn trading partners for erecting barriers to U.S. goods, yet they abandon these principles when powerful U.S. interest groups are threatened by foreign competition" (99).

This unbalanced framework was recently burdened with a financial and economic crisis that emerged from the neoliberal system. The crisis is pushed by both market failures and state, or regulatory, failures. Stanley Hoffmann (1995) argues that "a huge zone of irresponsibility" has been created:

> The global economy is literally out of control, not subject to the rules of accountability and principles of legitimacy that apply to relations between individuals and the state. States hesitate to impose their own rules unilaterally, out of fear of inefficiency and self-damage. The liberalism, successful in reducing the state's power, has created a formidable anonymous new power. (166)

Three major problems impede the establishment of a stable liberal world economy; first, the lack of a robust state-market matrix that both supports economic globalization on more equal terms and has enough flexibility to be applicable to different economic challenges; second, the lack of a new set of coherent strategies for confronting transnational bads; and third, the lack of a liberal state, or coalition of states, able and willing to take the lead in consistent economic policymaking with universal appeal. A new, serious economic downturn is now on the horizon, this time with countries rather than banks defaulting on debts (*Economist* 2010). Liberal states are comprehensively unready to face the challenge.

There is no easy way of going back to a Liberalism of Restraint order in the economic sphere, because at high levels of cross-border integration significant coordination of policies is required. One observer argues that the world should not strive for maximum economic openness in trade and finance. We should rather aim for levels of openness that "leave room for the pursuit of domestic social and economic objectives in rich and poor countries alike. The best way to save globalization is to not push it too far" (Rodrik 2009). But there is no consensus about the road to reform, and leading liberal countries, including the United States and the United Kingdom, want to preserve the major elements of the neoliberal system that supported their role as leading centers of finance.

Again, the situation reflects deeper tensions in liberalism. In one major strand of liberal thought, greed is good; when self-seeking individuals pursue their interests in the marketplace, the larger economic public interest is served as well, aided by the "unseen hand" of market supply and demand (A. Smith 1976). Another major strand of liberal thought claims that human beings are guided by reason and compelled to pursue the moral progress of mankind. Self-perfection comes from "acting as a member of a social organization in which each contributes to the better-being of all the rest" (Green 1941: 32). Liberal states have basically run the global economy on the principle that self-seeking actors will contribute to the greater good. This has helped foster economic growth, but it also led to great inequalities and a number of transnational bads. The challenge for liberal states is to construct a more stable system with better possibilities for benefits for all.

International Institutions and Liberal World Order

International institutions are central elements in a liberal world order, but liberal states support two different approaches to international institutions: one pluralist and the other nonpluralist. The pluralist approach envisages universal institutions with membership for all sovereign states, such as the UN General Assembly. The nonpluralist approach emphasizes international institutions based on member countries that are democratic and respect the human rights of their citizens. The pluralist attitude leads toward a Liberalism of Restraint order where all sovereign states have a voice in international institutions, irrespective of the substance of their domestic political orders. The nonpluralist attitude leads toward a Liberalism of Imposition order where liberal states take the lead and define the appropriate rules for others.

The George W. Bush administrations leaned toward an Impositionist order based on a "coalition of the willing." It was an order that left the United States relatively unconstrained and required commitments to rules from everybody else. That led to a system that not even the close allies of the United States were ready to accept; nor would other great powers. But what is the alternative? There is no simple way of constructing a reformed Liberalism of Restraint order. On the one hand, there appears to be dwindling domestic support in the United States for liberal internationalism. On the other hand, leading liberal states are not at all in agreement about the reform of international institutions, and it will not be an easy task to include nondemocratic great powers as major stakeholders in the system.

Beneath these issues is a tension between legitimacy and effectiveness. The ambition of liberal states must be to work toward international institutions that are both legitimate and effective, but in the real world one of these priorities most often comes at the expense of the other. The United Nations with its universal membership is considered a highly legitimate organization by many, but it is also known as highly ineffective, especially the forum with most legitimacy, the General Assembly. Decisions in the General Assembly are taken on the basis of consensus; that means concrete plans with precise demands on specific states play no part in the decisions. Instead, consensus is reached by making plans for the future that are extremely ambitious and noncommitting. Members are aware that the lofty principles will not be translated into concrete action. Coalitions of the willing, by contrast, may not hold great legitimacy in the eyes of international society, but they can make concrete decisions and proceed toward getting the job done. At the same time, such coalitions may exercise arbitrary power that will be perceived by others as liberal imperialism.

It is a further complication that much-debated reforms of international institutions may do little to solve the problem. For example, there is a large debate about a reform of the UN Security Council because the current great power membership reflects the world anno 1945 (J. Paul and Nahory 2005). A frequent suggestion is to include Brazil, India, Germany, and Japan as new permanent members. This may well give the council a higher degree of legitimacy, but it will not necessarily make it a more effective decision-making body.

Finally, the legitimacy of international institutions is not neatly aligned with democracy at home. The UN General Assembly may be seen as legitimate because of the universal membership of all sovereign states, but it lacks legitimacy in the sense that many of these member states are nondemocratic. Liberal theory has only tentatively begun to speculate what democracy should mean in an increasingly globalized world where there is a growing demand for governance above the level of the single sovereign state. In liberal thought, the independent state was always the given context for liberal democracy. The liberal tradition is strongly in favor of international cooperation, but the more demanding versions of that cooperation have consequences for democracy at home that have not been thought through.

Liberal Values and World Order

Liberals believe in the possibility of a better world but have often placed too much faith in the certainty of progress. That leads toward a liberal idealism that expects major political and economic problems to be resolved in due course when liberal principles come to fruition everywhere. In the real world, however, progress is much less secure and the future considerably more uncertain. Under such conditions, liberal principles must always develop in response to new and old challenges; should they fail to do so, the liberal project may be in jeopardy.

The road to modern, effective, democratic, and economically robust statehood in Europe and North America has not been replicated in many parts of the world. Instead, a different kind of state formation has taken place that has often led to the creation of weak states. Many weak states are not on the road to modernity; they are dominated by social forces and political groups that are not interested in effective state formation or in development and modernity.

In short, liberal optimism might fail miserably, and that prospect is not only connected to weak states. Successful modernizers, such as China, may be developing new models that include capitalism but not liberal democracy. And in the heartland of consolidated liberal states, the earlier chapters have uncovered a host of political, economic, and institutional challenges to the liberal project.

Liberal values have been strengthened in the world but are far from firmly entrenched. The promotion of such values is bound to be met with strong skepticism from many quarters. I have argued that this is related to an identity challenge and a power challenge that emerge from the insistence on universal values, in spite of local traditions and customs.

Liberals are compelled to show respect for other values; that is a core principle of the Liberalism of Restraint. But they cannot embrace such values without qualification or they end up denying that there are universal values valid for all human beings, irrespective of local traditions and customs. Yet it is the endorsement of these universal values that is perceived by skeptical groups as liberal imperialism. This is especially the case when the implementation of universal values takes place by means that have very little to do with equal rights and participation and much more to do with power and coercion.

In the sphere of international institutions, the insistence on liberal democracy as the appropriate basis for legitimacy becomes a power challenge because it excludes others and regards them as illegitimate. Two consequences follow. On the one hand, nondemocratic powers are encouraged to chart their own course. Charles Kupchan (2008) notes that "Russia's blustery reactions to the enlargement of NATO and Kosovo's independence from Serbia, its forceful intervention in Georgia this past summer, and its teamwork with China to form the Shanghai Cooperation Organization are a hint of what might be in store" (101).[1] On the other hand, nondemocratic states

---

1. Indications of a more aggressive Chinese stance were mentioned in chapter 6.

will question the claim of liberal democratic legitimacy because it serves to exclude and thereby disenfranchise more than half of the world's population from international affairs.

In the economic sphere, the power challenge emerges from the attempt by liberal states to impose neoliberal principles on others, which narrows the development options for latecomers and does not reflect the development experience of the liberal states themselves. In that way, the supposedly level playing field is tilted in favor of further economic upgrading of the advanced liberal states themselves and against the development aspirations of the latecomers.

In sum, liberal states must respect other values. In a world of sovereign states, the principle of nonintervention is the formal expression of the autonomy that liberal states must afford others. At the same time, the principle of universal values valid for all is of increasing importance in international society, and liberal states must be committed to support and strengthen such values. In doing so, liberal states are open to charges of hypocrisy because those at the receiving end can often point to a gap between their rhetorical commitment to equal benefits for all and their actual deeds that reflect their particular material interests.

The Prospects for Liberal World Order Reconsidered

History is not predetermined in a way that guarantees development in a liberal direction. That is to say, history needs a helping hand if it is going to produce liberal progress; that helping hand must primarily come from liberal states. What can these states then do in order to successfully push local, national, regional, and global developments in a liberal direction? We have learned that the answer is far from simple and straightforward; we have also learned that liberal states need to confront a number of problems, tensions, difficulties, and dilemmas, of which the most important ones have been analyzed in this book. It has already been indicated that these issues cannot be solved once and for all; they can be more or less adequately managed.

What liberal states can and will do is heavily influenced by their perceived position in the global system of power. Liberal victory in the Cold War changed the constellation in the favor of liberal states (see chapter 6). The full recognition of this came with the United States National Security Strategy (NSS) of 2002. It underlined that the new situation of U.S. primacy created "a moment of opportunity to extend the benefits of freedom across the globe.... [The United States] will actively work to bring the hope of democracy, development, free markets, and free trade to every corner of the

world." Robert Kagan (2003) spoke of U.S. power as "the sole pillar upholding a liberal world order that is conducive to the principles [the United
States] believes in."

Charles Krauthammer, writing in 2004, claims that the West, and in particular the United States, is more powerful than ever. "We are in a unipolar
world dominated by a single superpower unchecked by any rival and with
decisive reach in every corner of the globe" (1). He wants to pursue a "democratic globalism" that seeks to spread Western values, especially democracy,
because that is an "indispensable means for securing American interests"
(9). In that sense, the U.S. national interest and what John Kennedy called
"the success of liberty" are one and the same. But even a superpower cannot
spread democracy everywhere; its strongest efforts should be directed "where
it counts" (Krauthammer 2004: 9) to combat global threats to freedom; at the
time of writing that was Afghanistan and Iraq.[2]

In short, a perceived position of liberal strength in the world leads toward
preference for an interventionist strategy of Imposition, and a perceived position of liberal weakness leads toward preference for a noninterventionist
strategy of Restraint. Samuel Huntington (1996), for example, strongly believes that the West is a civilization in decline. The West is powerful, even
dominant right now, but the power of the West will continue to decline.
Much of its power will "simply evaporate," whereas the "most significant
increases in power are accruing and will accrue to Asian civilizations, with
China gradually emerging as the society most likely to challenge the West for
global influence. These shifts in power among civilizations are leading and
will lead to the revival and increased cultural assertiveness of non-Western
societies and to their increasing rejection of Western culture" (82–83). In this
situation, says Huntington, the prudent way for the West is to "endure the
miseries, moderate its ventures, and safeguard its culture" (311). The best way
to accomplish that is intensified cooperation across the Atlantic with the aim
of preserving technological and military superiority, combined with a strict
policy of avoiding "intervention in the affairs of other civilizations" (312).

These views can be seen as radical versions of a Liberalism of Imposition
and a Liberalism of Restraint, respectively. The liberal dilemma is that both
of these postures contain problems that threaten to undercut liberal advance.
A radical strategy of Imposition risks being received as liberal imperialism
that sabotages liberal progress because other peoples and states see it as an
exercise of arbitrary power with no respect for local interests and values.

---

2. Irving Kristol and Robert Kagan have supported a similar view; see Fukuyama (2006).

When outsiders dominate insiders, liberal values of freedom and equality are easily undermined.

A radical strategy of Restraint will emphasize nonintervention, tolerance, and respect for sovereignty. But in a globalized world plagued by weak and failing states, by comprehensive economic crisis, by ineffective international institutions in need of reform, by a looming environmental crisis, and by flagging support for liberal values among nonliberal peoples and states, a radical strategy of Restraint is not enough. It will do much too little, and that will be harmful to liberal progress.

In that way, liberal strength leads toward Imposition, which threatens to undercut liberal advance; and liberal weakness leads toward Restraint, which, at least in the present situation of global challenges, threatens to undercut liberal advance. Liberal progress in the world is by no means assured or guaranteed.

Take the weak states. Their historical development has differed from that of the successful modernizers; their futures are likely to be different also. It is not a law of history that all states will successfully modernize, even if there are some successful cases, in particular in Latin America and East Asia. This gloomy prospect touches upon a fundamental element in the liberal vision of world order: the notion that an ever increasing number of states will develop liberal democratic institutions and thus become key forces for the growth of a liberal order. As noted in chapter 3, many weak states experienced democratic openings after the end of the Cold War. These openings have been replaced by standstill; despite having acquired some components of a democratic system and having held decent elections, these countries have little political participation, their elites remain corrupt and self-interested, there is no rule of law, no free press, and no effective institutions. Because the conditions for further democratic advancement are so poor, the weak states are likely to remain in a gray area between semidemocracy and outright authoritarianism. According to Thomas Carothers (2002), this gray area is "not an exceptional category to be defined only in terms of its not being one thing or the other; it is a state of normality for many societies, for better or for worse" (18).

The persistence of weak statehood, even combined with some of the trappings of democracy, means that the liberal benefits expected from a process of democratization will not be forthcoming. This results in the liberal dilemma, where both Imposition and Restraint have proven ineffective remedies.

In the economic sphere, the neoliberal Imposition system is plagued by both market failures and regulatory failures, as evidenced in the current economic crisis. On the one hand, market players overreacted or underreacted and made irrational decisions based on imperfect information. On the other hand, regulators were too inactive because they placed excessive trust in the notions of rational market actors and perfect markets. One commentator talked about "the biggest regulatory failure in modern history" (Wade 2008). The crisis exemplifies how the global economy produces, not only transnational goods, but also transnational bads.

There is no easy path to a Restraint system. In the aftermath of World War II, the United States took the lead in establishing an economic Liberalism of Restraint system for the OECD-world that combined open markets with domestic autonomy concerning the promotion of social welfare and economic standards. Such leadership is lacking today, because leading liberal states are focused on their own problems and are less willing to accept global responsibility. This happens at a point in time where a long period of intense economic globalization has sharply increased the demand for the regulation of economic activities across borders in order to avoid or minimize a series of potentially disruptive transnational bads.

We have also entered a period of more preponderant nondemocratic great powers, first and foremost China. It was argued earlier (chapter 6) that a reformed liberal Restraint order will be less effective because of the tension between the increasing demands for regulation on the one hand and China's emphasis on traditional values of sovereignty and nonintervention on the other. John Ikenberry (2008) claims that the existing Western order has a "remarkable capacity to accommodate rising powers" (31), including China. But he also emphasizes that success in this area requires the United States and other liberal states to reform, support, and develop the existing institutional order. Chapter 6 underlined the severe obstacles to a reformed, stable, liberal Restraint order.

When liberals insist on the universal validity of their values, they also pose a power challenge and an identity challenge to others that risks undermining liberal ambitions; instead of the inclusion of others, the gulf between insiders and outsiders opens up even more. Afghanistan provides a recent example. The grand assembly of traditional Afghan leaders, the Loya Jirga, voted by a two-thirds majority in favor of making the aging King Zaher Shah the interim head of state in 2002. It took comprehensive U.S. interference behind the scenes, including "bribes, secret deals and arm twisting" (Johnson and Mason 2009), to install the U.S. candidate, Hamid Karzai, instead. The result was a strong reaction against the United States. Thomas Johnson and Chris Mason (2009) explain why:

An American cannot declare himself king and be seen as legitimate: monarchy is not a source of legitimacy of governance in America.

Similarly, a man cannot be voted president in Afghanistan and be perceived as legitimate. Systems of government normally grow from existing traditions, as they did in the U.S. after the Revolutionary War, for example. In Afghanistan, they were imposed externally. Representative democracy is simply not a source of legitimacy in Afghanistan at this point in its development. This explains in no small measure why a religious source of legitimacy in the form of the hated Taliban is making such a powerful comeback.

If liberal value Imposition is too much, liberal Restraint will be too little. When the promotion of liberal values is set aside to the benefit of a "strategic partnership" (chapter 6) with China, for example, it must strengthen those domestic forces that want to combine capitalism with authoritarianism in a nonliberal path to modernity.

These reflections underline the problems connected with radical versions of Imposition and Restraint. At the same time, proponents of radical Restraint (e.g., Huntington) tend to underestimate Western power, and proponents of radical Imposition (e.g., Kagan) tend to overestimate it. On the one hand, the West dominates economic and institutional networks in which other countries want to participate because it is to their advantage. Huntington rejects any possibility for sustained cooperation across civilizational divides, but that is an exaggeration of enmity between different cultures. For example, both Russia and China have, after all, embraced capitalism and favor intense participation in economic globalization. On the other hand, the West cannot dictate terms to others and dominate them through sheer power. Military and other hard power will not produce support for liberal values around the world unless there is sufficient local demand for moving in a liberal direction. When such demand is missing, "democratic globalism" falters and must face charges of liberal imperialism.

This is a more benign and interdependent world than the postwar world. The Western position remains strong, but it is not all-powerful, and it is constrained in several ways in the promotion of liberal values.[3] What can liberal states then do? There are several paths between the Scylla of Imposition and the Charybdis of Restraint, but I will argue that each of them is plagued by problems related to negotiating the tensions in liberalism.

---

3. There is a large debate on the standing of liberal states in the world. See for example Mahbubani (2008); Ikenberry (2008); Zakaria (2008a, 2008b); Haas (2008); Bernstein and Pauly (2007); Drezner (2007); Shapiro (2008).

Liberal Principles Reconsidered

Is there a pragmatic, "in-between" liberal strategy that avoids the problems connected with more radical versions of Imposition and Restraint? In principle yes, in practice no, for reasons discussed below. My premise is that a stable and strong liberal world order must be able to offer to the world a substantial promise of improvements on core liberal values: freedom, order, tolerance, and equality of opportunity. In a globalized world, it is not sufficient that these values are satisfied in the core countries of the West, the OECD-world. They must show real promise in modernizing and weak states as well, that is, on a global scale, because that makes up the fundamental motive for supporting a liberal order everywhere.[4] To what extent is this the case, or to what extent does this promise to be the case in a not too distant future? Let us visit each of the four areas of liberal concern discussed in this book.

First, in order to confront the problem of weak states, liberal *theory* needs to come to terms with the ambiguous institution of sovereignty. Sovereignty is a precondition for freedom, but sovereignty is also a vehicle for taking away freedom from large groups of people; it is an insecurity container that leaves the populations in weak states at the mercy of self-seeking elites and exposed to a perennial threat of violent domestic conflict.

Liberal *politics* needs adjustment as well. A radical Liberalism of Restraint presents no viable solution: millions of people cannot be left to perish because the world has decided that they have a sovereign right to solve their own problems. Nor does a radical Liberalism of Imposition present a solution: recolonization is not on the agenda. The only way forward is a clearer definition of the conditions under which international society will intervene in weak states, combined with the buildup of robust capacities for undertaking such intervention. James Fearon and David Laitin (2004) have helpfully discussed these issues under the headings of *recruitment, coordination, accountability,* and *exit.* A move in this direction would, it is to be hoped, have a disciplining effect on elites in weak states; they would have to expect external intervention in situations short of complete state collapse.

What has actually happened in this area? One major way of approaching that problem was set forth in 2005 under the label of "responsibility to protect" (R2P). The UN General Assembly emphasized the responsibility of sovereign states to protect their populations from "genocide, war crimes,

---

4. For a rigorous investigation of norm evolution, see Kelley (2008).

ethnic cleansing and crimes against humanity" and stated its readiness to "take collective action" when states manifestly fail in that responsibility (UNGA 2005; see also chapter 3). The R2P can be seen as a solution to the tension between too much Restraint and too much Imposition. On the one hand, it establishes a platform for action by international society when innocent people suffer. On the other hand, it does so within a rule-based framework requiring Security Council authorization.

But R2P is a solution only if it can actually be implemented. Effective implementation requires political will, legitimate authority, and operational capacity; there are major problems in all three areas. This was made abundantly clear in the UN General Assembly's recent (fall 2009) debate about R2P, which took place on the basis of a report from the secretary general on its implementation (UNGA 2009). Political will runs up against skepticism in many countries in the South that R2P will be an instrument of the strong against the weak and that it may undermine respect for international law. It also confronts hesitation in the North concerning obligations to undertake the missions and provide the capacity to do so. There is no multinational standing force, and several Western countries are militarily strained by operations in Afghanistan and Iraq. As for authority, Security Council authorization cannot be obtained if consent is lacking from the five permanent veto powers. The original R2P Report (G. Evans and Sahnoun 2001) suggests a modified veto system to address that problem, but such a system must await the larger debate about UN reform. The conclusion of the recent General Assembly debate was that R2P remains an "aspirational goal" to be achieved only "when all elements are in place" (closing comment by General Assembly president). R2P is based on a principle of taking collective action against genocide, war crimes, ethnic cleansing, and crimes against humanity only on a "case-by-case basis and in cooperation with relevant regional organizations as appropriate" (UNGA 2009). The current situation, then, is better described as one of "inhumanitarian nonintervention" (T. Weiss 2006: 746). Even if the R2P became effective, it would address only the tip of the iceberg in weak states: flagrant cases of genocide, war crimes, ethnic cleansing and crimes against humanity. It would not speak to the root causes of underdevelopment and weak statehood.

We move to the liberal world economy. Here, liberal *theory* must recognize that minimally regulated free markets produce transnational bads as well as transnational goods. This needs to be followed up by reflections on how best to confront transnational bads. Liberal *politics,* therefore, needs to follow reformed principles. They include (a) restoring the balance between market and government (avoiding excessive deregulation); (b) making short-run actions consistent with long-run visions; (c) being attentive to distributive impacts (avoiding exacerbating wealth and income inequalities); and (d) avoiding an increase in global imbalances and asymmetries.[5]

Successfully confronting the current financial and economic crisis requires a turn away from a neoliberal system emphasizing unregulated markets toward a system where social objectives worldwide are given a higher priority. Former Brazilian president Fernando Henrique Cardoso (2009a) calls this "globalized social democracy." It involves "economic integration with the global market combined with relative national autonomy in decision-making, a more competent State that is capable of implementing active social policies, and a framework of democratic rules promoting partnerships between government and civil society" (454). The turn away from a neoliberal Imposition system toward a reformed Restraint system requires a reconstruction of global market rules in four areas: trade rules, "investors' rights," global property rights rules, and financial market rules (Cardoso 2009a: 454; P. Evans 2009: 324). Details of these problems were set forth in chapter 5. What are the prospects for reform? Not very good.

Comprehensive reform is up against vested interests in the North combined with an ever-increasing diversity in the South that makes any collective action by the South a complicated task (P. Evans 2009: 333). As indicated above, a wide-ranging agenda for reform was set forth by a UN commission on the economic crisis headed by Joseph Stiglitz (Stiglitz et al. 2009). The commission proposed reforms of the global financial system, a new global reserve system to replace the dollar as reserve currency, comprehensive financial market regulation, governance reforms of the World Bank and IMF, and an alternative forum to the G20, a Global Economic Council. The proposals have been largely ignored by the G20 (*Canberra Times* 2009).[6] Meanwhile, the G7 countries go against any proposals for wide-ranging reform (Wu 2009); at the same time, the financial bailouts to private banks and firms combined with stimulus programs in the developed countries distort the playing field the same way as tariffs do (Stiglitz 2009). The South is hit harder by economic crisis than the North and has fewer possibilities for response.

In order to confront the problems of international institutions, liberal *theory* must seek to mitigate the tension inherent in the combined endorsement

---

5. Selective summary from Stiglitz et al. (2009: 18–20).

6. The commission of experts, headed by Joseph Stiglitz, that reported to the UN General Assembly in September 2009, noted that "countries that have held themselves out as models of best practices have been shown to have had deeply flawed macroeconomic policies and institutions and to have suffered from major shortfalls in transparency" (Stiglitz et al. 2009: 20).

of pluralist and nonpluralist approaches. Liberal theory favors a pluralism that includes all sovereign states and a nonpluralism that excludes nondemocracies. Both are respectable liberal goals, but they cannot both be pursued with full force simultaneously. Liberal *politics* must overcome, as David Held (2007) says, "institutional competition, overlapping jurisdictions, the excessive costs of inaction, and the failures of accountability" (249). That points toward three types of measures: first, promoting coordinated state action to tackle common problems; second, reinforcing those international institutions that can function effectively; and third, developing multilateral rules and procedures that lock all powers, small and major, into an accountable multilateral framework (Held 2007: 249).

A decisive element is this regard is the positive commitment by liberal governments and liberal electorates to more effective and legitimate international institutions. It is a precarious balance both to take the lead and to relinquish traditional ambitions of liberal hegemony. What are the prospects for institutional reform? I will focus on the Bretton Woods institutions, which are indeed in need of reform. Cardoso (2009b) speaks of the "fragility" of the IMF and the World Bank: "they are clearly incapable of managing the dynamism of the global economy and the multinational corporations as well as balancing the growth of emerging economies" (299). But a new global pact with reformed institutions will not emerge easily. Leading liberal states have a two-sided collective action problem in this regard: On the one hand, their room for maneuver is constrained by strong private interest groups—especially in the financial sectors of their economies—who are against reform. According to one observer, the states are "incapable of securing even reconstructions that are in their own immediate interests... [due to] entrenched private resistance" (P. Evans 2009: 333). On the other hand, both large-deficit and large-surplus states are against ceding power to global institutions, because bilateral arrangements increase their scope of control. In effect, the United States will not and cannot (for lack of political and economic capital) push a fundamental reform of Bretton Woods; nor will China, who is more focused on bilateral relations with the United States (and does not have the power to set global rules). The EU does not have such power either. That pushes the prospects for a new global pact into the future.

Finally, in order to confront the problem of liberal values in the world, liberal *theory* must recognize the tension between one version of liberal freedom that emphasizes autonomy, self-determination, and the right to chart your own course, as an individual or as a society, and another version of liberal freedom that emphasizes the universal validity of rights to life, liberty, security of the person, and protection against discrimination relevant for all people and societies. This problem is especially acute because this tension plays out in a situation where there is no guarantee of liberal progress. As far as liberal *politics* is concerned, Namit Arora (2009) recently speculated about acting in a world where there is a plurality of values but relativism cannot be justified because humans "share a common humanity and many common values." Two principles stand out:

> I have to take seriously at least what I hold to be the core values of my liberalism, such as commitment to try and understand others and to modify my opinions in lights of new discoveries. Indeed, the only path open to me as a pluralist *and* a liberal is to try to persuade others of my subjective values and to put my weight behind ideas and policies that appeal to my liberalism.... Last but not least, I should try to persuade others without being self-righteous or hypocritical. (3–4)[7]

Nothing of this will be easy when pursued by liberal states that have a precisely defined set of obligations to their own citizens and operate in an international system where rules and authority are not precisely defined. We have seen how attempts at promoting liberal values have produced skepticism and resistance in many places. I have claimed that real progress in the support for liberal values will hinge on the extent to which the forces behind liberalism can help produce tangible results for the skeptic peoples on the ground. Previous chapters have explained the complexity of such an undertaking in great detail. In Afghanistan in 2009, liberal states felt compelled to support the election of Hamid Karzai for president, even if the election was "a foreseeable train wreck" with "one in three votes for Karzai fraudulent" (*Guardian* 2009),[8] according to UN diplomat Peter Galbraith. In contrast to Galbraith, the Western-led UN mission in the country believes that Karzai is the best bet for creating some order and stability. But the support for Karzai will hardly boost the support for liberal values among the Afghan population. It is no simple matter to define liberal policies that will, with great certainty, improve the standing of liberal values in the world. The above examples concerning weak states and R2P, the financial and economic crisis, and the issue of institutional reform point in the same direction.

Other commentators have been more optimistic concerning the prospects for a reformed liberal order. Reflecting on U.S. foreign policy in particular,

---

7. Habermas (1984) makes a similar point.

8. The 2010 parliamentary election was also plagued by widespread fraud, see *New York Times* (2010).

Francis Fukuyama (writing in 2006) proposes a *"realistic* Wilsonianism that recognizes the importance to world order of what goes on *inside* states and that better matches the available tools to the achievement of democratic ends" (184, italics in original). First and foremost, that leads to a recommendation of "dramatic demilitarization of American foreign policy" (184). Preventive war should be seen as an extreme measure, and the rhetoric about a global war on terror should cease. There should be higher emphasis on promotion of economic and political development in the world, by means of soft power; legitimacy must be sought by working through and shaping international institutions. Unchecked power, including U.S. power, is dangerous, because hegemony has to be "not just well-intentioned but also prudent and smart in its exercise of power" (193).

A similar kind of realistic Wilsonianism was proposed by Joseph Nye in 2002. He urges the United States to view international order as a public good and to pursue "a strategy based on public goods" (147). This is sensible advice. It corresponds well with the analysis of the future liberal world order by John Ikenberry (2009). He foresees that a reformed liberal order will "need to become more universal and less hierarchical—that is, the United States will need to cede authority and control to a wider set of states and give up some of its hegemonic rights and privileges" (80). The precise character of such an order will of course depend on the extent to which the United States will be willing to combine a continued provision of public goods with reduced hegemonic rights and privileges. It will also depend on the extent of cooperation, support, and willingness to follow shared norms and rules on the part of other states in the system.

But any version of realistic Wilsonianism will have to negotiate the tensions in liberalism analyzed here, and neither Fukuyama nor Nye says much about how to do that beyond the sound recommendation to be less impositionist and more cooperative than the George W. Bush administrations. The underlying problems remain: We live in an international society of sovereign states. Sovereignty is an appropriate condition of freedom, provided states have constitutional government. But this is absent in many countries and shows no promise of emerging anytime soon. Instead, self-seeking state elites are protected by sovereignty. We live in a world of free markets that should provide economic growth and prosperity for all. They do for some, but they also bring huge inequalities and insufficient improvement for at least half of the world's population. We live in a world of strong international institutions, but they are rarely able to combine legitimacy and effectiveness, and liberal states much prefer "institution-shopping" (Fukuyama 2006: 155–80) rather than confronting the problem. All this puts pressure on liberal values, and the conditions for promoting such values appear increasingly adverse today. Additional liberal progress will most probably have to involve a rethinking of several basic liberal principles, and the prospects in this regard are not bright. Thus the reasons for my pessimism: strong and self-confident liberal states will have a tendency to lean toward radical Imposition and do too much; weakened and unsure liberal states will lean toward radical Restraint and do too little.

But maybe I am asking too much of liberalism and liberal states. In macrohistorical terms, the progress in liberal values has certainly been impressive, even more so considering the adverse circumstances of earlier days. A large number of small changes combined can produce substantial and significant reform. Minor changes matter; President Cardoso (2009a) would rather fight for improvements in "certain rules of the game" than try to "change the game altogether" (454). And individuals matter; when Americans elected Barack Obama as president, they also significantly altered the U.S. approach to liberal world order.

Albert Hirschman was animated by a "bias for hope" when addressing the problems of the developing world. He emphasized that when looking for large-scale social change, one must be guided by what Danish philosopher Søren Kirkegaard called "the passion for what is possible." "Possibilism" (Hirschman 1971: 28) shies away from revolutionary or utopian proposals but also entertains the ambition of going beyond strictly incremental change. Possibilism may be the best road forward for liberal states as well as for liberal individuals. The tensions between Restraint and Imposition will not go away, but possibilism appears to be a sensible tool for handling them. In spite of past achievement, liberal progress will not take place automatically; it will depend on individuals and states that help move liberal world order in the right direction. Western democracies, however, face tensions and dilemmas that undercut liberal progress.

◼ ABBREVIATIONS

BJP	Bharatiya Janata Party
CIA	Central Intelligence Agency
CIS	Commonwealth of Independent States
CCP	Chinese Communist Party
CFSP	Common Foreign and Security Policy
CPA	Coalition Provisional Authority
DSB	Defense Science Board
ECB	European Central Bank
EU	European Union
FDI	foreign direct investment
GATS	General Agreement on Trade in Services
GATT	General Agreement on Tariffs and Trade
GDP	gross domestic product
GP	government procurement
G20	The Group of 20 (finance ministers and central bank governors from 19 countries plus the European Union)
ICC	International Criminal Court
IGO	international governmental organization
IMF	International Monetary Fund
INGO	international nongovernmental Organization
IR	international relations
MFA	Multi Fiber Agreement
NAFTA	North American Free Trade Agreement
NATO	North Atlantic Treaty Organization
NDCs	now developed countries
NGO	nongovernmental organization
NSS	National Security Strategy
ODA	Official Development Assistance
OECD	Organisation for Economic Co-operation and Development
OSCE	Organization for Security and Co-operation in Europe
R2P	Responsibility to Protect
SAP	Structural Adjustment Program

TRIMS   Trade-Related Investment Measures
TRIPS   Trade-Related Aspects of International Property Rights
UK   United Kingdom
UN   United Nations
UNGA   United Nations General Assembly
WMD   weapons of mass destruction
WOMP   World Order Models Project
WTO   World Trade Organization

◼ References

Acemoglu, Daron, Simon Johnson, and James A. Robinson (2003). "An African Success Story: Botswana." In *In Search of Prosperity: Analytical Narrative on Economic Growth,* edited by Dani Rodrik, 80–119. Princeton: Princeton University Press.

Adler, Emanuel, and Michael Barnett (eds.) (1998). *Security Communities.* Cambridge: Cambridge University Press.

Alavi, Hamza, and Theodor Shanin (1982). *Introduction to the Sociology of "Developing Societies."* Basingstoke: Palgrave Macmillan.

Allison, Graham (2004). *Nuclear Terrorism: The Ultimate Preventable Catastrophe.* New York: Times Books.

Amsden, Alice, and Wan-Wen Chu (2003). *Beyond Late Development: Taiwan's Upgrading Policies.* Cambridge: MIT Press.

Andersen, Eva (2009). "Den (u)demokratiske verdensorden." Unpublished paper, Department of Political Science, Aarhus University.

Angell, Norman (1909). *The Great Illusion.* London: Weidenfeld & Nicolson.

Annan, Kofi (2003). "Do We Still Have Universal Values?" 3rd Global Ethic Lecture of the Global Ethic Foundation, University of Tübingen, December 12. http://www.paep.ca/en/CIYL/2006/doc/Global%20Ethics%20-%20Do%20We%20Still%20Have%20Universal%20Values%20-%20Kofi%20A.%20Annan.pdf.

Applebaum, Anne (2010). "China's Quiet Power Grab." http://www.washingtonpost.com/wp-dyn/content/article/2010/09/27/AR2010092704658.html. September 28.

Arnson, C. J., and I. W. Zartman (eds.) (2005). *Rethinking the Economics of War.* Baltimore: Johns Hopkins University Press.

Arora, Namit (2009). "Being Liberal in a Plural World." February 2. http://www.3quarksdaily.com/3quarksdaily/2009/02/being-liberal-in-a-plural-world.html.

AsianOffbeat (2008). "93% Chinese support Hu Jintao." http://www.asianoffbeat.com/default.asp?Display=1841. June 23.

Atzili, Boaz (2006/7). "When Good Fences Make Bad Neighbors." *International Security* 31:3, 139–73.

Ayoob, Muhammed (2004). "Third World Perspectives on Humanitarian Intervention and International Administration." *Global Governance* 10:1, 83–98.

Bairoch, Paul (1993). *Economics and World History: Myths and Paradoxes.* Chicago: University of Chicago Press.

Barber, Benjamin R. (1995). *Jihad Versus McWorld.* New York: Random House.

Bayart, Jean-Francois (1993). *The State in Africa: The Politics of the Belly.* London: Longman.

Beck, Ulrich (1986). *Risikogesellschaft. Auf dem Weg in eine andere Moderne.* Frankfurt: Suhrkamp.

Beisheim, Marianne, Sabine Dreher, Gregor Walter, Bernhard Zangl, and Michael Zürn (1999). *Im Zeitalter der Globalisierung?* Baden-Baden: Nomos.

Beitz, Charles (2009). *The Idea of Human Rights.* New York: Oxford University Press.

Bellamy, Alex (2004). "Ethics and Intervention: The 'Humanitarian Exception' and the Problem of Abuse in the Case of Iraq." *Journal of Peace Research* 41:2, 131–47.

Belloni, Roberto (2007). "Rethinking 'Nation-Building': The Contradictions of the Neo-Wilsonian Approach to Democracy Promotion." *Whitehead Journal of Diplomacy and International Relations,* Spring/Winter, 97–109.

Bennett, Christopher (1995). *Yugoslavia's Bloody Collapse—Causes, Course, and Consequences.* London: Hurst.

Bentham, Jeremy (1927 [1789]). *Plan for an Universal and Perpetual Peace.* Introduction by C. John Colombos. Grotius Society Publications no. 6. London: Sweet and Maxwell.

Beran, Michael Knox (2006). "Was Liberalism's Philosopher-in-Chief a Conservative?" *http://www.city-journal.org/html/16_1_urbanities-isaiah_berlin.html.* Winter.

Berger, Peter L. (1999). "The Desecularization of the World." In *The Desecularization of the World,* edited by Peter L. Berger. Washington: W. B. Eerdmans. 1–19.

Berger, Thomas U. (1996). "Norms, Identity, and National Security in Germany and Japan." In *The Culture of National Security: Norms and Identity in World Politics,* edited by Peter J. Katzenstein. New York: Columbia University Press. 317–56.

Berlin, Isaiah (1969). *Four Essays on Liberty.* Oxford: Oxford University Press.

—— (1988). "On the Pursuit of the Ideal." *New York Review of Books* 35:4, 1–18.

Berman, Paul (2003). *Terror and Liberalism.* New York: W. W. Norton.

Bernstein, Steven F., and Louis W. Pauly (eds.) (2007). *Global Liberalism and Political Order: Toward a New Grand Compromise?* Albany: State University of New York Press.

Betts, Richard K. (2005). "The Political Support System for American Primacy." *International Affairs* 81:1, 1–14.

Bilgin, Pinar, and Adam Morton (2004). "From 'Rogue' to 'Failed' States? The Fallacy of Short-Termism." *Politics* 24:3, 169–80.

Blair, Tony (2007). "A Battle for Global Values." *Foreign Affairs* 86:1, 79–90.

Bloom, Allan (1989). "Response to Fukuyama." *National Interest* 16, 19–22.

Bluth, Christoph (1998) "The Post-Soviet Space and Europe." In *Security Dilemmas in Russia and Eurasia,* edited by Roy Allison and Christoph Bluth. London: Royal Institute of International Affairs. 323–42.

Bok, Sissela (1995). *Common Values.* Columbia: University of Missouri Press.

Boone, Jon (2009). "One in Three Votes for Karzai Fraudulent." http://www.guardian.co.uk/world/2009/oct/04/afghanistan-elections-peter-galbraith-un. October 4.

Booth, Ken, and Tim Dunne (eds.) (2002). *Worlds in Collision: Terror and the Future of Global Order.* Basingstoke: Palgrave Macmillan.

Bovard, James (2005). "Nonsense and the Inevitability of Democracy." *Freedom Daily.* http://www.fff.org/freedom/fd0605c.pdf. May.

Bowman, Steve (2002). *Weapons of Mass Destruction: The Terrorist Threat.* Washington, DC: CRS.

Bratton, Michael, and Nicholas van de Walle (1997). *Democratic Experiments in Africa.* Cambridge: Cambridge University Press.

Brilmayer, Lea (1994). *American Hegemony: Political Morality in a One Superpower World.* New Haven: Yale University Press.

Brook, Timothy, and Michael B. Frohlich (eds.) (1997). *Civil Society in China.* Armonk, NY: M. E. Sharpe.

Brownlee, Jason (2007). "Can America Nation-Build?" *World Politics* 59, 314–40.

Bull, Hedley (1995 [1977]). *The Anarchical Society: A Study of Order in World Politics.* Basingstoke: Macmillan.

Burton, John (1972). *World Society.* Cambridge: Cambridge University Press.

Busby, Joshua, and Jonathan Monten (2008). "Without Heirs? Assessing the Decline of Establishment Internationalism in U.S. Foreign Policy." *Perspectives on Politics* 6:3, 451–72.

Bush, George H. W. (1990). "A New World Order." Speech to Congress, September 11. In Eric A. Miller and Steve A. Yetiv, "The New World Order in Theory and Practice." *Presidential Studies Quarterly* 31:1, 56–68.

Bush, George W. (2002). Graduation speech at West Point. http://georgewbush-whitehouse.archives.gov/news/releases/2002/06/20020601-3.html. June 1.

Buzan, Barry (2004). *From International to World Society.* Cambridge: Cambridge University Press.

—— (2006). "Will the 'Global War on Terrorism' Be the New Cold War?" *International Affairs* 82:6, 1101–18.

Callaghy, Thomas M. (1991). "Africa and the World Economy: Caught between a Rock and a Hard Place." In *Africa in World Politics,* edited by John W. Harbeson and Donald Rotschild. Boulder: Westview. 39–69.

Campanella, Edoardo (2010). "The Triffin Dilemma Again." *Economics: The Open-Access, Open-Assessment E-Journal.* http://www.economics-ejournal.org/economics/journalarticles/2010–25. September 1.

Campbell, Ian (2004). "Retreat from Globalization." *National Interest* 75, 111–17.

Canberra Times (2009). "The G20's Missed Opportunity." http://www.jubileeaustralia.org/BlogRetrieve.aspx?BlogID=799&PostID=44232. August 24.

Cardoso, Fernando Henrique (2009a). "Response." *Studies in Comparative International Development* 44, 450–56.

—— (2009b). "New Paths: Globalization in Historical Perspective." *Studies in Comparative International Development* 44, 296–317.

194   **REFERENCES**

Carothers, Thomas (1997). "Democracy without Illusions." *Foreign Affairs* 76, 85–99.

—— (1999). *Aiding Democracy Abroad*. Washington, DC: Carnegie Endowment for International Peace.

—— (2002). "The End of the Transitions Paradigm." *Journal of Democracy* 13:1, 5–21.

Castells, Manuel (1998). *The Power of Identity,* Oxford: Basil Blackwell.

Cavallar, Georg (2001). "Kantian Perspectives on Democratic Peace: Alternatives to Doyle." *Review of International Studies* 27, 229–48.

Chabal, Patrick, and Jean-Pascal Daloz (1999). *Africa Works: The Political Instrumentalization of Disorder.* Bloomington: Indiana University Press.

Chalk, Peter (1998). "The Response to Terrorism as a Threat to Liberal Democracy." *Australian Journal of Politics and History* 44:3, 373–88.

Chandler, David (2006). "Back to the Future: The Limits of Neo-Wilsonian Ideals of Exporting Democracy." *Review of International Studies* 32:3, 475–94.

Chandra, Satish (1997). "The Indian Perspective." In *The New Realism: Perspectives on Multilateralism and World Order,* edited by Robert W. Cox. Basingstoke: Macmillan. 124–45.

Chang, Ha-Joon (2002). *Kicking Away the Ladder—Development Strategy in Historical Perspective.* London: Anthem Press.

—— (2003). "Kicking Away the Ladder: Infant Industry Promotion in Historical Perspective." *Oxford Development Studies* 31:1, 21–32.

Chaudoin, Stephen, Helen Milner, and Dustin Tingley (2010). "The Center Still Holds: Liberal Internationalism Survives." *International Security* 35:1, 75–94.

Chen, An (2003). "The New Inequality." *Journal of Democracy* 14:1, 51–59.

Chorev, Nitsan (2005). "The Institutional Project of Neo-liberal Globalism: The Case of the WTO." *Theory and Society* 34, 317–55.

Clapham, Christopher (1996). *Africa and the International System.* Cambridge: Cambridge University Press.

—— (1998). "Degrees of Statehood." *Review of International Studies* 24, 143–57.

Clinton, Hilary (2009). "Chinese Human Rights Can't Interfere with Other Crises." http://www.cnn.com/2009/POLITICS/02/21/clinton.china.asia/. February 22.

Cobden, Richard (1903). *Political Writings.* 2 vols. London: Fischer-Unwin.

Coker, Christopher (1992). "Postmodernity and the End of the Cold War." *Review of International Studies* 18:3, 189–98.

Commission on Growth and Development (Spence Commission) (2008). *The Growth Report: Strategies for Sustained Growth and Inclusive Development.* http://cgd.s3.amazonaws.com/GrowthReportComplete.pdf.

Cooper, Robert (1996). *The Post-Modern State and the World Order,* London: Demos.

Copson, Raymond (1994). *Africa's Wars and Prospects for Peace.* Armonk, NY: M. E. Sharpe.

Cox, Robert W. (1996). With T. J. Sinclair. *Approaches to World Order.* Cambridge: Cambridge University Press.

—— (2002). With M. J. Schechter. *The Political Economy of a Plural World.* London: Routledge.

Coyne, Christopher J. (2006a). "Reconstructing Weak and Failed States." *The Journal of Social, Political, and Economic Studies* 31:2, 143–62.

—— (2006b). "Reconstructing Weak and Failed States: Foreign Intervention and the Nirvana Fallacy." *Foreign Policy Analysis* 2, 343–60.

Crowder, George (2003). "Pluralism, Relativism and Liberalism in Isaiah Berlin." Conference, University of Tasmania, September 29–October 1.

Daalder, Ivo, and James Lindsay (2007). "Democracies of the World, Unite." *American Interest* 2:3, 1–10.

Dahl, Robert A. (1971). *Polyarchy: Participation and Opposition.* New Haven: Yale University Press.

—— (1985). *A Preface to Democratic Theory.* Chicago: University of Chicago Press.

—— (1989). *Democracy and Its Critics.* New Haven: Yale University Press.

—— (1999). "Can International Organizations Be Democratic? A Sceptic's View." In *Democracy's Edges,* edited by Ian Shapiro and Casiano Hacker-Cordón. Cambridge: Cambridge University Press. 19–37.

Dannreuther, Roland (2007). "War and Insecurity: Legacies of Northern and Southern State Formation." *Review of International Studies* 33, 307–26.

Daschle, Tom (1996). "The Water's Edge." *Foreign Policy* 103: Summer, 1–16.

David, Steven R. (1991). *Choosing Sides: Alignment and Realignment in the Third World.* Baltimore: Johns Hopkins University Press.

Delahunty, Robert, and John Yoo (2007). "Lines in the Sand." *National Interest* 87, 28–32.

Deller, Nicole, Arhun Makhijani, and John Burroughs (eds.) (2003). *Rule of Power or Rule of Law? An Assessment of US Policies and Actions regarding Security-Related Treaties.* New York: Apex Press.

Deng, Y. (1998). "The Chinese Conception of National Interests in International Relations." *China Quarterly* 154, 308–29.

Deudney, Daniel, and G. John Ikenberry (1999). "The Nature and Sources of Liberal International Order." *Review of International Studies* 25:2, 179–96.

—— (2009). "The Myth of the Autocratic Revival: Why Liberal Democracy Will Prevail." *Foreign Affairs* 88:1, 77–94.

Deutsch, Karl W., et al. (1957). *Political Community and the North Atlantic Area.* Princeton: Princeton University Press.

Diamond, Larry (2002). "Thinking about Hybrid Regimes." *Journal of Democracy* 13:2, 21–35.

—— (2005). "Lessons from Iraq." *Journal of Democracy* 6:1, 9–23.

Dicken, Peter (2003). *Global Shift: Reshaping the Global Economic Map in the 21st Century.* London: Sage.

Dobbins, James, et al. (2003). *America's Role in Nation-Building: From Germany to Iraq.* Santa Monica: Rand.

Donnelly, Jack (1993). *International Human Rights.* Boulder: Westview.

Donohue, Laura K. (2008). *The Cost of Counterterrorism.* Cambridge: Cambridge University Press.

Doyle, Michael W. (1983). "Kant, Liberal Legacies and Foreign Affairs," pts. 1 and 2. *Philosophy and Public Affairs* 12:3, 205–35, and 12:4, 323–54.

—— (1986). "Liberalism and World Politics." *American Political Science Review* 84:4, 1151–69.

—— (1997). *Ways of War and Peace.* New York: W. W. Norton.

Drezner, Daniel W. (2007). "The New World Order." *Foreign Affairs* 86:2, 14–28.

Ebeling, Richard (1991). "A Liberal World Order." Future Freedom Foundation. http://www.fff.org/freedom/0991b.asp. September.

Economist, The (2008). "Finance and Economics: But Will It Work? Rescuing the Banks." October 18.

—— (2010). "New Dangers for the World Economy." February 11.

Edwards, Sebastian (1993). "Openness, Trade Liberalization, and Growth in Developing Countries." *Journal of Economic Literature* 31, 1358–93.

Eizenstat, Stuart E., et al. (2005). "Rebuilding Weak States." *Foreign Affairs* 84:1, 134–46.

Elklit, Jørgen (1999). "Electoral Institutional Change and Democratization: You Can Lead a Horse to Water, but You Can't Make It Drink." *Democratization* 6:4, 28–51.

Englebert, Pierre (2009). *Unity, Sovereignty and Sorrow.* Boulder: Lynne Rienner.

Englebert, Pierre, and Rebecca Hummel (2005). "Let's Stick Together: Understanding Africa's Secessionist Deficit." *African Affairs* 104, 399–427.

Englebert, Pierre, and Denis M. Tull (2008). "Postconflict Reconstruction in Africa." *International Security* 32:4, 106–39.

Eriksen, Stein Sundstøl (2005). "The Politics of State Formation: Contradictions and Conditions of Possibility." *European Journal of Development Research* 17:3, 396–410.

European Union (2010). "Common Foreign and Security Policy for the European Union." http://ec.europa.eu/external_relations/cfsp/index_en.htm.

Evans, Gareth, and Mohamed Sahnoun (co-chairs) (2001). *The Responsibility to Protect.* Report of the International Commission on Intervention and State Sovereignty. Ottawa: International Development Research Centre.

Evans, Peter (2009). "From Situations of Dependency to Globalized Social Democracy." *Studies in Comparative International Development* 44, 318–36.

Falk, Richard A. (1987). *The Promise of World Order: Essays in Normative International Relations.* Philadelphia: Temple University Press.

Farer, Tom J. (2003). "Humanitarian Intervention before and after 9/11." In *Humanitarian Intervention: Ethical, Legal and Political Dilemmas,* edited by J. L. Holzgrefe and Robert O. Keohane. New York: Cambridge University Press. 53–90.

Fearon, James D., and David Laitin (2004). "Neotrusteeships and the Problem of Weak States." *International Security* 28, 5–43.

Fearon, James D. (2007). "Iraq's Civil War." *Foreign Affairs* 86:2, 1–12.

Fettweis, Christopher J. (2004). "Evaluating IR's Crystal Balls: How Predictions of the Future Have Withstood Fourteen Years of Unipolarity." *International Studies Review* 6:1, 79–105.

Foreign Policy (2005). "The Failed States Index." 149: July–August, 56–65.

—— (2007). "The Globalization Index." 163: November–December, 68–76.

—— (2008). "The Failed States Index." http://www.foreignpolicy.com/story/cms. php?story_id=4350. July.

Franceschet, Antonio (2001). "Sovereignty and Freedom: Immanuel Kant's Liberal Internationalist 'Legacy.'" *Review of International Studies* 27, 209–28.

Fraser, Derek (2007). "Failed States: Why They Matter and What We Should Do about Them." *International Insights, CIIA/ICAI* 5:2, 1–6.

Freeden, Michael (2008). "European Liberalisms: An Essay in Comparative Political Thought." *Political Theory* 7:1, 9–30.

Freedom House (2010). *Freedom in the World 2010.* Lanham, MD: Rowman and Littlefield.

Fukuyama, Francis (1989). "The End of History." *National Interest* 16, 3–18.

—— (1992). *The End of History and the Last Man.* New York: Avon Books.

—— (2004). *State Building: Governance and World Order in the Twenty-First Century.* London: Profile Books.

—— (2006). *America at the Crossroads: Democracy, Power, and the Neoconservative Legacy.* New Haven: Yale University Press.

Galbraith, John Kenneth (1994). *A Journey through Economic Time.* Boston: Houghton Mifflin.

Gallie, Walter B. (1978). *Philosophers of Peace and War: Kant, Clausewitz, Marx, Engels, and Tolstoy.* Cambridge: Cambridge University Press.

Garrett, Banning (2001). "China Faces, Debates, the Contradictions of Globalization." *Asian Survey* 41:3, 409–27.

Gat, Azar (2007). "The Return of Authoritarian Great Powers." *Foreign Affairs* 86:4, 59–63.

Giddens, Anthony (1999). *Runaway World.* London: Profile.

Gilpin, Robert (1987). *The Political Economy of International Relations.* Princeton: Princeton University Press.

Gizelis, Theodore-Ismene, and Kristin E. Kosek (2005). "Why Humanitarian Interventions Succeed or Fail." *Cooperation and Conflict* 40:4, 363–83.

Gold, Thomas B. (1986). *State and Society in the Taiwan Miracle.* New York: East Gate Books.

Goldsmith, Arthur A. (2004). "Predatory versus Developmental Rule in Africa." *Democratization* 11:3, 88–110.

Gong, Gerrit W. (1984). *The Standard of "Civilization" in International Society.* Oxford: Oxford University Press.

Goodrich, Leland M., et al. (1969). *Charter of the United Nations.* New York: Columbia University Press.

Gray, John (1995). *Liberalism: Essays in Political Philosophy.* 2nd ed. London: Routledge.

—— (2000). *Two Faces of Liberalism.* Cambridge, UK: Polity.

Green, Thomas Hill (1941). *Lectures on the Principles of Political Obligation.* London: Longmans Green.

Gruber, Lloyd (2005). "Power Politics and the Institutionalization of International Relations." In *Power in Global Governance,* edited by Michael Barnett and Raymond Duvall. Cambridge: Cambridge University Press. 102–30.

Gurr, Ted Robert (1994). "Peoples against States: Ethnopolitical Conflict and the Changing World System." *International Studies Quarterly* 38: Fall, 347–77.

Gurr, Ted Robert, and Barbara Harff (2003). *Ethnic Conflict in World Politics.* Boulder: Westview.

Haas, Richard N. (2008). "The Age of Nonpolarity." *Foreign Affairs* 87:3, 44–56.

Habermas, Jürgen (1984). *The Theory of Communicative Action.* Vol. 1. Boston: Beacon Press.

Harbom, Lotta, and Peter Wallensteen (2009). "Armed Conflicts 1946–2008." *Journal of Peace Research* 46:4, 577–87.

Hardy, Henry (2003). "Taking Pluralism Seriously." http://berlin.wolf.ox.ac.uk/writings_on_ib/hhonib/taking_pluralism_seriously.html.

Held, David (1995). *Democracy and the Global Order.* Cambridge, UK: Polity Press.

—— (2006). *Models of Democracy.* 3rd ed. Cambridge, UK: Polity Press.

—— (2007). "Reframing Global Governance: Apocalypse Soon or Reform." In *Globalization Theory: Approaches and Controversies,* edited by David Held and Anthony McGrew. Cambridge, UK: Polity Press. 240–61.

Held, David, Anthony McGrew, David Gloldblatt, and Jonathan Perraton (1999). *Global Transformations: Politics, Economics and Culture.* Cambridge: Cambridge University Press.

Helleiner, Eric (2005). "The Evolution of the International Monetary and Financial System." In *Global Political Economy,* edited by John Ravenhill. Oxford: Oxford University Press. 151–76.

Hellmann, Joel S. (1998). "Winners Take All: The Politics of Partial Reform in Post-Communist Transitions." *World Politics* 50, 203–34.

Helman, Gerald B., and Steven R. Ratner (1992). "Saving Failed States." *Foreign Policy* 89, 3–20.

Herbst, Jeffrey (1996–97). "Responding to State Failure in Africa." *International Security* 21:3, 120–44.

—— (1997). "Correspondence." *International Security* 22:2, 175–84.

Hirschman, Albert (1971). *A Bias for Hope: Essays on Development and Latin America.* New Haven: Yale University Press.

Hobbes, Thomas (1946). *Leviathan.* Oxford: Blackwell.

Hobhouse, L. T. (1916). *Questions of War and Peace.* London: T. Fisher Unwin.

Hobson, John A. (1915). "The International Mind." *Nation,* August 14.

Hoffmann, Stanley (1995). "The Crisis of Liberal Internationalism." *Foreign Policy* 98: 159–78.

—— (1998). *World Disorders.* Lanham, MD: Rowman and Littlefield.

Holbraad, Carsten (2003). *Internationalism and Nationalism in European Political Thought.* Basingstoke: Palgrave Macmillan.

Holm, Hans Henrik, and Georg Sørensen (eds.) (1995). *Whose World Order? Uneven Globalization and the End of the Cold War.* Boulder: Westview.

Homer-Dixon, Thomas (1991). "On the Threshold: Environmental Changes as Causes of Acute Conflict." *International Security* 16:2, 76–116.

Hoogvelt, Ankie (1997). *Globalisation and the Postcolonial World.* Basingstoke: Macmillan.

Howard, Michael (1978). *War and the Liberal Conscience.* New Brunswick: Rutgers University Press.

Hughes, Christopher (2002). "China and Global Liberalism." In *The Globalization of Liberalism,* edited by Eivind Hovden and Edward Keene. Basingstoke: Palgrave. 193–218.

Human Rights Watch (2009). "China: Government Rebuffs UN Human Rights Council." http://www.hrw.org/en/news/2009/06/10/china-government-rebuffs-un-human-rights-council. June 11.

—— (2010). "China: Chokehold on Civil Society Intensifies." http://www.hrw.org/en/news/2010/04/11/china-chokehold-civil-society-intensifies. April 12.

Huntington, Samuel P. (1993). "The Clash of Civilizations?." *Foreign Affairs* 72:3, 22–49.

—— (1996). *The Clash of Civilizations and the Remaking of World Order.* New York: Simon and Schuster.

—— (1999). "The Lonely Superpower." *Foreign Affairs* 78:2, 35–44.

—— (2007). "Interview." *New Perspectives Quarterly* 24:1. http://www.digitalnpq.org/archive/2007_winter/14_huntington.html.

Hurrell, Andrew (1990). "Kant and the Kantian Paradigm in International Relations." *Review of International Studies* 16:3, 183–205.

—— (2006). *On Global Order: Power, Values, and the Constitution of International Society.* Oxford: Oxford University Press.

Ignatieff, Michael (2003). *Empire Lite: Nation-Building in Bosnia, Kosovo, and Afghanistan.* London: Vintage.

Ikenberry, G. John (1996). "The Myth of Post–Cold War Chaos." *Foreign Affairs* 75:3, 79–91.

—— (2001). *After Victory: Institutions, Strategic Restraint, and the Rebuilding of Order after Major Wars.* Princeton: Princeton University Press.

—— (ed.) (2002a). *America Unrivaled: The Future of the Balance of Power.* Ithaca: Cornell University Press.

—— (2002b). "America's Imperial Ambition." *Foreign Affairs* 81:5, 44–60.

—— (2004). "The End of the Neo-Conservative Moment." *Survival* 46:1, 7–22.

—— (2005). "Creating America's World: The Sources of Postwar Liberal Internationalism." Unpublished paper.

—— (2008). "The Rise of China and the Future of the West: Can the Liberal System Survive?" *Foreign Affairs* 87:1, 23–37.

—— (2009). "Liberal Internationalism 3.0: America and the Dilemmas of Liberal World Order." *Perspectives on Politics* 7:1, 71–87.

—— (2011). *Liberal Leviathan: The Rise, Triumph, Crisis, and Transformation of the American World Order.* Princeton: Princeton University Press.

Ikenberry, G. John, Michael Mastanduno, and William C. Wohlforth (2009). "Unipolarity, State Behavior, and Systemic Consequences." *World Politics* 61:1, 1–27.

Inglehart, Ronald, and Christian Welzel (2005). "Inglehart-Welzel Cultural Map of the World." http://www.worldvaluessurvey.org/wvs/articles/folder_published/article_base_54.

Inglehart, Ronald, and Christian Welzel (2009). "How Development Leads to Democracy." *Foreign Affairs* 88:2, 33–49.

Ingram, Derek (1995). "NGOs Keep the Pressure Up on Bureaucrats." *Bangkok Post,* July 21.

Inoguchi, Takashi, and Paul Bacon (2005). "Empire, Hierarchy, and Hegemony: American Grand Strategy and the Construction of Order in the Asia-Pacific." *International Relations of the Asia-Pacific* 5:2, 117–32.

International Civil Society (2010). "Sign-On Statement for a Global Leaders Forum." http://www.halifaxinitiative.org/content/towards-a-global-leaders-forum.

International Commission (ICISS) (2001). *The Responsibility to Protect.* Ottawa: International Development Research Centre.

Jackson, Andrew (1837). "Eternal Vigilance." http://freedomkeys.com/vigil.htm.

Jackson, Robert (1993). *Quasi-states: Sovereignty, International Relations and the Third World.* Cambridge: Cambridge University Press.

—— (1994). "International Boundaries in Theory and Practice." Paper for Sixteenth World Congress of the International Political Science Association, Berlin, August 21–25.

—— (1995). "International Community beyond the Cold War." In *Beyond Westphalia? State Sovereignty and International Intervention,* edited by Gene M. Lyons and Michael Mastanduno. Baltimore: Johns Hopkins University Press, 59–87.

—— (2000). *The Global Covenant: Human Conduct in a World of States.* Oxford: Oxford University Press.

Jackson, Robert, and Carl Rosberg (1994). "The Political Economy of African Personal Rule." In *Political Development and the New Realism in Sub-Saharan Africa,* edited by David E. Apter and Carl G. Rosberg. Charlottesville: University Press of Virginia. 291–325.

Jackson, Robert, and Georg Sørensen (2010). *Introduction to International Relations: Theories and Approaches.* 4th ed. Oxford: Oxford University Press.

Jahn, Beate (2005). "Kant, Mill, and Illiberal Legacies in International Affairs." *International Organization* 59, 177–207.

Jakobsen, Peter Viggo (1996). "National Interest, Humanitarianism, or CNN: What Triggers UN Peace Enforcement after the Cold War?" *Journal of Peace Research* 33:2, 205–15.

Jenkins, Kate, and William Plowden (2006). *Governance and Nationbuilding: The Failure of International Intervention.* Cheltenham, UK: Edward Elgar.

Jentleson, Bruce (2007). "Yet Again: Humanitarian Intervention and the Challenges of 'Never Again.'" In *Leashing the Dogs of War: Conflict Management in a Divided World,* edited by Chester Crocker et al. Washington, DC: Institute of Peace. 277–97.

Jervis, Robert (1978). "Cooperation under the Security Dilemma." *World Politics* 30: January, 167–214.

—— (2003). "The Compulsive Empire." *Foreign Policy* 137, 83–87.

Job, Brian (ed.) (1992). *The Insecurity Dilemma: National Security of Third World States.* Boulder: Lynne Rienner.

Johnson, Thomas H., and M. Chris Mason (2009). "Democracy in Afghanistan Is Wishful Thinking." http://www.csmonitor.com/Commentary/Opinion/2009/0820/p09s01-coop.html. August 20.

Joseph, Richard (1998). "Africa, 1990–1997: From *Abertura* to Closure." *Journal of Democracy* 9:2, 3–17.

Kagan, Robert (2003). "Looking for Legitimacy in All the Wrong Places." *Foreign Policy* 137, 70–72.

—— (2007). "End of Dreams, Return of History." *Policy Review* 144, August–September. http://www.hoover.org/publications/policy-review/article/6136.

Kaldor, Mary, Helmut Anheier, and Marlies Glasius (2003). "Global Civil Society in an Era of Regressive Globalisation: The State of Global Civil Society in 2003." In *Global Civil Society 2003,* edited by Kaldor, Anheier, and Glasius. Oxford: Oxford University Press. 1–19.

Kant, Immanuel (1992). *Kant's Political Writings.* Edited by H. Reiss. Cambridge: Cambridge University Press.

Kaplan, Robert D. (1994). "The Coming Anarchy." *Atlantic Monthly* 273:2, 44–76.

—— (2000). *The Coming Anarchy: Shattering the Dreams of the Post Cold War.* New York: Random House.

Katzenstein, Peter (ed.) (2009). *Civilizations in World Politics: Plural and Pluralist Perspectives.* London: Routledge.

Keene, Edward (2002). *Beyond the Anarchical Society: Grotius, Colonialism and the Order in World Politics.* Cambridge: Cambridge University Press.

Kelley, Judith (2008). "Assessing the Complex Evolution of Norms: The Rise of International Election Monitoring." *International Organization* 62:2, 221–55.

Kelly, Sean (1993). *America's Tyrant: The CIA and Mobutu of Zaire.* Washington, DC: American University Press.

Kennedy, John F. (1960). "Acceptance of the New York Liberal Party Nomination." http://www.pbs.org/wgbh/amex/presidents/35_kennedy/psources/ps_nyliberal.html. September 14.

Kennedy-Pipe, Caroline, and Nicholas Rengger (2006). "Apocalypse Now? Continuities or Disjunctions in World Politics after 9/11." *International Affairs* 82:6, 539–52.

Keohane, Robert O. (1984). *After Hegemony: Cooperation and Discord in the World Political Economy.* Princeton: Princeton University Press.

—— (1989). *International Institutions and State Power: Essays in International Relations Theory.* Boulder: Westview.

—— (1990). "Multilateralism: An Agenda for Research." *International Journal,* 45: 731–64.

—— (1998). "International Institutions: Can Interdependence Work?" *Foreign Policy* 110: Spring, 82–96.

Keohane, Robert O., and Joseph Nye Jr. (eds.) (1971). *Transnational Relations and World Politics.* Cambridge: Harvard University Press.

—— (1977). *Power and Interdependence: World Politics in Transition.* Boston: Little Brown.

Keohane, Robert O., Joseph S. Nye, and Stanley Hoffmann (eds.) (1993). *After the Cold War: International Institutions and State Strategies in Europe, 1989–1991.* Cambridge: Harvard University Press.

Kindleberger, Charles P. (1973). *The World in Depression, 1929–1939.* Berkeley: University of California Press.

Kingston-Mann, Esther (1999). *In Search of the True West: Culture, Economies, and Problems of Russian Development.* Princeton: Princeton University Press.

Kleinwächter, Lutz, and Raimund Krämer (2011). "Der Aufstand des Jahres 1432," *Welt Trends,* Spezial 1, 1–8.

Kohli, Atul (2001). *The Success of India's Democracy.* Cambridge: Cambridge University Press.

—— (2004). *State-Directed Development: Political Power and Industrialization in the Global Periphery.* Cambridge: Cambridge University Press.

Krasner, Stephen D. (1982). "American Power and Global Economic Stability." In *America in a Changing World Political Economy,* edited by William P. Avery and David Rapkin. New York: Longman. 29–48.

Krasner, Stephen D. (1992). "Realism, Imperialism, and Democracy: A Response to Gilbert." *Political Theory* 20:1, 38–52.

—— (2001). "Abiding Sovereignty." *International Political Science Review* 22:3, 229–51.

—— (2004). "Sharing Sovereignty: New Institutes for Collapsed and Failing States." *International Security* 29:2, 85–120.

Krauthammer, Charles (2001). "The New Unilateralism." *Washington Post,* June 8.

—— (2004). *Democratic Realism: An American Foreign Policy for a Unipolar World.* Washington, DC: AEI Press.

Krugman, Paul (1995). "Dutch Tulips and Emerging Markets." *Foreign Affairs* 78:4, 28–44.

—— (2008a). "Moment of Truth." *New York Times,* October 10.

—— (2008b). "Let's Get Fiscal." *New York Times,* October 17.

Kupchan, Charles A. (2002). *The End of the American Era.* New York: Knopf.

—— (2008). "Minor League, Major Problems." *Foreign Affairs* 87:6, 96–110.

Kupchan, Charles A., and Peter L. Trubowitz (2007). "Dead Center: The Demise of Liberal Internationalism in the United States." *International Security* 32:2, 7–44.

Kymlicka, Will (1999). "Citizenship in an Era of Globalization." In *Democracy's Edges,* edited by Ian Shapiro and Casiano Hacker-Cordón. Cambridge: Cambridge University Press. 112–27.

Lampton, David M. (2008). *The Three Faces of Chinese Power: Might, Money, and Minds.* Berkeley: University of California Press.

Lang, Susan (2007). "Water, Air, and Soil Pollution Causes 40 Percent of Deaths Worldwide." *Cornell University Chronicle Online.* http://www.news.cornell.edu/stories/Aug07/moreDiseases.sl.html. August 2.

Latham, Robert (1997). *The Liberal Moment: Modernity, Security and the Making of Postwar International Order.* New York: Columbia University Press.

Layne, Christopher (2006). "The Unipolar Illusion Revisited: The Coming End of the United States' Unipolar Moment." *International Security* 31:2, 6–41.

Leonard, David, and Scott Straus (2003). *Africa's Stalled Development: International Causes and Cures.* Boulder: Lynne Rienner.

Liberal International (1997). "The Liberal Agenda for the 21st Century: The Quality of Liberty in Open Civic Societies." Oxford: Congress of Liberal International. http://www.liberal-international.org/editorial.asp?ia_id=537.

Linz, Juan J. (1990). "Transitions to Democracy." *Washington Quarterly* 13, 143–64.

List, Friedrich (1966 [1885]). *The National System of Political Economy.* New York: Kelley.

Little, Richard (1996). "The Growing Relevance of Pluralism?" In *International Theory: Positivism and Beyond,* edited by Steve Smith, Ken Booth, and Marysia Zalewski. Cambridge: Cambridge University Press. 66–86.

Locke, John (1965). *Two Treatises on Government.* New York: Mentor Books.

Loewenberg, Jacob (ed.) (1929). *Hegel: Selections.* New York: Scribner's.

Logan, Justin, and Christopher Preble (2006). "Failed States and Flawed Logic: The Case against a Standing Nation-Building Office." *Policy Analysis* 560, January 11.

Lundestad, Geir (1986). "Empire by Invitation? The United States and Western Europe, 1945–52." *Journal of Peace Research* 23:3, 1–21.

Luttwak, Edward (1999). "Give War a Chance." *Foreign Affairs* 78:4, 36–44.

Lyons, Terrence (2004). "Post-conflict Elections and the Process of Demilitarizing Politics: The Role of Electoral Administration." *Democratization* 11:3, 6–62.

Mahbubani, Kishore (2008). "The Case against the West." *Foreign Affairs* 87:3, 108–24.

Mainwaring, Scott, and Timothy R. Scully (eds.) (1995). *Building Democratic Institutions: Party Systems in Latin America.* Stanford: Stanford University Press.

Malone, Andrew (2008). "How China's Taking Over Africa." http://www.dailymail.co.uk/news/worldnews/article-1036105/How-Chinas-taking-Africa-West-VERY-worried.html. July 18.

Mandelbaum, Michael (2003). *The Ideas That Conquered the World.* New York: Public Affairs.

Mann, Michael (2003). *Incoherent Empire.* London: Verso.

Mansfield, Edward, and Jack Snyder (2005). *Electing to Fight: Why Emerging Democracies Go to War.* Cambridge: MIT Press.

Manuel, Trevor (2003). "Africa and the Washington Consensus: Finding the Right Path." *Finance and Development,* September, 18–20.

Mastanduno, Michael (2005). "US Foreign Policy and the Pragmatic Use of International Institutions." *Australian Journal of International Affairs* 59:3, 317–33.

—— (2008). "System Maker and Privilege Taker: U.S. Power and the International Political Economy." *World Politics* 61:1, 121–54.

McKinlay, Robert, and Richard Little (1986). *Global Problems and World Order.* London: Frances Pinter.

Mearsheimer, John J. (2001). *The Tragedy of Great Power Politics.* New York: W. W. Norton.

Menkhaus, Kenneth (2004). *Somalia: State Collapse and the Threat of Terrorism.* London: IISS.

Mill, John Stuart (1984 [1859]). "A Few Words on Non-Intervention." In *The Collected Works of John Stuart Mill,* Vol. 21: *Essays on Equality, Law and Education,* edited by John M. Robson. Toronto: University of Toronto Press. 109–24.

Moffitt, Michael (1987). "Shocks, Deadlocks, and Scorched Earth: Reaganomics and the Decline of U.S. Hegemony." *World Policy Journal* 4: Fall, 559–79.

Monten, Jonathan (2005). "The Roots of the Bush Doctrine: Power, Nationalism, and Democracy Promotion in U.S. Strategy." *International Security* 29:4, 112–56.

—— (2007). "Primacy and Grand Strategic Beliefs in US Unilateralism." *Global Governance* 13, 119–38.

Moore, Barrington, Jr. (1966). *Social Origins of Dictatorship and Democracy.* Harmondsworth: Penguin.

Moravcsik, Andrew (1997). "Taking Preferences Seriously: A Liberal Theory of International Politics." *International Organization* 51:4, 513–53.

Mowle, Thomas S., and David H. Sacko (2007). *The Unipolar World: An Unbalanced Future.* Basingstoke: Palgrave Macmillan.

Mueller, John (2004). *The Remnants of War.* Ithaca: Cornell University Press.

—— (2006). "Is There Still a Terrorist Threat? The Myth of the Omnipresent Enemy." *Foreign Affairs,* September/October, 2–12.

Müller, Harald (2003). *Amerika Schlägt Zurück. Die Weltordnung nach dem 11. September.* Frankfurt am Main: Fischer.

—— (2009). *Building a New World Order: Sustainable Policies for the Future.* London: Haus.

Müller, Jan-Werner (2008). "Fear and Freedom: On 'Cold War Liberalism.'" *European Journal of Political Theory* 7:1, 45–64.

Münkler, Herfried (2005). *Imperien—Die Logik der Weltherrschaft vom Alten Rom bis zu den Vereinigten Staaten.* Berlin: Rowohlt.

Murphy, Craig N. (2000). "The Limited Prospects for UN Reform Created by the Ambivalence and Disunity of the Group of 7." Wellesley, MA: Wellesley College.

Nadia, Ghia (1996). "How Different Are Postcommunist Transitions." *Journal of Democracy* 7:4, 15–29.

Ndegwa, Stephen N. (1997). "Citizenship and Ethnicity: An Examination of Two Transition Moments in Kenyan Politics." *American Political Science Review* 19:3, 599–617.

Nelson, Brian R. (1982). *Western Political Thought.* Englewood Cliffs: Prentice

Nicholls, David (1974). *Three Varieties of Pluralism.* Basingstoke: Macmillan.

Nisbet, Robert (1979). *Social Change and History: Aspects of the Western Theory of Development.* Oxford: Oxford University Press.

North, Douglas C. (1990). *Institutions, Institutional Change and Economic Performance.* Cambridge: Cambridge University Press.

Nozzel, Susanne (2004). "Smart Power." *Foreign Affairs* 83:2, 131–42.

NSS (2002). *The National Security Strategy of the United States of America.* Washington, DC: The White House, Office of the President of the United States.

Nye, Joseph S., Jr. (1988). "Neorealism and Neoliberalism." *World Politics* 40:2, 235–51.

—— (1990). *Bound to Lead: The Changing Nature of American Power.* New York: Basic Books.

—— (2002). *The Paradox of American Power: Why the World's Only Superpower Can't Go It Alone.* Oxford: Oxford University Press.

—— (2003). "US Power and Strategy after Iraq." *Washington Post,* May 5.

Nyerere, Julius (1980). "Nyerere and the IMF." http://taifaletu.blogspot.com/2009/03/nyerere-and-imf-will-our-leaders.html.

Oakeshott, Michael (1975). *Hobbes on Civil Association.* Oxford: Blackwell.

Ottaway, Marina (2005). "Iraq: Without Consensus, Democracy Is Not the Answer." Policy Brief, Carnegie Endowment.

Packenham, Robert (1973). *Liberal America and the Third World.* Princeton: Princeton University Press.

Paine, Thomas (1995). "The Rights of Man." In *Complete Writings,* edited by Eric Foner. New York: Oxford University Press.

Papagianni, Katia (2007). "State Building and Transitional Politics in Iraq: The Perils of a Top-Down Transition." *International Studies Perspectives* 8:3, 253–71.

Paris, Roland (2004). *At War's End: Building Peace after Civil Conflict.* Cambridge: Cambridge University Press.

Patrick, Stewart (2006). "Weak States and Global Threats: Fact or Fiction." *Washington Quarterly* 29:2, 27–53.

Paul, James, and Céline Nahory (2005). "Theses Towards a Democratic Reform of the UN Security Council." *Global Policy Forum.* http://www.globalpolicy.org/component/content/article/200/41131.html. July 13.

Paul, T. V. (2004). Introduction. In *Balance of Power: Theory and Practice in the 21st Century,* edited by T. V. Paul, James J. Wirtz, and Michael Fortmann. Stanford: Stanford University Press. 1–29.

Paul, T. V., James J. Wirtz, and Michael Fortmann (eds.) (2004). *Balance of Power: Theory and Practice in the 21st Century.* Stanford: Stanford University Press.

Pauly, Louis W. (2005). "The Political Economy of International Financial Crises." In *Global Political Economy,* edited by John Ravenhill. Oxford: Oxford University Press. 177–203.

Pei, Minxin (2005). "Statement to Senate Foreign Relations Committee." http://carnegieendowment.org/files/PeiTestimony050607.pdf. June 7.

Peterson, Richard T. (2004). "Human Rights and Cultural Conflict." *Human Rights Review,* April–June, 22–32.

Plattner, Marc (2005). "Two Kinds of Internationalism," *National Interest,* Spring: 79, 84–92.S

Polanyi, Karl (1957 [1944]). *The Great Transformation: The Political and Economic Origins of Our Time.* Boston: Beacon Books.

Pollard, Sidney (1971). *The Idea of Progress.* Harmondsworth: Penguin.

Portes, Richard (1998). "An Analysis of Financial Crisis: Lessons for the International Financial System." Conference paper, FRB Chicago/IMF Conference, Chicago, October 8–10.

Posen, Barry (2003). "Command of the Commons: The Military Foundation of U.S. Hegemony." *International Security* 28:1, 5–46.

Princeton Project (2006). *Forging a World of Liberty under Law.* G. John Ikenberry and Anne-Marie Slaughter, co-directors. Princeton: Woodrow Wilson School.

Putnam, Robert D. (1995). "Bowling Alone: America's Declining Social Capital." *Journal of Democracy* 5:1, 65–78.

Reinicke, Wolfgang (2000). "The Other World Wide Web: Public Policy Networks." *Foreign Policy* 117, 44–57.

Reno, William (2000). "Sovereignty and Personal Rule in Zaire." *African Studies Quarterly.* http://web.africa.ufl.edu/asq/v1/3/4.htm.

Rice, Condoleezza (2005). "The Promise of Democratic Peace." *Washington Post,* December 11, B07.

Rice, Susan E., and Stewart Patrick (2008). *Index on State Weakness.* http://www.brookings.edu/reports/2008/02_weak_states_index.aspx. February 14.

Rittberger, Volker, and Bernhard Zangl (2003). *Internationale Organisationen—Politik und Geschichte.* 3rd ed. Opladen: Leske und Budrich.

Robinson, William (1996). *Promoting Polyarchy: Globalization, US Intervention, and Hegemony.* Cambridge: Cambridge University Press.

Rocha Menocal, Alina (2004). "And If There Was No State? Critical Reflections on Bates, Polanyi and Evans on the Role of the State in Promoting Development." *Third World Quarterly* 25:4, 765–77.

Rodrik, Dani (2006). "Goodbye Washington Consensus, Hello Washington Confusion?" Harvard University, January.

Rodrik, Dani (2008). "No More Laundry Lists." http://www.guardian.co.uk/commentisfree/2008/jul/10/economics.development/print. July 10.

—— (2009). "Saving Globalization from Its Cheerleaders." http://rodrik.typepad.com/dani_rodriks_weblog/2007/07/saving-globaliz.html. July 30.

Roosevelt, Franklin D. (1941). "The Four Freedoms." http://usinfo.org/facts/speech/fdr.html. January 6.

Rosecrance, Richard (1986). *The Rise of the Trading State: Commerce and Conquest in the Modern World.* New York: Basic Books.

—— (1999). *The Rise of the Virtual State.* New York: Basic Books.

Rosenau, James N. (1990). *Turbulence in World Politics: A Theory of Change and Continuity.* Princeton: Princeton University Press.

—— (1992). "Citizenship in a Changing Global Order." In *Governance without Government: Order and Change in World Politics,* edited by J. N. Rosenau and E. O. Czempiel. Cambridge: Cambridge University Press. 272–94.

Rosenblum, Nancy L. (1978). *Bentham's Theory of the Modern State.* Cambridge: Harvard University Press.

Ross, Robert S., and Zhu Feng (eds.) (2008). *China's Ascent: Power, Security, and the Future of International Politics.* Ithaca: Cornell University Press.

Rubin, Alissa J., and Carlotta Gall (2010). "Widespread Fraud Seen in Latest Afghan Elections." http://www.nytimes.com/2010/09/25/world/asia/25afghan.html?_r=2. September 14.

Ruggie, John G. (1982). "International Regimes, Transactions, and Change: Embedded Liberalism in the Postwar Economic Order." *International Organization* 36:2, 195–231.

Russett, Bruce, John Oneal, and Michaelene Cox (2000). "Clash of Civilizations or Realism and Liberalism Dejà Vu? Some Evidence." *Journal of Peace Research* 37:5, 583–608.

Rustow, Dankwart (1970). "Transitions to Democracy: Towards a Dynamic Model." *Comparative Politics* 2:3, 337–63.

Saideman, Stephen M., Daniel J. Lanoue, Michael Campenni, and Samuel Stanton (2002). "Democratization, Political Institutions, and Ethnic Conflict: A Pooled Time-Series Analysis, 1985–1998." *Comparative Political Studies* 35:1, 103–29.

Samuels, Richard J. (1994). *"Rich Nation, Strong Army": National Security and the Technological Transformation of Japan.* Ithaca: Cornell University Press.

Sandbrook, Richard (1985). *The Politics of Africa's Economic Stagnation.* Cambridge: Cambridge University Press.

Schaller, Michael (1997). *Altered States: The United States and Japan since the Occupation.* New York: Oxford University Press.

Schatz, Sayre P. (1994). "Structural Adjustment in Africa: A Failing Grade So Far." *Journal of Modern African Studies* 32:4, 679–92.

Schimmelfennig, Frank (1996). "Legitimate Rule in the European Union." *Working Paper 1.45.* Berkeley: University of California, Center for European Studies.

Scholte, Jan Aart (2005). *Globalization—A Critical Introduction.* 2nd ed. Basingstoke: Palgrave Macmillan.

Schraeder, Peter J. (2004). *African Politics and Society.* Belmont, CA: Wadsworth.

Schumpeter, Joseph (1955 [1919]). "The Sociology of Imperialisms." *Imperialism and Social Classes.* Cleveland: World.

Schwarzenberger, Georg (1936). *League of Nations and World Order.* London: Constable.

Schweller, Randall L. (2001). "The Problem of International Order Revisited: A Review Essay." *International Security* 26:1, 161–86.

Senghaas, Dieter (1998). *Zivilisierung wider Willen. Der Konflikt der Kulturen mit sich selbst.* Frankfurt: Suhrkamp.

Shapiro, Ian (2008). *Containment: Rebuilding a Strategy against Global Terror.* Princeton: Princeton University Press.

Shklar, Judith (1989). "The Liberalism of Fear." In *Liberalism and the Moral Life,* edited by Nancy Rosenblum. Cambridge: Harvard University Press. 21–38.

Simpson, Gerry (2001). "Two Liberalisms." *European Journal of International Law* 12:3, 537–71.

Skowronek, Stephen (2006). "The Reassociation of Ideas and Purposes: Racism, Liberalism, and the American Political Tradition." *American Political Science Review* 100:3, 385–401.

Slaughter, Anne-Marie (1997). "The Real New World Order." *Foreign Affairs* 76, 183–98.

—— (2004). *A New World Order.* Princeton: Princeton University Press.

Smith, Adam (1976 [1776]). *Wealth of Nations.* Edited by Roy H. Campbell and Andrew S. Skinner. Oxford: Oxford University Press.

Smith, Tony (1994). *America's Mission: The United States and the Worldwide Struggle for Democracy in the Twentieth Century.* Princeton: Princeton University Press.

Sørensen, Georg (1991). "Strategies and Structures of Development: The New 'Consensus' and the Limits to Its Promises." *European Journal of Development Research* 3:3, 121–45.

—— (1996). "Individual Security and National Security: The State Remains the Principal Problem." *Security Dialogue* 27:4, 371–87.

—— (1999). "Sovereignty: Change and Continuity in a Fundamental Institution." *Political Studies* 47:3, 590–604.

—— (2001). *Changes in Statehood: The Transformation of International Relations.* Basingstoke: Palgrave Macmillan.

—— (2004). *The Transformation of the State: Beyond the Myth of Retreat.* Basingstoke: Palgrave Macmillan.

—— (2006a). "What Kind of World Order? The International System in the New Millennium." *Cooperation and Conflict* 41:4, 343–64.

—— (2006b). "Liberalism of Restraint and Liberalism of Imposition: Liberal Values and World Order in the New Millennium." *International Relations* 20:3, 251–72.

—— (2007). "After the Security Dilemma: The Challenge of Insecurity in Weak States and the Dilemma of Liberal Values." *Security Dialogue* 38:3, 357–78.

—— (2008). *Democracy and Democratization: Processes and Prospects in a Changing World.* 3rd ed. Boulder: Westview.

Spero, Joan E., and Jeffrey A. Hart (1997). *The Politics of International Economic Relations.* 5th ed. New York: St. Martin's Press.

Steil, Benn (2010). "China, the Dollar, and the Return of the Triffin Dilemma." http://whatmatters.mckinseydigital.com/currencies/china-the-dollar-and-the-return-of-the-triffin-dilemma. January 12.

Stiglitz, Joseph E. (2001). "Whither Reform? Ten Years of Transition." In *The Rebel Within: Joseph Stiglitz and the World Bank,* edited by Ha-Joon Chang. London: Anthem. 127–71.

—— (2009). "Nationalized Banks Are 'Only Answer.'" http://www.dw-world.de/dw/article/0,,4005355,00.html. June 2.

Stiglitz, Joseph E., and Linda J. Bilmes (2008). *The Three Trillion Dollar War—The True Cost of the Iraq Conflict.* New York: W. W. Norton.

Stiglitz, Joseph E., et al. (2009). *Report of the Commission of Experts of the President of the United Nations General Assembly on Reforms of the International Monetary and Financial System.* http://www.un.org/ga/president/63/interactive/financialcrisis/PreliminaryReport210509.pdf. June 24–26.

Strange, Susan (1986). *Casino Capitalism.* Oxford: Basil Blackwell.

—— (1987). "The Persistent Myth of Lost Hegemony." *International Organization* 41, 551–74.

Talentino, Andrea Kathryn (2007). "Perceptions of Peacebuilding: The Dynamic of Imposer and Imposed Upon." *International Studies Perspectives* 8:2, 152–71.

Talisse, Robert B. (2000). "Two-Faced Liberalism: John Gray's Pluralist Politics and the Reinstatement of Enlightenment Liberalism." *Critical Review* 14:4, 441–58.

Taylor, Lance (1997). "The Revival of the Liberal Creed—The IMF and the World Bank in a Globalized Economy." *World Development* 25:2, 145–52.

Tepperman, Jonathan D. (2004). "Some Hard Truths about Multilateralism." *World Policy Journal* 21:2, 27–36.

Teschke, Benno (2003). *The Myth of 1648: Class, Geopolitics and the Making of Modern International Relations.* London: Verso.

Tilly, Charles (1985). "War Making and State Making as Organized Crime." In *Bringing the State Back In,* edited by Peter Evans, Dietrich Rueschemeyer, and Theda Skocpol. Cambridge: Cambridge University Press. 169–91.

—— (1990). *Coercion, Capital, and European States, AD 990–1990.* Cambridge: Basil Blackwell.

Time Magazine (2007). "Person of the Year." http://www.time.com/time/specials/2007/personoftheyear/article/0,28804,1690753_1690757,00.html.

Tønnesson, Stein (2004). "The Imperial Temptation." *Security Dialogue* 35:3, 329–43.

Toulmin, Stephen (1990). *Cosmopolis: The Hidden Agenda of Modernity.* Chicago: University of Chicago Press.

Toye, John (1987). *Dilemmas of Development.* Oxford: Blackwell.

—— (ed.) (2003). *Trade and Development.* Cheltenham, UK: Edward Elgar.

Trachtenberg, Marc (1999). *A Constructed Peace: The Making of the European Settlement, 1945–1963.* Princeton: Princeton University Press.

Underhill, Geoffrey (2000). "Global Money and the Decline of State Power." paper for ISA Annual Meeting, Los Angeles, March 14–19.

United Nations (1945). Charter. http://www.un.org/en/documents/charter/index.shtml. June 26.

—— (1993). *Vienna Declaration and Programme of Action.* A/CONF; 157/23. New York: UN.

—— (2000). *United Nations Millennium Declaration.* Resolution 55/2 adopted by the General Assembly. New York: UN.

United Nations General Assembly (UNGA) (2005). "World Summit Outcome 2005. Assembly Resolution A/RES/60/1. October 24, 2005.

—— (2009). "Debate on R2P." http://www.responsibilitytoprotect.org/index.php/component/content/article/35-r2pcs-topics/2493-general-assembly-debate-on-the-responsibility-to-protect-and-informal-interactive-dialogue-.

Van de Walle, Nicolas (2001). *African Economies and the Politics of Permanent Crisis.* Cambridge: Cambridge University Press.

Vasquez, John A. (ed.) (1996). *Classics of International Relations.* Chicago: Prentice Hall.

Voeten, Erik (2004). "Resisting the Lonely Superpower: Responses of States in the United Nations to U.S. Dominance." *Journal of Politics* 66, 729–54.

Wade, Robert Hunter (1998). "The Asian Debt-and-Development Crisis of 1997–?: Causes and Consequences." *World Development* 26:8, 1535–53.

—— (2003). "What Strategies Are Available for Developing Countries Today? The World Trade Organization and the Shrinking of 'Development Space.'" *Review of International Political Economy* 10:4, 621–44.

—— (2008). "Financial Regime Change?" *New Left Review* 53: September–October.

Waldron, Jeremy (2003). "Security and Liberty: The Image of Balance." *Journal of Political Philosophy* 11:2, 191–210.

Wallerstein, Immanuel (1995). "The Agonies of Liberalism: What Hope Progress?" In *After Liberalism*. New York: W. W. Norton. 252–72.

Walt, Stephen (2005). *Taming American Power: The Global Response to U.S. Primacy.* New York: W. W. Norton.

Waltz, Kenneth N. (1979). *Theory of International Politics.* Reading: Addison-Wesley.

—— (1986). "Reflections on *Theory of International Politics:* A Response to My Critics." In *Neorealism and Its Critics,* edited by Robert O. Keohane. New York: Columbia University Press. 322–47.

—— (1993). "The Emerging Structure of International Politics." *International Security* 18:2, 44–79.

—— (2002). "Structural Realism after the Cold War." In *America Unrivaled: The Future of the Balance of Power,* edited by G. John Ikenberry. Ithaca: Cornell University Press. 29–68.

Watson, Adam (1992). *The Evolution of International Society.* London: Routledge.

Weigel, George (1991). "Religion and Peace: An Argument Complexified." *Washington Quarterly* 14:2, 27–42.

Weinstein, Jeremy M. (2007). "Africa's Revolutionary Deficit." *Foreign Policy,* July–August, 70–71.

Weinstein, Jeremy M., John Edward Porter, and Stuart E. Eizenstat (2004). *On the Brink: Weak States and U.S. National Security.* Washington: Center for Global Development.

Weiss, Linda (2005a). "America Inc. Breaking New Ground or Breaking the Rules?" Paper for ISA Convention, Honolulu, Hawaii.

—— (2005b). "Global Governance, National Strategies: How Industrialized States Make Room to Move under the WTO." *Review of International Political Economy* 12:5, 723–49.

Weiss, Linda, and Elizabeth Thurbon (2006). "The Business of Buying American: Public Procurement as Trade Strategy in the USA." *Review of International Political Economy* 13:5, 701–24.

Weiss, Thomas G. (2006). "R2P after 9–11 and the World Summit." *Wisconsin International Law Journal* 24:3, 741–60.

Weiss, Thomas G., and Karen E. Young (2005). "Compromise and Credibility: UN Security Council Reform?" *Security Dialogue* 36:2, 131–54.

Wen, Dale (2005). *China Copes with Globalization.* San Francisco: International Forum on Globalization.

Wheeler, Nick, and Ken Booth (1992). "The Security Dilemma." In *Dilemmas of World Politics,* edited by John Baylis and Nicholas J. Rengger. Oxford: Clarendon. 29–61.

Wiarda, Howard, with Esther M. Skelley (2006). *The Crisis of American Foreign Policy.* Lanham, MD: Rowman and Littlefield.

Wight, Martin (1977). *Systems of States.* Leicester: Leicester University Press.

Williamson, John (1990). "What Washington Means by Policy Reform." In *Latin American Adjustment: How Much Has Happened?* edited by John Williamson. Washington, DC: Institute for International Economics. Chap. 2.

—— (2002). "Did the Washington Consensus Fail?" Outline of speech. http://www. iie.com/publications/papers/paper.cfm?ResearchID=488. November 6.

Wivel, Anders (2008). "Balancing against Threats or Bandwagoning with Power? Europe and the Transatlantic Relationship after the Cold War." *Cambridge Review of International Affairs* 21:3, 289–305.

Wohlforth, William C. (2002). "U.S. Strategy in a Unipolar World." In *America Unrivaled: The Future of the Balance of Power,* edited by G. John Ikenberry. Ithaca: Cornell University Press. 98–121.

Woodruff, David (1999). *Money Unmade: Barter and the Fate of Russian Capitalism.* Ithaca: Cornell University Press.

Woolcock, Michael, and Lant Pritchett (2002). *Solutions When the Solution Is the Problem: Arraying the Disarray in Development.* Washington, DC: Center for Global Development Paper 10.

World Bank (1994). *Adjustment in Africa: Reforms, Results, and the Road Ahead.* New York: Oxford University Press.

—— (1996). *World Development Report 1996.* New York: Oxford University Press.

—— (1997). *World Development Report 1997.* New York: Oxford University Press.

—— (2000). *Entering the 21st Century: World Development Report 1999/2000.* New York: Oxford University Press.

—— (2005). *Economic Growth in the 1990s: Learning from a Decade of Reform.* Washington, DC: World Bank.

Wu, Brandon (2009). "Obama Administration Blocking Reform at the UN Financial Crisis Summit?" http://citizen.typepad.com/eyesontrade/2009/06/obama-administration-blocking-reform-at-the-un-financial-crisis-summit.html. June 23.

Young, Crawford, and Thomas Turner (1985). *The Rise and Decline of the Zairian State.* Madison: University of Wisconsin Press.

Zacher, Mark W. (2001). "The Territorial Integrity Norm: International Boundaries and the Use of Force." *International Organization* 55:2, 215–50.

Zacher, Mark W., and Richard A. Matthew (1995). "Liberal International Theory: Common Threads, Divergent Strands." In *Controversies in International Relations: Realism and the Neoliberal Challenge,* edited by Charles W. Kegley Jr. New York: St. Martin's Press. 107–50.

Zakaria, Fareed (2008a). "The Future of American Power: How America Can Survive the Rise of the Rest." *Foreign Affairs* 87:3, 32–43.

—— (2008b). *The Post-American World.* New York: W. W. Norton.

Zartmann, I. William (1995). "Putting Things Back Together." In *Collapsed States,* edited by I. William Zartmann. Boulder: Lynne Rienner. 267–75.

Zielonka, Jan (1998). *Euro-Paralysis: Why Europe Is Unable to Act in International Politics.* Basingstoke: Macmillan.

Zimmern, Alfred (1918). "Capitalism and International Relations." Reprinted in *Nationality and Government and Other War-time Essays,* by Alfred Zimmern. London: Chatto & Windus.

Zürn, Michael (1998). *Regieren jenseits des Nationaalstaates. Globalisierung und Dena-
tionalisiering als Chance.* Frankfurt am Main: Suhrkamp.

—— (2002). "From Interdependence to Globalisation." In *Handbook of International
Relations,* edited by Walter Carlsnaes et al. London: Sage. 23–51.

—— (2004). "Global Governance and Legitimacy Problems." *Government and Opposition* 39:2, 260–87.

Zürn, Michael, Martin Binder, Matthias Ecker-Ehrhardt, and Katrin Radtke (2006).
*Politische Ordnungsbildung wider Willen—Ein Forschungsprogramm zu transna-
tionalen Konflikten und Institutionen.* Berlin: Wissenschaftszentrum Berlin für
Sozialforschung.

Zürn, Michael, and Stephan Leibfried (2005). "Reconfiguring the National Constellation." In *Transformations of the State?* edited by Stephan Leibfried and Michael Zürn. Cambridge: Cambridge University Press. Chap. 1.

◼ INDEX